The Q&A WAY *in* CHESS

BRUCE PANDOLFINI

RANDOM HOUSE
PUZZLES & GAMES

NEW YORK   TORONTO   LONDON   SYDNEY   AUCKLAND

TABLE OF CONTENTS

Introduction   v

Chapter 1: Class Struggles   1

Chapter 2: Teaching or Preaching   38

Chapter 3: Chess Through the Ages   75

Chapter 4: Mind Play   107

Chapter 5: Tech Games   143

Chapter 6: Culture, Place, and Time   175

Chapter 7: Going Through a Phase   214

Chapter 8: Mishegaas: Rules, Etiquette, Notation,
            and More   248

Index   285

Acknowledgments   291

INTRODUCTION

Teach for an hour, and you'll find you've been asked at least a few good questions. Teach for a lifetime, and you'll lose track.

Different students have similar needs. They all want to learn how to play chess better. They all want to raise their rating. They all want to find the right book, or the perfect online site. They all want to study in the proper way. They all want to get more out of their favorite game. They want the answer to everything chess, and they want it now.

The material in *The Q&A Way in Chess* comes from a monthly column I have written since 1999 for the online site Chesscafe.com. Shortly before the turn of the century I chose a question-and-answer format. Hanon Russell, the editor and founder of the Web site, agreed.

More than 200 questions have been arranged in eight chapters. Where to place a specific question wasn't necessarily easy to decide. Many of the questions could have found a home in several sections, and a good chunk of the emails I received actually contained several questions masquerading as one. Moreover, some of the questions weren't even questions. They were more like statements, where my task was to figure out what was driving the writer. In some cases I kept the statements entwined with the questions, even when they weren't very relevant, because they influenced my answer. I felt that editing them out would have changed the meaning or flavor of my response. Besides, the unclear lead-ins and disguised questions were especially fun—they gave me a puzzle, and the chess player in me loves to figure things out.

In cases where I would have had to write a book to answer an email, I singled out a particular issue that I deemed most appealing to the reader. That didn't always work. Nor did I always know what to say, though I usually said it anyway. Those were often the answers I'd get the most feedback on. Not all feedback is positive, and occasionally I'd have to emend my ways in later columns. I hoped *Q&A* was a learning experience for my readers. It certainly turned out to be one for me.

I omitted the writers' identities for each question but kept the country of origin. Questions came in from all over the world (a few seemed to come from other worlds), but many of them sounded as if they came from the same place, in chess terms.

The most common questions focused on personal improvement. Chess players asked how to get their rating up, or they needed advice on the most efficient way to move from one playing class to the next higher one. The first chapter, "Class Struggles," is all about getting better and higher-rated.

Subsequent chapters include questions on teaching and the chess profession (how to become a teacher, how to coach); age (from problems of the young to problems of the old); chess thinking (including analysis, visualization, calculation, and elements of psychology); the three phases of the game (opening, middlegame, and endgame); new technology and other forms of chess (computers, the Internet, software, speed chess); rules, problems, and specific tasks; and a final chapter of hard-to-classify questions, along with some questions from each of the earlier categories, just to round things off.

As a rule, I gave the same type of advice I'd give to my own students in private and classroom situations. I tried to get people focused on the most relevant features of a problem. I kept stressing becoming more self-reliant. It's natural to turn to experts for all kinds of help. But they can't make our moves for us. We have to learn to think for ourselves, and I consistently placed that message in answer after answer. I hoped to convince my readers to trust their own judgments. I argued that they didn't need the teacher to learn. If it put me out of business, I reasoned I could always go back to teaching chemistry.

Some of the questions raised additional questions. They couldn't be answered without further specification or clarification. So I often asked certain rhetorical questions back. They would serve as a prelude to explain why I chose to answer the way I did.

Naturally, I enjoyed the questions from those who didn't know what they wanted to ask. It gave me an opportunity to tell them what they were thinking. Some readers wanted me to give thoughtful answers before they had taken the time to formulate thoughtful questions. Maybe it's a sign of our times, which doesn't mean it's not a sign of all times. It's natural to react without too much thought when we feel impassioned.

What applies to the readership applies to me, too. Whether due to onrushing deadlines or plain old poor judgment on my part, some of my answers were a bit too impulsive. They left me shuddering afterward. In a number of cases I seemed to be offering the same advice. As a teacher, I kept some of that repetition to drive home the importance of specific points, and perhaps I tried to relieve possible monotony with an occasional joke.

Once it's in print, however, it's out there forever, so I've been stuck with having said some very silly things. Fortunately, this is a book, and with the benefit of hindsight, I've been given the chance to tone down a few of the outrageous things I've written—but not all. Therefore, where my answers have fallen short, or simply failed to meet a high standard, I beg the forgiveness and indulgence of you, the reader. I meant to do a better job. I simply screwed up. I wanted to preserve the feel of the original columns. I hope that keeping the character of the column intact will be viewed more as a virtue than a shortcoming, but in the end, none of that is for me to say.

Obviously, though, not everything in *The Q&A Way in Chess* appears as it did originally. Typos and grammatical errors were corrected, and some of the answers were modified to avoid redundancy from comparable questions. Indeed, many of the questions appear cut from the same cloth. Now and then, everyone should change his or her garb. I also added a few diagrams, just to make ideas more vivid. I may have taken liberty with some of the diagrams, in that here and there I included a couple of illustrations that showed the very opposite of the point being made. I justified it in my own mind because they supported the underlying nature of the column, which blends instruction with my odd sense of humor. But there are no chess variations or long strings of notation here, and none of the diagrams are necessary to understand the answers anyway. As in the real column, I have relied on language to express concepts, not symbols or pictures. Most ideas that can be expressed can be explained in words, and chess is no different.

The chief message I've tried to get across in my teachings, my columns, and in this book, is the value of doing things for the right reason. The right reason to play chess is not to get better at chess (not that there's anything too wrong with that). The main reason to play chess, it seems to me, is to find stimulating leisure time that adds to the quality of our lives. When we place the emphasis solely on nuts-and-bolts improvement, we may be missing the point.

So, if there's an overarching theme to the book, it's to get more of us to appreciate that chess can be great fun. You don't have to be a grandmaster to play chess for sheer pleasure. I'm not even sure that for them it's play at all. But fun it should be, and that's the one thing chess offers us all.

The
Q&A
WAY *in*
CHESS

CHAPTER 1

Class Struggles

Questions about improvement fill this first chapter. Chess players ask how they can reach the next rating class or the next level of understanding. There are questions about what to study, which books to read, how often to practice, the proper speed of play, the right kind of opposition, training systems, tournament play, clock management, and suitable curricula.

Self-doubt, lack of confidence, nerves, anxiety, lack of patience, and unreasonable expectations are issues that crop up regularly. Some people wanted to know how to get past a period of stagnation. Others watched their ratings fall and thought of giving up the game. Some never seemed to improve at all.

There were even a few who were so strong and successful that I had to wonder why they wrote at all. Maybe they just wanted to see their names in print, or maybe the joke was on me. I tried my best to make sure it wasn't on you, but you never know. A couple of the wiser questioners realized they were in it for the right purpose: for mental stimulation and pure enjoyment. I hope this first selection leaves the reader feeling much the same way.

STUDY TIME

Q. I have only five to ten hours a week to study chess. How can I compete with people who study ten hours every day? Isn't it hopeless?
—*Ireland*

A. I understand your concern. It's hard to compete with people who study six, eight, or ten hours a day, when you have only a few hours for the entire week. In fact, it's virtually impossible to compete successfully with those full-time students of the game, not that there are many of them.

Let's consider a few things. Do you really think that full-time students study all day long at maximum intensity? Isn't it likely that the law of marginal returns will go into effect, and as time passes, less will be obtained from comparable labor? With prolonged, unbroken study, isn't it probable that some of the effort might be purposeless, wasteful, or even counterproductive?

You don't have to answer those questions, of course. But they do suggest how to compensate for having less study time than others. You can obtain more from your efforts, countering time discrepancies and restraints, by working at full capacity for a certain critical period (however long that should be). The point is that some kinds of learning are not necessarily functions of time. Instead, they are more dependent on intensity of concentration. Unless a specific threshold of attention is reached, in just the right way, the secrets of the given level might not be revealed, regardless of how long you sit at the chessboard. The full-time student may have opportunities to learn more, but the student who works harder for shorter stretches may, in some cases, have chances to learn *better*. Still, I do see your point, which could explain my sudden sense of despair.

CLOCK MANAGEMENT

Q. I find myself getting into time trouble a lot in league games (35 moves in 1.75 hours). If I speed up too much, I tend to miss elements of the position, including tactics. Any advice on how to manage my clock better?
—*United Kingdom*

A. You certainly don't want to move too quickly at any point, but you shouldn't be wasting time on obvious moves, such as opening variations you're quite familiar with and responses you know to be forced. But be careful—even in the most innocent situations, taking a little more time initially could save time later on, especially when a thoughtless response might lead down the wrong path.

Perhaps you're wasting time considering irrelevant options. Try to determine what's germane and keep your analysis centered on the most attractive possibilities. You might consider practicing with a quicker time control, experimenting with different ones to see which give you the right blend of exercise and time to think. If you play enough games under faster conditions, the experience may carry over naturally, so that you cope better with the time allotted in league action.

In such competitions, it could also be advantageous to divide your score sheets into parts before starting play. Simply draw lines under key moves so that you can monitor early enough if you're on track not to overstep. Since 35 moves in 1.75 hours works out to five moves for every 15 minutes, you might want to partition your score sheet for five-move intervals. Try to play the first ten moves in 20 minutes (instead of in 30 minutes), then follow the formula we've just outlined, and you'll have ten minutes of safety built in. Of course, in any particular game, the demands of the position may cause you to break away from this plan. But if it helps you even slightly, it's worth it. This is a game where little things, like clock management, truly affect big things, like results.

It could be that the real solution might be improving your concentration. If you can stay attentive for longer periods, you'll be more alert and see more. You'll also save time, avoiding waste and reducing the effort you must make to re-enter the analytic forum. Every instant you let your mind meander inadvertently, or you get up from the board (not that you do this), you consume additional time just to get back to the game. Of course, we all need to take breaks during riveting contests, but these lulls should be enjoyed judiciously, when they're most needed.

TACTICAL IMPROVEMENT

Q. I am a French chess player rated 1710 ELO. I try to improve my tactical ability by solving tactical chess puzzles. But, by repeating the exercises at different times, I noticed that I am still not able to solve the problems I didn't solve six months ago. So, it seems that I am not making any progress and that my methodology is not the right one. Could you propose another regimen that would be more efficient? Please take into account that, as an engineer with a family, I have not a lot of time (about four hours per week) to devote to chess instruction.
—France

A. If you're not solving certain problems now, what makes you think you'll be able to solve them in the future if you don't try to work on them in the interim? Try to figure out what level of problem you're comfortable with. Look at books that grade or organize problems by degree of difficulty. Once you've found your comfort level, keep solving problems (over the course of weeks and possibly months) until you no longer have any trouble with them. At that point, your tactical ability should show real growth and you'll be ready to move up to the next level.

SELF-DOUBT

Q. I'm about a USCF Class B player. I've been at this level for a few years. I'm not expecting miracles, or for you to give me a whole course of study, like many people ask for. I'm not concerned with particular opening variations or what books to read. I know it's not about how many hours I study, because I study enough, maybe too much. I also don't think it's about time and the clock, because I've tried all kinds of time controls. I've tried many different steps and I'm beginning to think it's a matter of attitude. Maybe I'm not positive enough, or I have too many doubts. What should I do? Can you make any suggestions?
—USA

A. I can suggest a lot, but let's just concentrate on this: In chess it's essential to have confidence. Distrust your own thinking and you're as good as lost.

Lose subjectivity and acquire objectivity. Get into the habit of basing all decisions on your analysis of the position before you. I know it's not possible to leave all your emotions at home. But somehow you have to exclude them from the equation or your solutions will be contaminated. (Actually, if we're going to be fair about it, even grandmasters find themselves making some key chess decisions for emotional reasons.)

Take this approach beyond the conclusion of particular games. If you have an unsuccessful result, don't walk away from the board crestfallen. Use the same critical powers you tried to tap during the game to comprehend afterward why you actually lost. That's the only reliable way to bring about any advancement, whether it makes you a superior player or merely enables you to better understand chess and how to get more from it. What should you do? Be positive, be determined, be objective, and most of all, enjoy being all three.

CONFIDENCE

Q. My problem is that I don't believe in myself. I'm an 1800 player, and whether I play against higher or lower rated players, I don't have any confidence to win at all. I keep thinking that they are better than me and that affects my game so that I don't play my usual style. Could you give me advice? I'll never improve without it.
—*USA*

A. I'd worry less about losing and focus more on having pure fun. Just play your usual style. I believe in you, no matter whom you play or how well you do. Now go out and gain a couple of hundred rating points for the Gipper.

NERVES

Q. I have been playing competitive chess for 30 years, but I now find that I am becoming increasingly tense and nervous while playing, and am now reduced to playing ten-minute games on the Internet. This nervousness and lack of confidence in my own ability have been affecting me for the last ten years, and although I have taken breaks from playing, the situation has not improved. I am losing to players who are weaker than me. My British rating grade is 142. Three years ago I was 163 and that was

my highest grade ever. Thirty years ago I was grade 140. Any suggestions? I play bridge on the Internet and have no such problems.
—*England*

A. Why are you reduced to playing ten-minute games on the Internet? You can play games with longer time controls, so that you feel less pressured and have more time to think.

I wonder if you're placing emphasis on the wrong things, such as rating points. Stop focusing so much on ratings (and victories) and start savoring the simple experience of playing. That is, try to revel in the game's beauty: in its logic, patterns, themes, and ideas. Besides, results don't always tell the story, especially in chess, where you can play a good game and lose, or a bad game and nonetheless win. Obviously, it's great to be a winner, but it's no great thrill to win if you don't deserve it.

Neither ratings nor results are totally reliable measures of playing strength. Perhaps you actually have been playing beneath your level, possibly because of anxiety or something like it, or maybe those "weaker" players who've been beating you are in reality stronger than you think, even with their abysmal ratings. No matter what, it's clear you need a change in viewpoint.

Instead of becoming stultified over the loss of games and rating points, start playing more for the sheer amusement of it. You might consider taking another break from competition. But this time, after you come back refreshed and eager for action, why don't you play some casual chess across from human beings and without an interface? Perhaps with nothing serious at stake, under light and social circumstances, your nervousness will abate and you'll once again begin to appreciate chess as the stimulating pastime it really is. And if you can't quite do that, and remain too anxious, you can always take solace in your other love, namely bridge. Apparently you have no such problems there, and that's also a wonderful game. (I know too many bridge masters to say otherwise.)

GYMNASTIC CHESS

Q. I get too nervous while playing chess. In order to fix it I began to practice gymnastics (!) while playing long standard games (usually 40 min-

utes per side). I put it into practice last 31 December. In exactly one month, my standard rating rose from 1500 to 1975! Could you share any thoughts or suggestions about it!? Thank you.
—*Brazil*

A. I'm not certain I'd recommend your approach to others, particularly for standard tournament settings. I'd have to know which calisthenics you're talking about. I could see finger exercises, dynamic tension, and that kind of thing, where you can continue to sit at the board and annoy your opponent without breaking any rules. But headstands, though also very disturbing, might be a little difficult for average readers to execute, especially when short of time, or when they can't get a crazy position out of their mind and have to take it to the bathroom, the water cooler, or other places itinerant thinkers usually go. Still, your rating gain is impressive, and for many readers, a rating point takes priority over everything else there is or ever could be. So, I will print it, hoping the editor sees the point and lets it go anyway.

PATIENCE

Q. I apologize in advance for not using the correct terms, but I'm somewhat confused. I have no idea what my rating is, but as a guideline, I win about half my games on Yahoo.com against players of about 1200 (I know this doesn't tell you much but it's all I have). I have found dozens of books that describe the basics, and piles of them that discuss openings, etc., but even the texts that claim to be "intermediate" seem to assume that I know what a Sicilian opening is (or is that a defense?). My chess game is much like my golf game, in that I go out and hack away without really going to the driving range to learn the strokes. I read a book that describes a game that was previously played by a master, and annotates the "why" behind his/her moves, but after a list of three to four moves I can't visualize the board in my head any longer. I do have Chess-Master software, and that has a large number of games in it, but somehow I'm not even sure how to analyze them. Again, I'm sorry for being so basic, but I seem to have hit a block on how to become a better player. Watching out for potential skewers, forks, etc., is fairly straightforward

(not that I catch them all the time), and I can formulate an attack without leaving myself too exposed, but beyond that I get a little lost. I see mention of how d4 vs. e4 can lead to an open or closed board, and I can't even see that. I'm not opposed to doing some studying or reading, but I feel it should be of some value or I'd rather just sit and enjoy a game. I think I'm on the verge of taking my game to the next level of understanding, but I need some guidance.
—USA

A. The secret is not to obsess about what you're doing, but to enjoy it. The more you enjoy, the better you'll become, and that's true even for chess. Genuine growth takes time. Always try to keep the big picture in mind by centering on the small. Be willing to settle for tiny but certain advances, and stay context based. If you blow a particular endgame, try to find out why. If you mishandle an opening, try to learn how you could have managed it better. Be specific, with no immediate urgency to solve a larger problem. Just keep taking things in stride and eventually real gains will be made. By sheer accumulation of experience, parts will begin to fit into place naturally, without your having to put them anywhere.

A much greater power, more potent than our own controlling consciousness, insures that each cog turns the wheel the way it works best. I suspect wisdom has already informed you of this. As the sage says: "To everyone is given the key to the gates of heaven; the same key opens the gates of hell."

FUN

Q. I have been playing for about a year now. I mostly play because I enjoy the game, but I do like to win occasionally too. I don't spend a lot of time studying books or opening variations. I learned the basic principles of opening play, and rather than playing a move by reflex, I like to play based on those principles. Sometimes I fall victim to various traps and tricks, but I find after I fall for a trap a couple of times, I tend to recognize it in the future. I realize that if you want to achieve master level, then eventually you will need to engage in endless study, but for the ca-

sual (semi-serious) player, isn't there definitely something to be said for just learning good fundamentals, and simply playing?
—*USA*

A. There's always something to be said for learning the ground rules and applying them. Even masters do that. There's also something to be said for "simply playing." Masters do that, too. Chess survives because it's a game that millions of mortals play for their own reasons, one of the most common being simple enjoyment. If it had been left only to those who spend their every waking hour studying its intricacies—the so-called chess gods—it would have vied with the dodo bird for extinction. We don't need wings to sense the supremacy of flight.

BECOMING MORE ACTIVE

Q. I really appreciate your efforts to help the great unwashed masses. I hit the wall several years ago around 1700 USCF, and I can't seem to progress. I find in looking over my past games and in playing new games that I inevitably drift into passive positions. Training texts provide numerous examples of how to proceed from a strong position, but I seem to be missing something between the opening and the kinds of positions from which middlegame book exercises begin. It happens even against weaker players. I feel as though, in trying to respond reasonably to my opponent's threats, I can never identify active choices. I also feel no matter how aggressive an opening is, I can't develop attacking chances unless the book line comprises an actual attack. Perhaps this is a problem common to many class B players, and I (we) would greatly appreciate any advice that you can offer.
—*USA*

A. Your difficulties appear to be twofold. Your play seems to lack spark, and you tend to lose your way if there's nothing clear and definite to do. The latter can be among the hardest situations to play from, so it's not surprising that you're having trouble with them. Grandmasters sometimes lose their way in such circumstances, too. There are no panaceas, no Band-Aids. You simply have to get stronger.

9

There are some things you can try. Play over games that usually last between 15 and 25 moves, and do as many tactical, real-game problems as you can. In this regard, and with respect to either of these two tasks, it's not as necessary to analyze exhaustively, not that I'm trying to discourage you from doing what I practically always seem to recommend. But since you appear to be more concerned with your general lack of activity, it makes sense, for now, to focus on what's active and what's not, rather than placing all your emphasis on developing your analytic skills (though you shouldn't neglect those either).

It might help to plan weekly marathon sessions, say two to four hours, where you try to play over dozens, if not hundreds, of shorter games at high speed. You can do this better on your computer, but it could also be performed over the board. To make it more engaging, you can try it with a friend, and that should slightly decrease the number of missed mistakes and slightly increase the number of useful pointers seen and noted. You can become more active by playing a lot of speed chess, and also just by trying to think "active." If you stay mindful of a problem, you have a much better chance to tackle and eventually correct it. Maybe this advice will help you somewhat, though I question its value to the "great unwashed." They have their own ways of thinking, and I'd prefer that they stayed inactive (one can hope), possibly not even going to tournaments at all. I admit that the game would lose some quality productions, but the whole chess world would smell so much sweeter.

STARTING AGAIN

Q. Well, I learnt how to play chess five months ago, and I just love this game. I want to improve more and more. I read *My System* by Nimzowitsch three times, and then *Chess Praxis*. Well, there lies the problem: I got to be a positional player, so I get into the middlegame quite well, and I have almost always a plan, but when I don't have one, my plan is to direct all my attention to the center of the board, and amazingly I always achieve my goal of "taking the center." But, when I achieve the domination of the center and I have a winning position, I don't know what to do next. Maybe I need to learn how to mobilize my pieces. A friend of mine, a very strong player, told me that I don't know what to do when I get the

rooks in the center and need to control them. I'm a perfectionist, neither an attacking nor a defensive player. I don't have a rating yet, but I can beat a 1700 ChessMaster 9000 rated player quite easily, and I beat a 2000 yesterday. What should I do to improve my play? Should I worry about the lack of plans in the ending? I don't study chess by obligation, I just sit in front of the PC and study four hours a day. I really love it.
—*Brazil*

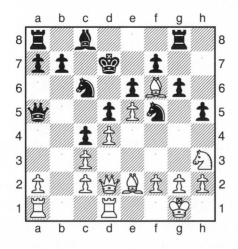

Kmoch-Nimzowitsch, Bad Niendorf 1927
Black shows us how it's done after a mere 47 moves more.

A. You've entered the building by skipping the ground floor. I know Superman can do that but I'm not sure about chess players. It appears that you've been dealing with advanced subjects (planning and other sophisticated positional themes) before you've built up a foundation on which to base your thinking and judgment. I recommend that you go back to fundamentals. Make sure you really grasp opening essentials (the principles governing development, the fight for the center, king safety, the control and use of open lines, seizing and maintaining the initiative, and how to win a won game). Any of the classic texts will do here, such as Capablanca's *Chess Fundamentals* or Tarrasch's *The Game of Chess*.

But perhaps even more than learning opening principles you've got to concentrate on tactics—all kinds of tactics—including mating tactics, non-mating tactics, and all their various implementations throughout the phases. And there never can come a point when you know enough that you no longer have to keep your mind active and sharp by solving such practical problems. It goes on forever, but you shouldn't mind, for it's clear you love the game and its move-by-move challenges.

LOSING INTEREST

Q. I have been playing chess for more than 20 years (gosh, where has the time gone?). I reached a rating of 1820 (Welsh chess union—I guess this is about 1920 USCF) but now I am slowly going downhill. I am about 25 points lower every year. Being semi-retired, I now spend about 15 hours a week studying chess. I identified my two biggest weaknesses, opening play and tactics, and I concentrate on these. I play against my computer at home, other people in the chess club once a week, and play in four tournaments a year, which amounts to about 100 rated games a year.

The problem is this: When I sit down to play a game I have no "fear factor." There is no "kick," no thrill anymore. It is just not exciting. I usually play opponents in the range 1500 to 2000, and I can win against a 2000 and lose against a 1500. I can play brilliantly one game and terribly the next; I have lost all reliability. I find it almost impossible to concentrate on the game. I find that the result of a game is not the most important thing anymore. If I play well then I am happy (even if I lose), but if I play badly then I am ashamed about the way I played (even if I win). After a bad game I say to myself "I *know* that I am better than this, so why do I play such rubbish?" During a game that I am playing badly, I will talk to myself and try to raise my game, but I just cannot "lift" myself back to a level that I know I am capable of! It has become so bad that I am thinking about giving up the game. Have I overdosed on chess? A friend suggested that I try to play opponents a class higher. What do you think?
—*USA*

A. The last thing you want to do is play against opponents who could kick your butt all the time, unless you find some personal pleasure in being crushed more efficiently. (Are you sure the advice came from a friend?) It does seem as if you need a holiday. I propose that you take a vacation from chess for a while, in spite of its tempting appeal. Then stand firm. Don't re-enter the combat zone until further resistance is impossible, and you simply must play chess.

At that point you should go back to the board and start chessing, without the slightest regard for anything other than pure entertainment. If playing still isn't any fun, why bother to persist? How many lives do you have to waste? Find something else to amuse yourself with and be happy that the game has provided you with a valuable life lesson, that you're not a pawn and chess isn't the only way to advance to happiness. All right, maybe it is, but the last time I said that I got letters.

LOWERING THE CHESS HANDICAP

Q. I am a novice female player. About seven months ago I started playing chess at a nearby chess club. I had not played since I was a teen but thought it would be fun and a nice social outlet. I was given a novice rating of 750 and placed on the club's ladder (literally at the bottom) for weekly play. I became totally enthralled with the game and spent hours on my computer with ChessMaster, studied openings, your endgame book and tactical puzzle books. After all of this I believe I understand the game much better and, in spite of the fact I very seldom win, I enjoy it. Nevertheless, my interest is beginning to wane as I have made no progress in playing better and my rating is now 745. I don't need a chess teacher—I need a chess therapist! Can you offer any encouragement for those of us who are starting out but apparently don't have an aptitude for the game? I went through this same process when I took up golf. I am now an 11 handicap, so I know that somewhere along the line I will break through in chess (particularly since my goals are modest). When does that usually happen? What should I do to keep my enthusiasm up?
—*USA*

A. Chess improvement doesn't happen just like that, and seven months isn't necessarily a long time to wait to see results. Sometimes advancement can take years. I'm sure you experienced this at golf. It helps that your goals are reasonable and modest. If you stay with competition, think less about how you fare against others and more about getting something out of the experience to better yourself.

Right now you're probably on a learning plateau, where you're steadily acquiring ideas and techniques that won't manifest themselves until you reach the end of the plateau. At that point you'll be able to see the next level, with a realistic chance to jump ahead, but before then it might seem as if you're not making any gains at all, even though you're clearly learning and encountering new challenges.

I suggest that you stay with the game, continuing to do those things that have given you pleasure, rather than seeking panaceas and setting yourself lots of burdensome tasks. So just keep playing ChessMaster. It's perfectly satisfactory to study openings, endgames, and tactics, if these activities afford you real intellectual excitement. When you love something, it usually loves you back, and if you continue doing chess for the right reason, because it pleases you, it's certain that you'll climb the ladder of life if not the ladder in your unsympathetic chess club.

REGIMEN

Q. I need some help! I am a beginner chess player (Under 1300). I live in a very small town (Lunenburg, Nova Scotia), and have no access to a chess club or instructors. I have purchased ChessMaster 9000, and also your book *The Chess Doctor*. I also play on the Internet, usually longer games. I find the more I learn, the less I know about what I thought I knew and sometimes my game (if I ever had one) really falls apart. There is so much information out there, but where to start? Even with Chess-Master it is hard to know how to pace oneself. Do you have any advice for setting up a basic self-training regimen? Some basic formula for going from step one to perhaps getting to the point where I should start studying openings?
—*Canada*

A. Chess players typically ponder such questions at some point or another. Most of us are used to following a stepwise regimen that begins with small and defined building blocks and moves toward more complex models. We start by learning the verb, then how it's conjugated.

But chess doesn't have a step one. To improve at the game, one doesn't need to follow a particular path and I don't teach that way. I try to take into account that every student is different—in who they are, what they already know, how they learn, and what they like to study. So to offer a definite course or procedure, without respect to the total picture, regardless of the student's human qualities, would actually defy everything I've believed, practiced, and professed in the teaching trade.

Still, I understand why you are feeling overwhelmed. Even a grand chess thinker can feel that way now and then (some explain the sentiment by comparing chess to art, or even to life itself, or to something analogous and equally humorous). Begin where there's a situation that piques your interest. It could be a particular opening, or a king-and-pawn ending you've found perplexing or intriguing. More important than what you focus on is how you focus on it—naturally, with zeal and a desire to learn.

It would be easy to list several books you could consult. But that wouldn't mean that other books aren't at least as good or even better. I may not know of the other volumes, I may have forgotten them, I might not think of them while in the moving vehicle I may at that moment be occupying, or I may have misjudged them or you altogether. That's why I recommend you go to cornucopian sources and judge for yourself. Compare numerous manuals and you'll be able to tell firsthand which ones you're likely to enjoy reading. You might make a mistake, and choose a book you've over-appreciated, but such errors provide powerful hands-on experience for subsequent decision making. The best learning is self-learning, even when selecting books you know little about.

Nevertheless, here's a practical suggestion. On a daily basis, solve a certain number of tactical chess problems—those that might apply to real games. Take them from books you've picked yourself. Don't set the problems up on a board. Do them in your head, no matter how hard. If you move the pieces, you're getting away with murder: your own. I'm not suggesting that you stay with some of the trickier problems forever, but make sure you invest enough time—time you can live with—before checking the answer. You'll want to reach a point when confirmation is unnecessary, because you'll have the confidence to know you're right.

In addition to working on your tactics, you might want to play over game collections with annotations. Games played by any of the world champions or top players are a good place to begin, but even more important are the annotations. You should scan them, and they should clearly summarize in practical words the essence of what's happening. That way you have the option of skipping the note if it's needless or not particularly helpful.

Finally, play challenging opposition as often, fearlessly, and exuberantly as you can. Chess and learning are games that prosper on bravery. You obviously have passion for the game. Before there were chess teachers and learning programs, the desire and will to succeed were all most of us had. I suspect they'll still work even in today's high-tech, circuit-driven chess rain forest.

BREAKING BAD HABITS

Q. I am a 30-year-old who has been playing chess off and on for 20 years. I understand the basics (I know a skewer from a pin) but I don't seem to have any sort of ability to really understand the game. From time to time I've tried reading books, playing through games, and I've memorized a few openings here and there, but I get frustrated at my almost glacial progress and I'm still a patzer at best. I would absolutely love to become a chess player rather than just pushing wood around. Is it possible to gain seriousness after 20 years of bad habits? Or should I stick with the novice setting on my chess program? If it isn't too late, can you recommend any training programs that might lead to a better understanding of chess?
—*USA*

A. It's never too late to improve, especially if you love chess as much as your email suggests. You might start by getting your game critiqued, to see expressly what's wrong with it and what should be overhauled. It's always best to identify problems before attempting to solve them, and too often general advice applies more to abstract concepts than to individual people.

If you can, take a few sessions with a chess teacher or strong player aimed mainly at understanding how you might proceed—two to four meetings should suffice. Ask your instructor to spell out a course of study you could pursue on your own, primarily with books and software, over the next six months or so. You can always go back when the time is fitting for follow-up.

If that's not feasible, try to obtain chess software with tests that claim to assess your strengths and weaknesses, while judging the level of your overall play. I suppose even crude evaluations are better than nothing, although this is just a supposition. Once you get some system feedback, you can supplement your efforts with literature designed to deal with the areas of your greatest apparent need. The front and back covers of chess books can help you pick out volumes that might be pertinent (that's where I get some of my best ideas).

Other than that, you could review annotated games contested by strong players, solve lots of tactical, real-game problems (making sure not to move the pieces), and play as often as you can against strong opposition, especially those who think a lot about their own play and want you to know it. They have the potential to say wondrous things, and some of the commentary might even be instructive. Good luck, and may you enjoy the quest no matter the results, since that's the truest path to happiness and time well spent.

PLATEAUS

Q. I was wondering what you'd recommend for the discouragement that you feel when you plateau, not that *you* ever do, but most of us are mere mortals. You mentioned at some point that chess learning is often a quantum process, with little improvement for periods of time followed by sudden jumps. Undeniably, though, the periods of stagnation suck. I follow a regimented training schedule involving lots of tactical exercises with some theory thrown in. Do you have any suggestions how I can get through periods in which I feel I'm going nowhere?
—*Canada*

A. I know of no immediate solution to your problem. You're going to have to ride it out and survive. Sometimes, in order to do that, we have to take a break. That's why vacations were invented. Possibly, if you can find some other activities to engage your interest, or even if you simply do nothing other than rest, you might whet your appetite for further involvement and come back with just enough renewed vigor to lift you to the next echelon. Besides, even when we stop thinking about a situation consciously our minds still pursue things unconsciously. So why not apply a little enforced relaxation to the problem? See some movies you've wanted to see, or read some books you've wanted to read. None of them have to be about chess or anything remotely like it (which is the way some people look at this column).

COUNTERATTACK

Q. I'm 25 years old. Last year I rediscovered the game of chess, having not played more than half a dozen games in the last ten years. I bought a load of books and chess software and really started studying chess seriously for the first time. While I'm not completely dissatisfied with my progress, I came across a big problem. I am happy when my opponent plays attacking chess and I am defending and counterattacking. But when I play a player similar to myself (i.e., a counterattacker) I'm rarely able to win. My skills in planning and executing an attack on the opponent's position seem to be underdeveloped. Are there any books on the subject you could recommend?
—*The Netherlands*

A. I'm going to advise you to study game collections of great players known for their counterattacking skills rather than suggest a particular book on the subject. This method takes into account all the different styles that a counterattacker might have to face, and is, therefore, more complete. If you examine hundreds and maybe even thousands of such examples, you should develop an increased sensitivity for the critical small points on which such positions hinge. You can best do this with software, though literature can do the job, albeit more slowly and with greater labor on your part.

For this enterprise, two counterattackers come to mind, and each is radically different from the other. They are Korchnoi and Karpov. Certainly, there are other players who would serve your needs nicely and adequately, but in the games of these two giants there is a full range of challenging circumstances. Use them, and you will sharpen your own play on the cutting edge of developing chess theory.

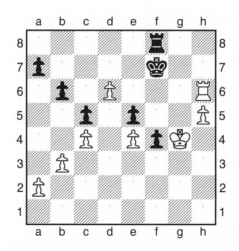

Petrosian-Korchnoi, USSR 1963
Black wins with the unexpected counterattack 1. ... f3!.

STRENGTHENING YOUR WEAKNESSES

Q. My name is Josh and I'm 17 years old. I am from San Antonio, Texas, and I'm not a prodigy or a great chess player, but I do love chess. I know you are probably sick of answering questions, so I will make it short. Other than paying for a tutor, how can I find out what I need to work on as a chess player? I have no problem reading up on chess or studying matches but how do I know what to work on without knowing what my weaknesses are? Any help would be appreciated.
—USA

A. The most accurate indicator of what you need to do is your own play. Here's what I'd do if I were you. I'd play as much serious chess as I could, against the best players available. I'd approach each game with total concentration, as if the future of humanity depended on my efforts, just as any artist should in any discipline. After each contest I'd try to understand why things happened and how I could have done them better. If necessary, I'd ask every good player I could corral what he or she thought of this and that.

If I were to read books, and certainly I would, I'd turn to collections of annotated games that would allow me to get inside the heads of top players, so I could be just a little bit more like them—those who've been through the wars and lived to tell about it. Overall, I'd give each game and every task my full heart, believing that our world is basically fair, and trusting that sincerity and dedication will bring insight and ultimate success.

BOARDING SCHOOL STUDY

Q. I'm 14 years old and have been playing chess seriously for about a year and a half. My rating is approximately 1400, but next week I am going to boarding school and am afraid I will not find many human opponents to practice against. Simply put, what methods would you suggest that I use when I can't find an opponent? Obviously, I can play on the Internet, but I would also appreciate hearing about any exercises I could use on my own.
—*USA*

A. As you've suggested, it can't hurt to solve tactical exercises daily. These should reflect real-game situations and present enough difficulty to make you work at finding the solution. Solve problems in your head, without moving the pieces, at least until the planet loses all its oxygen or there's peace on Earth, whichever comes first. Don't even bother to set up the positions. Just do the tactics directly from any book that appeals to you. This should force you to learn how to analyze in your head, if your progress is to be consequential.

If you've brought your set with you, or have access to a board on screen, you might be able to pursue another project: the creation of your own chess course, relying chiefly on game collections. As an inspiration, you could begin with something similar to the program that the late Jack Collins used to advocate. I think he called it his "world champions course," and many of his students benefited from it. If I understood it right, Jack would have his students play over 100 games of every world champion. This would now consist of 1500 first-class games. The program is compelling because you can see all the vital conceptions of an era reified by the game's leading exponents. The likely outcome is that you'll experience a profusion of outstanding chess while getting a sense for the evolutionary flow of chess thinking. And it can be great fun.

You could start with Steinitz, though it wouldn't hurt to throw An-

20

derssen and Morphy into the mix, to have a fuller picture. Moreover, you could settle on fewer games per player, say 20 or 25, and you could even concentrate on specific openings, as Imre Konig did in his classic *From Morphy to Botvinnik*. That is, if you're interested in the Ruy Lopez, for example, you could see how Morphy played it, how Steinitz differed or reinforced Morphy, what Lasker contributed to related lines, and so on, taking key variations right up to more recent times. You might even vary your regimen further, focusing on the great players who never became world champion, such as Tarrasch, Rubinstein, Reshevsky, Keres, Stein, Larsen, Korchnoi, and all the rest. Whatever you choose to do, it should serve as an adventure into the realms of chess theory and self-exploration.

If none of this seems exciting enough, there's always the usual fare, such as playing postal chess, taking individual lessons, founding a chess club on campus, working with software, or competing on the Internet. You might even be able to establish the basis of a chess book, regularly writing down your analysis of positions. You could also examine your own games, however they're played, no matter the circumstances. It's almost an argument in favor of going to boarding school, where I hope your gains in both chess and life are brought to fruition.

COLLINS PROGRAM

Q. I was reading your column where you answered the kid going to boarding school. I am just curious as to what exactly the program advocated by Jack Collins is? Could you give some information about the man and his plan, or tell me where I could find it?
—*New Zealand*

A. Mr. Collins passed away several years ago. He never really put his plan in print. In conversations with him and his students that spanned some 30 years, I deduced this much. The course consisted of between 1000 and 1500 games, from various texts. Essentially, the student had to play through 100 games of every world champion. If he couldn't come up with 100 games for a particular player, he'd go with whatever could be found.

In addition to the world champions, Collins tapped the games of Tarrasch, Rubinstein, Pillsbury, Marshall, Nimzowitsch, and other immortals. The course wasn't a rigorous one in the strictest sense. He didn't give any tests, and he didn't always use the same collections.

Despite Jack's encouragement, not every one of his students followed the program. Some even wondered what I was talking about when I brought it up, so I stopped mentioning it. Unfortunately, I put it in a column and now have to account for my words, ill-advised as they were. But I still think Jack had a wonderful idea.

GOALS

Q. I am a 1500 player from Tennessee. I played a lot of competitive chess in high school, but since college started, I haven't had the time to develop or practice. My goal in chess is to make it to 2150. Do you think this is possible if I don't start getting really serious until I'm 23, as I am 21 now and won't graduate for two more years? If it is possible, what is the best way to do it? Are there steps I should take?
—*USA*

A. School can be demanding, so I understand why you're considering putting serious chess out of the way until you get your degree. But unless you're committing the *Critique of Pure Reason* to memory (they didn't even try that in *Fahrenheit 451*), I see no reason you can't complete your academic requirements while continuing to improve your chess game. Sure, it's no easy task, but life doesn't necessarily become any easier. When you get out of school, you're still going to have to work. I've been told that's a fairly full-time activity too, so it's doubtful you're suddenly going to possess several unencumbered years for chess study.

Can a 1500 player put aside the game for a couple of years and pick it up at age 23, eventually to achieve a rating of 2150, whatever all those numbers purport to mean? Of course you can. You're clearly intelligent and motivated. Moreover, you won't be over the hill at 23 (don't, however, let it go to 24), and 2150 is surely not Mount Everest. (Why not something more reasonable, like 2140?)

What's the best way to get to 2150 once you get to 23? If I knew that I'd tell you. But since I don't, I'll have to offer the same advice I'd give myself, even though I wouldn't be any more likely to listen to me either.

Simply play regularly and often against the strongest opposition you can encounter, pursuing this stimulating task with the same passion—maybe even more—than you invest in your college career. Allow those games (not general guidelines and the stale advice of old maxims) to tell you what you need to study, and go from there. If you open your heart to Caissa, she's honor bound to pay back your commitment in the universal currencies of knowledge, skill, and lifelong pleasure. Well, that's what I picked up in college.

ANNOTATING CHESS GAMES

Q. Recently, I began a self-study program involving collecting a number of Morphy's games and annotating them. By performing this exercise a few times a week, I'm hoping to gradually improve my calculation and visualization skills. However, I've noticed that, when I'm annotating the games, I frequently consider poor candidate moves and variations that result in serious blunders. Much of my thinking time is spent pondering poor or irrelevant moves and variations, a practice that strikes me as a serious liability in a real tournament game. In your experience, is this typical for an average player, or does one usually learn how to weed out poor variations more quickly as time goes on?
—*USA*

A. You are to be commended. Regularly annotating quality chess games is a stellar way to improve your play. Obviously, no tack is likely to be effective right away. Efficiency at any endeavor is a result of layered expertise. Expertise develops from practice. Keep at it, and you'll inevitably sharpen your diagnostic tools so that you can eventually focus on relevant moves efficiently from the start of any analysis. You shouldn't be astonished if you soon manifest solid progress, and other than those you surpass, who wouldn't be pleased by that kind of surprise?

GAME COLLECTIONS

Q. In a previous column, you mentioned a beginning player should play through *The ABC's of Chess*—the game collections of Alekhine, Botvinnik, and Capablanca. Which of these players should I begin with? —*USA*

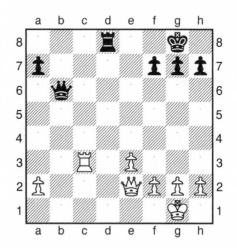

Bernstein-Capablanca, Moscow 1914
White resigned after Black played 1. ... Qb2.

A. You seem to be implying that you're a beginner. As I remember, the player who originally asked that question was not a beginner, but a 1300 player with a history. No matter. You have options. You could do it chronologically, starting with the world champion from Cuba (Capablanca). Or you could do it in terms of simplicity, starting with Capablanca. Or you could do it by the caprice of reverse alphabetical order, starting with the letter "C." All three of those approaches should work. But even better would be to circumvent the problem by commencing with Morphy, whether you're a 1300 player or you don't know all the rules and basics.

TRAINING SYSTEM

Q. I'm a 1620 player, having reached that level recently on the Internet. I'm not too bad with certain openings, though I sometimes blow the endgame. I admit I have some weaknesses in some endgames, but a teacher I know has told me I could be a quality endgame player if I studied with him every week, especially if he develops a special opening repertoire for me. He's an experienced Russian teacher who says he has a special system that he developed in the Soviet Union, not known to Americans, which is good for all the phases, so it will help my endgame. I was thinking, "What do you think of the White side of the Sicilian and the Black side of the King's Gambit, if I have the help of this teacher?"
—*USA*

A. Your question reminds me of an anecdote concerning the Viennese-born physicist Wolfgang Pauli (1900–1958), famous for his Exclusion Principle concerning electron orbits and spins. A graduate student had shown him a paper, wondering what the illustrious scientist thought of his unusual thesis. After scanning the paper, a confused Pauli supposedly said: "This isn't right. This isn't even wrong." I feel a little the same way about your question.

It's true that specific types of endgames are more likely to arise from certain opening variations, but studying the opening is not a sure way to improve a 1620 player's endgame, even if that particular four-digit number is achieved on the Internet, and despite the reassurances of an eminent trainer from a foreign land.

Then there's the matter of the opening phase you're going through. If you plan to play king-pawn openings for White, certainly you'll need to know how to cope when Black plays the Sicilian. But I'd be careful about investing all your marbles in the Black side of the King's Gambit, which is something you can't force because White doesn't have to start with a king-pawn opening (or move his f-pawn if he does). If White begins with a queen-pawn opening, responding with the King's Gambit could reduce you to the status of a chagrined graduate student trying to justify the impossible to Wolfgang Pauli.

Instead of worrying about chimerically phantasmagoric opening preparations, just look at your opponent's moves, answer them intelligently, and play chess. If that doesn't work, you can blame me. And if that doesn't work, there's always your acquaintance, the Russian trainer with the special system.

PLAYING DOWN

Q. I'm often bothered by ratings and how some players who aren't all that good get to be masters by winning lots of games against weaker players. I know this is true on the Internet where many A players beat up on C and B players. People won't even play you unless they think they can beat you or you are "chess challenged." Doesn't a player have an opportunity to get a higher rating just by winning 100 consecutive rated games against opposition a class beneath them?
—*USA*

A. Anyone who wins 100 rated games in a row has a real opportunity to gain rating points. We could also point out that some players won't even compete unless they have a good chance to win. But many other players are not afraid to "play up" because they realize that the competition is more challenging, they're going to learn more, and the payoff for winning is significantly greater.

It seems unfair that a player could garner a higher rating merely by winning many games against weaker opposition (possibly thereby increasing one's rating beyond his or her actual strength). But winning game after game is not a done deal. The possibility of losing or drawing an occasional game is very real, whether the opposition is a mere class below you or "chess challenged." Anyone can blunder, and if you keep playing weaker opposition, your zest for competition is likely to decrease. Meanwhile, a single letdown can cost you a batch of points, and you don't have to be outplayed to falter. You could be crushing your opponent, get cocky, and hang something, like the king. Or you could lose on time, since some unremarkable players can move remarkably rapidly.

Actually, anybody who wins 100 consecutive games against players a class lower is not only very lucky, he's probably very deserving of his higher rating. My advice to you is this: think less about the accuracy of your opponent's rating and more about the quality of your own moves. That will probably improve your numbers as well as your game.

SELF STUDY

Q. What is the best way for me to study my own games?
—*El Salvador*

A. There is no one best way to study your own games. To quote Monty Python, "We are all individuals." You're an individual, your games are individual to you, and your methods must therefore be individual. If there's a best way, it's merely the way that works best for you. Nonetheless, I will suggest a few things as a platform from which to springboard. You can modify what I outline here as you ascertain what appears to be more suitable to your personal needs.

Record your games somewhere, either in a notebook or, since you obviously have access to a computer, in an electronic file. If you can afford it, a tool like ChessBase would be ideal because of its ease of use, visual impact, and enormous databases.

After recording a particular game somewhere, play it over and write out your analysis. I would play through it at least twice, once from each side. You'd be amazed what can be discerned from another perspective, such as direct and potential threats.

Wherever you have doubts, make notes. Ask strong players about situations that stumped you. You can also send questions to various Web sites, such as Chesscafe.com, which has Gary Lane's excellent column on the openings. If it's feasible, you might consider having a few lessons from someone that can answer those annoying questions. It should be sufficient to take a session every month or so as material accumulates.

However you proceed, try to identify key moments when your games seemed to turn. Figure out, if you can, how you could have avoided unpleasant consequences by playing alternative moves that would have thwarted your opponents' threats. This way you'll tie your play and study together so that you're tackling relevant problems. The more diagrams and visual aids you can exploit the better. Fortunately, with many kinds of chess software, you can print out diagrams, so there's no need to draw them by hand. I would cut these out (the printed ones) and affix them to books, index cards, loose-leaf pages, and even walls or other surfaces that come under constant view.

Once you're able to determine a definite problem that pesters you, try to find illustrative paradigms from good players that cope with the same difficulties. How does Kasparov deal with that opening? How did Kramnik survive that assault? How had Anand played that ending? You can't cover everything. But if you try to find reasonable answers, and make useful associations, over time you'll add to your knowledge and gradually improve your play. So, there are many ways to go. Just stay alert and approach chess and its interplay with focus and an inquiring mind.

KEY MOMENTS

Q. I have been playing chess for years and recently turned to reading chess books. I like all kinds of chess books, even some of yours, though I think my favorite ones are game collections, especially of the great players. I've also noticed that in every game it seems there are key moments when you should start to think more. I must tell you that I have trouble figuring out when these moments are about to appear. Is there an exercise you could suggest to help me become better at recognizing them? *—USA*

A. I suppose you might become more receptive to those consequential junctures by focusing on the diagrams of annotated games. They're supposed to point out important moments during play. So take any typical game collection, go to game one, and concentrate on the first diagram. Try to guess the next move, and after a few minutes of pondering, check the subsequent text to see how well you did. Work through book after book this way, going from diagram to diagram, and it might make you slightly more attuned to those "key moments." It would help if you had a grandmaster willing to stand next to you and signal when those opportunities arise. But it's hard to get grandmasters to do that, so most of us just settle for doing the work ourselves, which also works, and it's a heck of a lot cheaper.

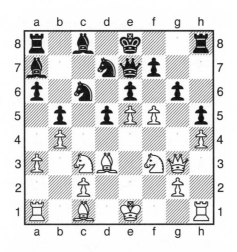

Spielmann-Keres, Noordwijk 1938
A typical key moment.
Black finds the brilliant defense, 1. ... Bb8!.

GETTING DIAGNOSED

Q. I am a 1650 player from Melbourne and have been playing for about 30 years. Perhaps an indication of my improvement is that over one ten-year stretch my rating went down one point! I play in regular Friday night tourneys and have a good grasp of openings, preferring tactics as opposed to positional style. However, my colleagues often comment that playing something like the Torre or Center Counter doesn't suit. The issue I have is that I seem to make simple mistakes against higher-rated players, which allow them to grind out the wins, and I often have difficulties with the lower-rated. Could you please give your thoughts on how a middle-ranked player like me could improve?
—Australia

A. Not to question any of your colleagues, but I'd look dubiously on opening recommendations offered by those who fail to discriminate between the Torre and the Center Counter. Maybe they have a reason to mislead you.

You write that you are losing to higher-rated players because you make simple mistakes. You might be committing the same types of errors against lower-rated players, too. Possibly, those lower-rated players lack the skills to take advantage of such errors, so it might appear as if you're not making the same kinds of mistakes when you actually are.

Nevertheless, I'm not even sure of this, and that's the point. I don't know enough about you to offer sound guidance, and you may not know enough about yourself to make objective statements about your own play. My advice is that you get your chess evaluated by a competent player, one at least 400 points stronger than you. (It shouldn't take more than a few sessions.) After your play is investigated and you hear the diagnosis, you'll have a better sense of why you've been at a standstill, and that's when you can take meaningful steps to remedy your situation. I'd also run a check on your colleagues.

CLASS A & B

Q. In one sense, when I look at games played by 1600 players and 1800 players, there doesn't seem to be much of a difference. Isn't the distinction a little bit arbitrary? Aren't the two rating classes (A and B) practically alike?
—USA

A. Try telling that to B players who continually lose to A players and see what they say. But actually, you have a point. Aside from an A player's undeniable superiority in opening knowledge, tactical awareness, endgame understanding, positional insight, analytic ability, and essentially more challenging experiences, the two classes are virtually indistinguishable.

WHAT TO BUY

Q. Yes . . . yes, I know it is a stupid question. But it seems to me no one is able to answer it: How can I improve? Should I study opening theory? Should I solve problems? Is there a book that can teach us 1800 players the way?
—Venezuela

A. If you're looking for *the* way, I suggest you turn to Lao-Tzu. The *Tao Te Ching* contains more valuable answers for 1800 players than you'll find in any chess book.

In fact, it's because no chess book has all the answers that some of us wind up buying hundreds of them. Many of these monographs actually do have something to offer, even when terribly written, as long as they contain at least one position we'd like to see a second time. It's nice to know that such a position is in a book sitting on our shelves, collecting dust with other positions and tomes.

You want to improve? My advice is to forget the printed word for now. Just play as often as you can, against the best competition you can find. You'll learn far more that way than from reading any one chess book. Now perhaps if you read two chess books . . .

SHOPPING FOR THE NEXT LEVEL

Q. I'm a 1900 USCF rated player and I just don't get any better. What suggestions do you have for me? I'm willing to buy the material that can get me to the next level.
—USA

A. There's nothing you can buy that will guarantee a gain in strength, so buy what you want, but buy for the right reasons. Buy chess books because you enjoy reading them. Buy chess software primarily because chess on computers stimulates you. Buy a chess teacher's time because you really want to understand the game. If you buy things for the right reasons your money will be well spent, and you'll have a good crack at achieving your subordinate goals, such as acquiring enough rating points to get to the next level. Why don't you play chess just to enjoy the pastime? That's the best way to get better at it. If you buy that, you don't have to buy anything else.

CLASS A TO EXPERT

Q. I have been "stuck" in Class A for more years than I care to remember. Yet, today I understand the game better, calculate deeper, read positions

better, and I'm now better at move selection than last year and find better tactical "shots" than in the past. Still the 2000 level eludes me. Every now and then I do poorly against lower-rated players (at some time during the tournament). My expert and master friends feel I should have a 2100 rating! Any thoughts? Any suggestions? What's the difference in Class A and Expert chess ability? It seems to be a thin mental line!
—*USA*

A. Ratings do mean something, but not everything. Some people excel in competition and others bomb. It would help if I understood what your friends mean when they say you play at the 2100 level. Do they truly feel you are a 2100 player, or that some aspects of your game are that good, or something else? If you really want to know where you stand, I recommend that you have your game evaluated by an experienced analyst. Find someone to judge your play objectively while making specific suggestions to propel you onward and in the right direction.

Admittedly, there is a difference between Class A (1800) and Expert (2000). Experts tend to be at least a little more careful, a little more knowledgeable, a little better prepared, and, perhaps, a little more experienced. It's often a matter of little things, but unfortunately, in this game, little things often matter. Factor in the mental line you mention, a line that may be thin but defiantly impenetrable, and no wonder headway can seem impossible. But it does appear that you're close. Get that assessment and have a course of action laid out for you. With a fresh start you'll feel inspired and be ready to move forward. Good luck on your purposeful adventure.

NUMERICAL ASSESSMENTS

Q. I just read your column for the first time and really enjoyed it. I currently play on the ICC (Internet Chess Club) and I am rated at around 1600, depending on the day. To give you some background, I started playing chess when I was five, won some tournaments and ended up quitting when I was nine. I am now 37 and have just started playing again for about the past year. What I am finding is that I am not improving much, so I have started to re-evaluate the way that I play. Here's where the question comes in. I am trying now to play my game based on the imbalances that I see on the board instead of a constant calculation mode. By imbalances, I mean that I take a step back and look at the entire picture, trying to evaluate the specifics of both players' pieces and play based on those imbalances (time, space, material, strong or weak minor pieces, etc). In constant calculation mode, my thoughts would instead follow, "I move, he moves, I take him, he takes me, etc." Will this work pay off in the end? I do say work because it requires a lot of concentration to understand an entire game from a picture and a list of moves. —*Canada*

A. You ask if I think the work you're doing will pay off in the end. I take this to mean it hasn't paid off yet. I won't pretend to comprehend your program, or quite what you're saying, but it seems as if you're attempting to assign numerical values to chess concepts and then basing your play on those assessments. That's the kind of thing computers do. Are you trying to think like a computer?

It might make more sense to find a chess teacher and let him or her evaluate your game, and maybe your thinking processes. See what the teacher thinks about the constant calculation mode before going any further (it may have already gone far enough). Not only are you possibly wasting time, but you may be on the verge of falling into a trap similar to the one that snared Franklin K. Young. Young, a chess innovator from bygone times, had many creative ideas, but few of them enabled people to improve their chess. So let's get back to reality. If you want to play chess better, try to understand your opponents' intentions before responding. Do that by analyzing moves, not by assigning values.

1600 TO EXPERT

Q. I have a question about a program for study. I am a 14-year-old player, obviously improving, as I have gone up in rating about 300 or 350 points over the past six months. I want to know how much study and play you think would be required to be an expert in a year, which is my

chess goal this year. Also, my coach who comes every week is a factor. (I'm 1600 right now.) I would like your master analysis to help me.
—*USA*

A. Chess improvement is not like that. There's no automatic formula for gaining 400 or more points in a year, such as for rising from Class B to Expert. But it's clear you have a passion for chess. So it probably doesn't matter what you do. You're bound to fly ahead merely on your love for the game. Nevertheless, if I were you, I'd try to find stimulating opponents who I could play seriously every week. Then I'd analyze those games with my teacher. That would likely aid your game a great deal. But you seem to be the type of kid who will forge his own path. Do it your way and make it work. Just remember Yogi Berra's sage advice, "If you come to a fork in the road, take it."

CLUB PLAY

Q. I am a strong beginning player with a rating of around 2100. I enjoy the competition of tournament chess, but am unsure of club chess. I have been to a couple of club meetings and I am unsure how this type of play will affect my strength. What do you think?
—*USA*

A. I don't know many beginning players who have ratings around 2100 (actually, you're the only one). I don't think it matters so much what your rating is, or where you play. What's important is who you play, and you can find challenging opponents practically anywhere, even at clubs. So if you're unconvinced about the caliber of opposition at your local chess club, just give it a try and see. If it proves not to be up to your plane, you can go back to tournaments all the wiser. Be warned, however, those ordinary 1600, 1700, and 1800 players can be amazingly good, even with unremarkable ratings.

SERIOUS PREPARATION

Q. I am a chess player with an ELO rating of 2000. In three months I will play in a very important tournament with rivals 200 points higher. How must I prepare? I want to win. Actually, I am playing twice per week, and solving tactical problems every day. Could you advise me on a method of training?

—*Chile*

A. Every other course of action pales before direct experience. The best way to prepare for upcoming games with 2200 players is to play 2200 players now. Furthermore, if you want to support your effort with study, it makes sense to analyze those training games afterward, preferably with the aid of a strong player, at least 2400 strength (2500 would be even better). The point is that your practice should simulate real-game conditions. With Armageddon only three months off, I'd start banging heads with chess masters before it's too late.

RATING DECLINE

Q. I have a rating of 2048 in the FIDE list (it has steadily declined from 2095). I don't play tournaments that regularly. People tell me (and I even believe) that I play much better in practice than in tournaments. I am prone to losing my nerve in the critical moment, especially in time pressure. I used to be a decent blitz player, but nowadays I have become terrible at it. In the early days (i.e., when I got a rating in 1994–1995) I liked playing in a flourishing style, wanting to attack and take risks all the time. But then *My System* hit me. It had a calming influence on my style. I read the book three times and also *Die Blockade*. I became an ardent follower of the great man (Nimzowitsch). I started to try to emulate him. There was some initial success, but later I realized in order to play the way he did one needs tactical and positional skills of the highest order together with a clear line of thinking. He used to bail himself out of difficult positions (if he got into one at all) through tactical skirmishes. A prominent player suggested to me that to understand the game better one has to study its evolution from Morphy's and Steinitz's days. I am 28 and this is all taking a long time. I earn my living by chess coaching, where I spend half of my productive time. I am sick and tired of being at this playing level. I want to rise. I will be really grateful if you suggest to me a training regimen, or whatever, that suits my condition.

—*India*

A. Allow me to reassure you. A drop of 47 points, from 2095 to 2048, shouldn't be cause for anxiety. Feel free to regard the two numbers as inconsequentially different. Frankly, ratings are hardly dependable measures of actual skill. You get a number, and it tells you little about the factors and conditions producing it. Be careful, because the number of numbers in today's world has gotten way out of hand.

It could be that your rating has simply gone back to where it should have been. Maybe you're still overrated, or perhaps you're actually underrated. We have no way of saying anything for sure. And since you aren't playing in tournaments regularly, your rating is even more likely to be unreliable, so you shouldn't place such emphasis on it. You wouldn't stress deleterious and erratic indicators with your students. Why do so with yourself?

You also point out that you're no longer a decent blitz player. But blitz, like ratings, shouldn't be considered a trustworthy gauge of genuine chess proficiency. Indeed, blitz tends to be superficial. Most blitz games hinge on playing threat after threat to force the opponent into time trouble. Your strategy depends on hoping that the other side blunders so you can clean up and win.

Let's not overlook the company you've been keeping. For some time you've been engrossed in Nimzowitsch and his awe-inspiring pronouncements. Naturally, in trying to grapple with his mind-blowing abstractions and stupefying concepts (often expressed as if the man wrote them in schizophrenic frenzy), you're more likely to get into time trouble and lose sight of ordinary things, such as your undefended b-pawn. Your adversaries will then be poised to take your b-pawn and plausibly some of its unsuspecting comrades. Suddenly, your opponents are the ones blessed with opportunities to clean up and deliver mate.

BECOMING AN IM

Q. I am a club player with an ELO 1850 (on the Internet, 2160). For a long time, I collected and worked on chess books, and studied articles by grandmasters in magazines. But because of my job, it is not possible for me to play in tournaments often. To be an International Master, which method or books would you recommend?

—*Turkey*

A. I don't necessarily prefer this method, but the only one that really works is to beat up on other good players in tournaments and practice sessions. I wish there were some easy way, such as reading a certain book or books or even performing a thought experiment, where the desired result is imagined and that's as good as actually doing it. There's no collection of books that can make you an International Master. (I'm surprised you haven't set your goals on the Grandmaster title, which is only a notch higher.) You must rely on real competition against formidable opposition, and even playing against stronger players might not work, since most of us don't have the talent to get that good. (I'm not saying that about you, of course.)

Now you say you can't play in tournaments because of your job. Does that mean your job doesn't afford you the time to play in tournaments? Or does it mean that your work times conflict with the usual times tournaments are held? If it's the former, there's nothing to be done, and it makes no sense to suggest anything because you don't have the physical time. If it's the latter, there's hope. It's called the Internet, which you already play on, as your 2160 rating indicates.

Instead of just playing on the Internet, however, why don't you play with greater purpose and enter Internet tournaments? But even if you decide otherwise, you can still set parameters that bring you into contact with stronger opposition. After losing a set of games, you can then go to your source materials (you may want to get some if you don't already have any, especially stuff on the openings). This process of playing and reviewing your own games may not make you an International Master, but it should make you a stronger player, and for most of us that's good enough.

CHAPTER 2

Teaching or Preaching

The art of teaching chess is a popular topic for coaches, teachers, organizers, and parents. My readers wanted to know where they could find teachers, which ones would work best for them, and what I thought about certain training methods. Some of the more intriguing queries focused on ethical issues, such as how to change teachers.

Many questions came from chess coaches. They asked all kinds of questions about techniques and approaches. They were curious about gaining control of a class, and what role they should play, if any, after lessons came to an end. Included in the mix are a few other questions about the chess profession in general.

One coach wrote in about a salient issue: he wanted to know if he should touch students as a sign of approval. I did my best to address this, and other controversial topics sincerely, but I confess I had my own doubts and questions as soon as my answers appeared. At times I wondered if I was sounding more like a therapist than a teacher. But there were some lighter moments, too. I especially enjoyed people asking me for advice they told me I was not qualified to give. Clearly, it's not that easy to make the best of one's idle time.

BEST APPROACH

Q. Has there ever been a study on what is the best approach to teach chess to children and/or adults? If so, what is it? Is the study available as a book, a paper, or online? Lastly, what is your assessment of the study? Thanks ever so much for your columns and books.
—*USA*

A. To my knowledge there are no such studies (there are many suggested programs, but I wouldn't call them studies), and if there were, their authors would be subject to verbal abuse from dissenting chess teachers. Most teachers will recommend their own systems, and that's that.

But that doesn't mean they don't agree on anything. Teachers generally think it's important to absorb basics, play regularly against good opposition, practice analyzing without moving the pieces, solve lots of tactical puzzles, work hard and stay focused while competing, and play the game for its challenge and fun. They may see eye to eye on a few more things too, but let's not press our luck.

FINDING A TEACHER

Q. How do I go about looking for a chess tutor in my city? There certainly aren't any in our Yellow Pages. Any tips as to where to start?
—*Canada*

A. I have a couple of suggestions. If you hear of an upcoming chess tournament in your area, go to the event and ask the organizers and players for references. You might even play a few games while you're at it (you never know where that will lead). I would visit nearby chess clubs and see what they have to offer. Scholastic chess clubs might also be worth checking out, even if you're not in school, because some youngsters have coaches or friends who take lessons. You could contact your own national chess federation. You could even go on the Internet and do a search for chess clubs. You'll find lots of helpful information there, including chess chat rooms where you can ask other fans who they know in your part of the world. If you're pesky enough, one of these approaches might succeed. You never know.

CHANGING TEACHERS

Q. I am a USCF expert and a chess teacher. I read your columns regularly and find your suggestions to be extremely insightful. My favorite books change almost daily, but the ones I recommend to my (usually advanced) students (1500–1800) include: *My System* by Nimzowitsch, *Think Like a Grandmaster* by Kotov, *My Best Games of Chess 1908–1937* by Alekhine, *My 60 Memorable Games* by Fischer, and my all-time favorite, *Zurich International Chess Tournament, 1953* by Bronstein. These are all classics, and I believe that beginning chess players should become familiar with these before they consider tackling more recent great books such as *Fire on Board* by Shirov, anything by Dvoretsky, or John Watson's *Secrets of Modern Chess Strategy*. However, the teacher should be very familiar with these and other resources, not only for the wealth of practical examples but also to help his or her students to understand and enjoy the complexities of the game. I also have a question. I have a student who has tremendous potential. She has blossomed under (or perhaps despite) my tutelage, and is now ready for more advanced training. I have recommended that she find a fairly strong master to help her in person, but she is having difficulty locating someone who is compatible with her personality and skills. She is a young teenager who has gained almost 600 rating points in three years to break 1900 USCF. If she decides to enlist the services of someone via the Internet, how would you recommend she select her next teacher?
—USA

A. Obviously, your student is quite talented, but I'm also sure she's benefited greatly from your expertise, your concern, and your sincerity. It takes a very wise and loving teacher to recognize that sometimes the best way to help a student is to help her move on. And this suggests an answer to your question.

You can feel free to take an active role in helping her find a new chess teacher, whether through the Internet or by some other means. As her teacher you're trying to counsel her, and finding a new teacher involves making some really difficult decisions. With her approval, and surely that of her parents, you could take the initiative in exploring new possibilities.

You could, for instance, conduct the interviews and make the introductions. You could ask the necessary questions to maintain continuity and insure a smooth transition. And you could help the student finalize the new alliance by reviewing the first couple of lessons and providing sincere feedback. After the new lessons assume their own life, there's no reason you couldn't check in now and then to see how things are going.

I'm not saying that you should interfere with the new teacher's lessons. That would be counterproductive and probaby injurious to the student. But it's perfectly reasonable to monitor how your former student is doing, maintaining your association as a kind of mentor, especially if the affiliation remains mutually beneficial to both of you. It's the natural outcome of any good teaching relationship: lifelong respect, support, and friendship. Surely the new teacher ought to understand that, since these are things he or she should want as well. Good luck. It may not be easy to find another you.

COACHES AND RATINGS

Q. My question regards coaching. My rating is around 1850. My performance for the past several months has been approximately 2100. My coach is about 100 points higher than me. Do you recommend I switch to a stronger coach?
—*USA*

A. You can still benefit from a teacher, coach, or trainer whose rating is barely higher than yours, but how much depends on several factors. The two primary ones would be how good you really are as a player and how good your coach is as a coach. Let's face it—ratings are meaningful but they aren't everything. Surely there are other considerations, too numerous to enumerate, that transcend mere numbers. Clearly, ratings can be ridiculously inflated or unfairly deflated by hundreds of points. Even the chess simians that think numerical index constitutes true worth as an individual—and I'm not suggesting you fall into this category—must admit that the numbers themselves are dubious. Can you really be certain that you're playing like a solid 2100 player? Some teachers automatically conclude that anyone posing such a question can't possibly be a member of the class to which their question refers. Of course, I'm not drawing this inference about you, your class, or your question.

If ratings were the only issue to be evaluated when selecting a coach, it would be a huge concession to work with anyone less qualified than Kasparov or Kramnik. I wonder how they feel hiring trainers 200 points below them in rating. It must be terribly demeaning. What could they possibly get from such people, who they could crush like a flea? Maybe they want some of the same things you try to obtain, albeit at a much lower level, from a coach merely possessing a 1950 rating. Maybe they just need another objective yet sympathetic voice. Maybe your own coach is so adept at coaching that he can actually help an 1850 player achieve a performance level of 2100 for several months when it's unclear that the results are merited. Or maybe the coach had nothing to do with it.

Certainly we all want our coaches to have a grasp of their subject matter, so that we can rely on what they're saying. Most of us also need a certain measure of encouragement, which can't be factored into a rating algorithm, to help us keep moving ahead. Some coaches are particularly good at this, and some aren't. In the end, switching coaches must come down to how you feel about your coach. If you have doubts about your relationship together, that's one thing. If you're thinking, however, of jettisoning him for a higher-priced mentor simply based on rating, you'd certainly never be accepted as a student by any coach I'd accept as an associate. But you decide, just as you must decide on your own moves, unless you can find a coach able to make them for you.

TWO COACHES

Q. I am writing about my son, who is eight years old and plays chess well for his age. He has been playing chess since the age of six, when my husband taught him how to play. However, from the very beginning my son has had a chess coach, which he found from his school. This man isn't a strong player, though he is a good coach, according to my son, and my

son and he get along. Anyway, we decided last year that my son needed opening lessons, to say the least, so we took on a new coach just for that, especially after we heard good things about him from people who should know, and even though his fee is high. This new coach is a great player, who knows all the openings, so we are not complaining about the fee. Now my son plays the Alekhine and Gruenfeld Defenses, neither of which he played before working with the new expensive coach, according to my husband! The old coach only showed pawn to e5 for black against e4, and nothing about d-pawn openings. Sometimes my son seems confused, but we think he is learning and he is getting better, thanks to the new coach, and my son has gained close to 100 rating points since last year alone (713 to 808, unofficially), according to my husband. We also think that the two coaches don't like each other and it's costing us a lot of money. Do you think we made a mistake? In other words, is it okay to have two coaches at the same time? What would you do?
—USA

A. First I'd hire a new coach after dismissing the other two. Is it okay to have two coaches at the same time? Sure, though the situation depends on a number of factors, from the age of the child, to how well the teachers work together, to whether you can afford two. Usually, the younger the child, the wiser it is to stay with just one coach. Older kids can handle divergent opinions better than younger ones. But even for older children, it's better if the coaches aren't competing with each other and particularly useful if they can avoid giving conflicting advice. If neither steps on the other's toes, and especially if one defers to the other on crucial issues, it might go smoothly.

In life we have many teachers, yet our most important teachers tend to be our parents. By nature there are two of them, and this is usually enough. It can be good when parents share certain views, and though disagreements are typical and natural, some clashes in viewpoint can be quite serious. But from your use of the word "we," it would seem that you and your husband are in marital harmony. So, after getting a third coach, you won't have to go out and get a third parent. It might make sense, nonetheless, to confine your efforts to raising a healthy child, while leaving chess lessons to the new coach.

EVALUATING A TEACHER

Q. My question concerns chess teachers. How do you define a good chess teacher? Rating of the teacher? Rating of the students? How long the students keep playing chess? How much the students enjoy chess (hard to measure)? Friends ask me to recommend a chess teacher for their children, and I don't know how to answer. There are several in the area (some of whom are not friends) and I don't know how to objectively decide who is a good teacher who is not so good.
—USA

A. Watch different teachers in action: do they tell the students the answers instead of posing a problem or a question and letting the students work out replies on their own? Do they lecture and demonstrate instead of asking kids to interact, debate, and explore ideas? One of the best teachers I ever knew was a master at doing just the latter. George Kane had the patience to let his students do the hard work of learning on their own. He was their guide, not their master. Tell students what you know, and they may not remember what you've said. Let them discover what you know, and they'll own it for life.

Ratings may determine something about how well someone plays the game, maybe. But they can't apprise you on how well someone teaches. So simply ask yourself a few questions. Is he or she the type of individual one could satisfactorily learn from? And, would I want anyone I care about sitting across a chessboard from such a person on a recurring basis? This approach might not get you the best teacher possible. But it should at least place you in the right school, if not the right classroom.

WHO IS QUALIFIED?

Q. To be a good teacher, you should be a good player, because if you are not, you have no business teaching. My question is, and very strong teachers (2500+) have confirmed this, can too much teaching hurt your playing? On the other hand, weak teachers (less than 1600), believe it or not, say that too much playing can hurt your teaching, which I find unbelievable and ridiculous. I am wondering if anyone, even you with your weird and

44

self-promoting reasoning (because you would like to make people believe that you are qualified to teach chess when you are not, forgetting about all the hype), can come up with an argument, no matter how fallacious, to justify how one's teaching could suffer from too much playing, when a person tries to do both at the same time. I know you won't print this because people like you only print complimentary questions that make them look good. If you do, I hope you at least address my question, if not my concern.
—USA

A. I see your point. Teachers in the 1601–2499 range must be average. Although it's not essential for teachers to play regularly in order to be successful as teachers, it might invigorate their lessons if they played a little tournament chess now and then, just to stay sharp and keep fresh in their minds the types of problems students are likely to face in over-the-board confrontation. But bear in mind that what works wonderfully for one relationship might fail miserably for another.

If you're a full-time teacher, and mainly tutor beginning and inexperienced players, it's natural to generalize a bit more than you'd like. That can't help your own play, since real contests require specific and pertinent thinking. Fall back on a platitude during actual battle, and you might find yourself hanging a pawn or two, if not mate. Furthermore, as a supportive teacher, it's typical to become sympathetic with your students, as you try to provide them with necessary encouragement. That same sensitivity, so valuable to good teaching, could spell death if it's not checked in your own tournament struggles. If any of that empathetic sentiment carried over to your own play, and your resolve were weakened even slightly, your ability to wage winning chess war might become seriously impaired.

Conversely, if you are a dedicated tournament contestant, and suddenly find yourself trying to teach someone, it would be easy to slip into competitive mode and forget that your ultimate aim is to assist the student. This problem is more likely to afflict coaches working with advanced talents, especially when the student is approaching the teacher's own playing strength and the teacher is prone to emotional insecurity. Some teachers who lack self-confidence become unwittingly defensive when they feel challenged.

The polarity is clear. When you teach, you're trying to help someone (the student), and when you play, you're trying to hurt someone (the opponent). Both adverse conditions—being too sympathetic while playing and becoming too antipathetic while teaching—are exacerbated by the fact that they tend to exist on the unconscious level.

You shouldn't aspire to serve two masters, even if both of them love chess, without expecting to make concessions. But you're welcome to try, whether or not you feel my response adequately addresses your question, if not your concern, and despite my tendentious reasoning, in all its misleading fallaciousness.

PLAYING STRENGTH

Q. Thank you for your excellent column at the Chesscafe! I always look forward to reading your updates. I have a question for you concerning chess classes. I am currently rated in the 1500s, and everything that I have learned has come from books and my computer. I have been considering going to a chess coach, but I come from a town that doesn't have a very large chess community. I know that there is one person who offers lessons, and he is rated around 2000. I realize that he can probably destroy me in every game, but do you feel that someone of his rating would have a good enough grasp on the game to be able to teach well? I am mostly interested in positional and strategic ideas, as I can practice tactics easily on my computer at home. Thanks very much for any advice that you would have about this!
—USA

A. There are strong players who can't teach and capable teachers who can't play. It doesn't automatically follow that if you can do one you can do the other, or that if you can't do one you can't do the other.

Generally, the first category of recognized "good player" is Class A. That is, an A player knows enough and has sufficient tools to be able to win a won game. The same really can't be said for players below 1800, though some 1799 players may want to mount a counterargument. There are simply too many ways to go wrong, and most of us, whether considering tactical or strategic questions, will find them. Accordingly, though not necessarily, most of us can derive value if our teacher possesses an established rating of 1800 or better, though some 1799 players may again differ(and some players with no rating can teach up a storm).

It's probably more important that one's mentor be a good teacher than a good player. Unfortunately, it's harder to quantify teaching ability. As a rule, an effective teacher should know his or her subject well enough to explain the fundamentals clearly and correctly. Beyond that, good teachers care about the quality of their work and what happens to their students. But these qualities don't lend themselves to numerical evaluation, so it may be tough to recognize them before you've spent some time in a person's presence.

Certainly, anyone who knows more than you do may be able to help you. But if we must talk numbers, as a rule it usually helps if the person trying to improve your play is at least two rungs of playing ability above you. Since USCF rating classes roughly correspond to levels of real understanding, veteran observers tend to recommend that one seek a teacher at least 400 rating points higher.

Nevertheless, I wouldn't follow this suggestion absolutely. People comparable to you in strength can still help because their experience may be greater than yours or they are really skilled at the teaching craft. Moreover, there are specialists who can help even though they are clearly weaker than the person they're trying to assist. Kasparov profits from trainers he could crush 6-0 in a match. But these situations are rare and not to be counted on.

Actually, I'd like to suggest another approach. Instead of focusing on ratings or how much stronger a teacher needs to be, why don't you take a lesson from this prospective teacher and see how you think about it afterward? If you feel it works, it probably has, and you've found yourself a coach. If it doesn't work, you should still have gotten something from it. Even a bad teacher has some gold to offer. Usually a few nuggets come out in that first session, when the teacher is trying to make a favorable impression.

If nothing else, that trial lesson should enable you to appreciate a good teacher when he or she eventually comes along, whether it's by direct contact or over a distance, like through the Internet. Ratings may express playing strengths, but that information can't replace your own judgment, which seems quite good and nicely articulated.

SILENCE

Q. I am a regular club player, to be sure, on the lower side of the bell curve regarding strength. Recently, after observing another member providing tuition to a gentleman new to chess, I was invited by the club member to provide a bit of tuition myself. The gentleman had a children's beginner's book, which explained the moves of the pieces, castling, fool's mate and some basic starts. My question: I felt that I overloaded the gentleman with information. Of course there is a lot about the game to learn. I talked about: in the opening, moving the minor pieces first and toward the center of the board; what are minor and major pieces; placing a piece so it has the greatest (or greater) scope for moving; trying to mate playing K vs. K & R and K vs. K & Q; counting how many pieces will cover a square for captures and defense; the relative values of the pieces; thinking of what your opponent may do first, then what you must do second; all this, and maybe a little more. He knew the pieces' moves—but not exactly their worth. So how should I start? I do not see myself in a career as a chess teacher, but it would be nice to know what is sensible. Also was there something basic that I missed in the above? We also played an instructive game where I suggested moves and discussed relative merit of positions. I closed by saying that the most that can be learned comes from playing.
—*Australia*

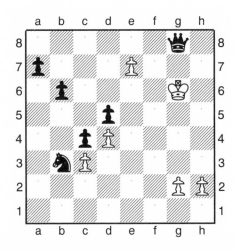

Botvinnik-Capablanca, Holland 1938 (variation)
White promotes next move, giving either a king
and queen mate or a king and rook mate.

A. You're right to be concerned about burdening the student with too much information. But I wouldn't be so troubled with your material or your method, since there are many things to teach in chess and just as many ways to teach them. Your regimen is fine and your approach seems honest. What's more, it's good to play your student to see directly how well he or she has absorbed what you've been teaching. If you should become more attracted to teaching, and would like to bone up on curriculum, you could turn to any number of excellent books that lay out full courses of study. Just go to a major bookstore, or check out any online service, and see what appeals to you.

Being a good teacher is not solely dependent on presenting correct information. Many prospective teachers assume that's all it is, and become discouraged when they feel their knowledge is inadequate. But this is patently false. If teaching were merely a matter of knowledge it would be reasonable to seek out the strongest player and get him or her to teach you. Yet the teacher can't make the moves for the student. And the teacher could never hope to show the student everything he or she knows anyway.

Developing your students' ability to think and analyze is more important than conveying information. Some of the best lessons contain a

49

lot of silence, where the teacher says just enough, allowing the student to ponder in peace. How else can one figure out what's going on? Nothing is more repugnant than a teacher who thinks he knows it all, who fills the hour with an intolerably incessant display of learning. I wouldn't be surprised if you already understood the value of timely silence. You may not want to teach again, but from the heartfelt and sincere way you've expressed yourself, I think you should consider giving it another try. My hunch is that you'd be good at it.

RATED TOO LOW

Q. I started playing chess a few months ago and I loved it. I'm 13 so apparently I took chess up quite old. I made good progress and progressed to the 1400 level in only a few weeks by reading books and doing exercises, etc. I thought that I would like to really improve so I asked my dad if we could hire a chess tutor and he thought it was a great idea. But when I went to find one they all refused to teach me because my rating was too low. What do I do from here? Can I utilize the Internet to improve to become a master? Does playing through master games (e.g., Garry Kasparov's games) really help improve my chess?
—*United Kingdom*

A. I too didn't take up chess until I was 13, so I know what you're talking about. And I must admit, I felt quite old at the time—forget about now.

Your initial success and decent starting rating are to be applauded. I find it astonishing, though, that there aren't any local chess teachers who'd want to help a player of your ability and obvious love for the game. It makes me wonder if the teachers you've encountered are really teachers.

I have a feeling, nevertheless, that you possess the independence to get by without any teacher at all. You're obviously very bright, and it's clear you truly love chess. As a result, you have so many options that it might not be sensible to recommend any of them over the others. The important thing is to keep playing and studying chess, however you do it.

If you had to work with any block of information, why don't you start with your own games? You could catalogue them, which is best done with software, such as ChessBase. Then you should subject those games to thorough analysis. Start by running searches to see which lines seem to achieve greater results, and find out which top players play the variations of special interest.

As a rule, to develop an opening repertoire, it's not a bad inspiration to adopt a leading player's lines. They will provide you with a sound and consistent catapult for your opening study. That's because most good players tend to sport a group of openings and defenses that are in harmony with a definite approach. Once you've found a player whose style you seem to admire, let that player be your guide—your Virgil. Allow him (or her) to do the preliminary work for you. Over time you can always modify your play to suit your own needs and tastes.

Input your openings into a program such as Fritz and see how it responds. Furthermore, you can use its appraising function to test your mental meanderings. You're still able to ask Fritz questions, as you would be able to with a teacher. It's just that Fritz (or any program like it) answers you more cogently—not in words, but in moves, the language that matters most on a chessboard. Naturally, using the tandem team of ChessBase and Fritz, your explorations needn't be restricted merely to the opening. There's no reason you can't also bolster your middlegame and endgame play by virtue of the same search and trial method.

So there you have it. All you need is a computer, the proper software, and a database of your own games, all propelled by your patent intellect and enthusiasm for chess. Once you realize you don't require a coach—that you are totally self-reliant and can indeed be your own best teacher—you're well on the way toward winning chess. And who knows? Someday you may have the opportunity to show those so-called chess teachers what they weren't capable of seeing in the first place.

TEACHING CLASS PLAYERS

Q. Hi, I am considering lessons/tutoring but I don't have a good idea of how to go about selecting an instructor/tutor. My experience in teaching other subjects persuades me that simply finding a strong player doesn't mean you've found a good instructor. So my question is this: What do you think a Class A/B/C player needs to look for in an instructor/tutor?

What are the telltale signs of someone who has given some thought to the question of how to teach effectively, and is there any way to objectively compare instructors? In short, how can the amateur shop for an instructor so as to reduce the chances of wasting time and money?
—*USA*

A. You should be looking for the same qualities in a chess coach you'd seek from coaches in other disciplines: expertise, experience, communication skills, solicitude, reliability, affordability, and preparedness. Be wary of hiring a coach who is overbooked or who has very important students. He or she might not be able to give you adequate time and consideration. I would also avoid teachers who present immutable systems. That usually means they are more concerned with displaying their own ideas than finding out about you as an individual. I suppose some concepts are set in stone, but people tend not to be, and teachers should never be.

If I were trying to find a teacher, I'd ask around. I'd try to locate current and former students and hear what they have to say. I'd also try to speak at least to a few different teachers themselves, and I'd probably pose some similar questions to compare their reactions. I'd ask about how they teach and I'd see what questions, if any, they ask me. I'd want a teacher who manifests interest in me as a person, one who is willing to deliver (or create) a program for my needs and within my budget. And if the teacher objects to answering my questions, or if he or she treats me like one of the herd, I'd drop him or her from my short list. Who needs to pay to be near someone like that?

But mistakes are still possible. You may engage the help of someone who seems promising but turns out wrong for you, or you may initially reject someone whose true worth doesn't show on first contact. Fortunately, you can give it a spanking new start and seek a different teacher (you have that right), now that you're armed with the knowledge of experience. You can even go back to a teacher that you rejected earlier, once you've seen the light. This time, though, you'll have a better notion of what not to do, as well as greater sensitivity for hidden qualities that you may have missed the first time around.

STUDYING THE COACH

Q. I'm 36 years old and live in Halifax, Nova Scotia. I've been playing chess competitively in Canada for eight years and my rating is around 1600 Canadian. My question is this: Is it better to study your own games or someone else's? I have a chess coach and our study method lately is for him to show me one of his games and assign me written homework questions about its strategies and tactics. We used to have me annotate one of my own games, but I've found that studying his games has made me sharper in my own! Maybe I'm wrong, but it sure seems that way. Any thoughts?
—Canada

A. Most teachers prefer reviewing their students' play and studying openings, examples, tactics, themes, and so on, germane to the students' apparent needs. Nevertheless, virtually any method or material can succeed when employed by a skilled teacher, so there's nothing inherently wrong with looking at your coach's games. And since you feel as if studying his play has actually helped, why risk changing things? If it's not broken, don't fix it.

INTERNET LESSONS

Q. This may be an unfair question if you personally give lessons over the Internet, but here goes anyway: What do you think of chess lessons over the Internet? Can they be as good as face-to-face lessons? Does it depend on the age of the student?
—USA

A. If one is going to take lessons, it makes more sense to do so in face-to-face situations. Subtle expressions and intonations are part of the learning process—and it's hard to absorb what you don't see or hear.

Chess lessons on the Internet also force players to expend considerable energy in typing out their thoughts and variations. Variant lines may cause confusion, and too much energy might be wasted on the wrong things. Of course, you can compensate for technical limitations. Speaking on the phone during the lesson or using written material and working out of a textbook beforehand can help. But even this broadened state of affairs is not quite comparable to having a live teacher in front of the student.

There are certain benefits to be obtained by working on the Internet. Players can study at unusual times and from faraway places, and young students will learn notation faster. Furthermore, almost any kind of lesson given by a good teacher is better than no lesson at all. But are Internet lessons likely to have the same impact as face-to-face lessons? Most chess educators will tell you no, though don't let this discourage you from using the Internet to connect to a great teacher, especially if there are no other practical ways to meet one directly.

SELF-RELIANCE

Q. I'm an enthusiastic 15-year-old chess player and I've recently begun studying chess very hard in order to improve my game. I'm about to compete in my first tournament. I play chess quite frequently on Yahoo! where my rating is about 1650–1700, and I also play in my local chess club. I seem to have come to a point where it is tough to improve any further without the guidance of an experienced chess coach, but the problem is lessons with a chess coach are just too expensive! I live in Abu Dhabi in the United Arab Emirates and I don't think there are any chess coaches available here. I know many coaches offer lessons through the Internet Chess Club but they charge about $50 per lesson, which would probably seem very unreasonable for my parents. I think that I really need a chess coach in order to help achieve my ambitions of becoming a professional chess player, so my question is this: Who would you recommend as a suitable coach who does not ask for such high rates? Also, what would be your advice to improve my game without the help of a chess coach?
—*United Arab Emirates*

A. It shouldn't impair your health to solve vast numbers of tactical problems, especially without moving the pieces unless absolutely necessary (and it never is). Reviewing annotated games contested by strong players should also help, as well as studying good books on particular areas of chess, such as clear texts on the middlegame and endgame, especially if they holistically integrate moves and explanations. And you don't need a coach to prosper from any of that, a truism most of us took for granted before the coaching discipline existed.

There are plenty of things you can do on your own, starting and finishing with playing lots of challenging chess games, against the strongest opposition you can find. Review those games and try to figure out how you could have done better—how you could have avoided problems, saved losing games, and made sure to win those winning ones you let get away. If you can't come up with a coach to fuel this process, you can use software, such as Fritz or ChessMaster. Simply input your moves and take note of the evaluations, hoping to make your plays either more positive or less negative. Eventually you should acquire greater understanding of your own games. Your play is likely to gain accordingly, with or without a coach. In fact, if you want to become a professional chess player, there's only one coach you should ever rely on anyway, and that's you. It's never too late to become self-sufficient, and it will probably cost you less than 50 bucks an hour.

PREACHING

Q. I recently had a conversation with a veteran grandmaster from Russia who asserted that no player who is less than a grandmaster should attempt to train talented young players. He argued that while not all grandmasters are good teachers, a player who is not a grandmaster lacks the necessary feel for how the pieces move to train a player to reach his full potential. He stated that Yusupov and Dolmatov, two of Mark Dvoretsky's most famous students, could have achieved even more than they did if their play had not been "sterilized" by an international master.

He compared teaching chess to teaching music. He said that an expert (but not great) musician may teach a student to play in a local bar, but that student would never be able to play in Carnegie Hall. Such a student would have to unlearn everything in order to learn the proper feel for the notes. To what extent do you agree with him? Should chess teachers who have truly gifted students recommend they start with grandmasters or should coaches work with young gifted players until they have taught

them as much as they can, and do you refer your very most gifted students to grandmasters for further training?
—*USA*

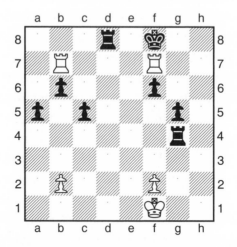

Yusupov-Dolmatov, Rapid Game 1991
Draw agreed. Imagine what might have happened
with different coaching.

A. Let me answer the last part of your question first. I try never to stay with a student beyond my ability to help. Once a student seems ready to move on, which might be determined fairly early in our relationship, I do what I can to find other teachers who can do a more appropriate job, including grandmasters.

Perhaps your veteran grandmaster is correct, but there's no way of knowing for sure. How would we test his hypothesis? Ask students to go back in time and live their lives twice, the second time studying with a grandmaster? If we could have two teachers who were virtual clones of each other, except for their chess ability, then we could make more definite statements—perhaps. For this analysis, if both teachers had an equally bright disposition, comparable knowledge about the art of teaching, pretty much the same degree of development in personal intelligence, practically the same dedication to the student and the enterprise, similar time to invest, and so on, then the playing skill of the teacher may mean quite a bit. In such a case, the stronger player might be the better teacher.

The real world, however, is not so ideal. I've never met a non-grandmaster who was a leading player, nor are there many grandmasters that seem to have a facility for teaching. If we want the teacher to impart factual knowledge about chess, then it's clearly better to have a grandmaster. But if we deem it wiser to empower the student to reach full potential on his or her own, then it makes more sense to stress teaching skill over playing strength. The grandmaster can't make your moves for you. The good teacher can inspire you to find the right ideas for yourself.

It's curious that so much emphasis is placed on the term grandmaster. What about those who are practically grandmasters? Are they likely to mislead their students with notions that would ultimately prevent them from reaching their full potential? Then there are all those ordinary grandmasters. In Voltaire's perfect world, how could they possibly teach as well as the super-grandmasters? Even super-grandmasters might pale before Garry Kasparov. What your grandmaster associate says about Mark Dvoretsky is patently unfair.

Did you consider that the grandmaster may have a personal grudge against Mark Dvoretsky? Maybe Dvoretsky once beat him in a meaningless game (which may have meant a lot to the grandmaster) or disagreed with one of his trivial or offhand comments (which also may have meant a lot to the grandmaster). I don't agree that the student might have to "unlearn everything." If you start down the wrong path, you'll learn a great deal from the process of getting back to the right one. I'd be willing, of course, to discuss all of these points with the grandmaster in question, though preferably over a few beers.

Maybe something is being missed here. What's the purpose of teaching—for teachers to show and tell students everything they know, or to help students develop so they can function without teachers? If we are to determine who should and shouldn't teach the young and talented, it seems we should answer this question before tackling anything else.

COACHLESS TEAM

Q. What kind of preparation plan do you recommend to a national team that doesn't have a coach and no grandmaster lives in the country? There is a continental tournament coming up soon, which will be 30 minutes per game. They also have a blitz tournament. The squad has a player who is a FIDE Master and three others have 2200 ELO ratings from two consecutive Olympiad appearances. There are two months before the tournament.

—*Ethiopia*

A. Without regard to how much time you have before the upcoming event, I recommend the following. Play regular round robin tournaments, preferably every week. Then have the team analyze the games in seminar sessions, where everyone tries to help everyone. Since you don't have a grandmaster coach, the group will have to coach itself. While no one could replace the world's best trainer, you'd be surprised how much could be realized by an assemblage of four to six really motivated people, all working in harmony for a common purpose. Moreover, fostering that all-for-one spirit beforehand naturally makes it easier to draw on it for the actual competition. It will already be there, which means all your squad has to do is play good moves as individuals.

MY METHODOLGY

Q. I love chess and hope to become a chess teacher. People tell me I would be considered a 1600 USCF player, though I am not officially rated. I need to create a teaching system or repertoire for my students, and I don't know where to start. Obviously, you have made a living in this area (everyone says this). How did you get started? Explaining what you did would be useful to me. I need to start somewhere, and I also worry about teaching chess as a business, since I lack the knowledge of how to do it. It would be all right to get one of your humorous answers.

—*USA*

A. When I first started in this business it wasn't a business. And personally I had no real talent for chess, teaching, commerce, or anything else. Actually, what I loved to do was read, though I didn't have much aptitude for that either. But it was 1972, Bobby Fischer was conquering the world, and it was one of those things where I happened to be at the right place at the right time, I guess. I was granted opportunities and worked hard to take advantage of them. Since I didn't know what I was talking about, or frankly how to teach at all, I started by consulting the few texts out there that seemed to organize lessons in a logical and stimulating way. You know, those by Fred Reinfeld and Irving Chernev, writers admired by every serious player.

I began collecting interesting didactic positions: examples that really illustrated useful points and did so in exciting but instructionally clear variations. It took a while, but as the positions accumulated, and my familiarity with them increased, the word got out and I began to attract more and more students. The situation fed off itself, and old students who should have despised me but didn't were encouraging new ones to seek me out. Soon it became possible to earn a living from doing what I realized I enjoyed doing the most.

Along the way I continued to improve my storylines while observing good teachers in action, to see if what they offered could be adapted to my own method. I'd say the teachers I learned the most from were Shelby Lyman, George Kane, Frank Thornally, Sal Matera, Julio Kaplan, Larry D. Evans, and Jack Collins, but certainly I benefited from many other fine teachers as well.

In due course I grew tired of hearing myself talk and elected to follow a new path. I decided to bring nothing prepackaged to lessons and assume that each student and situation would be truly unique. My teaching would stay fresh and challenging, and I could get by without having to prepare anything. My secret plan was to convince students that they could do it all on their own, without my help—in fact, that it would be to their advantage to get rid of me. Somehow this backfired and my dearth of true understanding became paradoxically appealing to them. Suddenly, I had more students than ever before. So you see, if you don't know how or what to teach but make your lack of knowledge a selling point, thereby turning a weakness into a strength, you'll have no trouble putting yourself over as a chess teacher. You might even make a living at it.

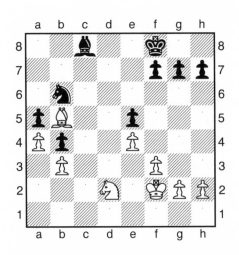

Reinfeld-Alekhine, Pasadena 1932
White holds the world champion to a draw.

CORE CURRICULUM

Q. I would like to work out an elaborate program (not a computer program, but rather a school program), which will be helpful to players from the green level (1000 ELO) to the master class (2000, 2200, or even 2400). I saw a few of them written by very good players, such as Kevin Spraggett, Michael de la Maza, etc. My question is simple: Is there any way to connect all programs to one, which will guarantee achieving great improvement to all students, or at least most of them? Maybe people are so different that it is impossible to make one program for all players. What do you think about it?
—*Poland*

A. It would be great to create a standardized curriculum. But people have different needs and learn in a variety of ways. Even where two or three bickering academics agree, two or three will debate over emphasis, order of presentation, choice of specific examples, and the division between theory and application. And that's before they get started.

I might also point out that many of the chessically learned vigorously dispute the value of certain authorities, styles of play, opening preferences, grading levels and rating correspondences, length of courses, the apportioning of study and practice, and reading lists. I'm sure I've forgotten something the enlightened wouldn't. Certainly, in trying to establish a core curriculum, you might face a battle comparable to meeting up with your worst opponent but many times exacerbated, multitudinously around the globe, by the interminable nattering of irritated, often mean-spirited disputants who produce an endless stream of ungrammatical, ill-conceived, poorly written, mistyped complaints and objections they deem essential to the advance of civilization. But you seem determined and sincere, and maybe those are the qualities needed to knock out the teeth of such imbecilic and unyielding chess types in countless academic forums worldwide.

PHONE LESSONS

Q. I have a talented eight-year-old son who wants to take chess lessons over the telephone. He is very curious and knows an incredible number of things. He loves gadgetry, computers, and all types of machines. He also loves nature and animals. He is also a brilliant musician who studies piano and voice, and he loves to sing Broadway show tunes. He is by far the best reader in his class and he is a wonderful problem solver. You should see him think and reason. His "problem" is that we live very far from the nearest city and can't meet with a chess teacher in person. What do you think about phone lessons? Do you know any chess teachers good enough who can do this? Do you think that these types of lessons can be effective, especially given the age of my son?
—*USA*

A. I wouldn't worry about your son's age or his ability to handle chess lessons over the phone. From your description of him I'm surprised he hasn't asked about early admission to Harvard (maybe *they* should be asking about *him*).

Sessions over the phone can work if both teacher and student are aware of the potential difficulties and prepare to meet them before starting. I realized this back in 1972 when I first began to teach students around the country.

But there is one prerequisite for telephone lessons: the student must be conversant with chess notation. Otherwise both student and teacher waste all sorts of time. The waste can be particularly silly, such as when the student doesn't know the names of the squares and has to depend on a grid. You'd be surprised how often phone lessons are halted or frustrated because the board is set up backward, with the higher numbers on White's side. Young children are prone to that mistake, though not as badly as their less knowledgeable parents or caregivers (the people who hurriedly set up the board to get things going).

Playing out variations is more difficult during phone lessons, and the student is often unable to get back to the original position without considerable loss of time. Occasionally, total confusion ensues and the game must be retraced back to the start. To avoid that problem, teachers who give phone lessons may require their students to use software instead of a chessboard, because navigating from point to point on a computer is far easier than trying to reconstruct a game by hand on an actual board. It saves time and the computer reduces the risk of impossible setups (it doesn't allow them).

Teachers who teach via phone often send their students an electronic file containing examples for upcoming sessions. That further decreases the possibility of errors while enabling the student to prepare ahead of time, so more can be learned from the material (let's hear it for preparation). In fact, many phone lessons simultaneously use the Internet, so that both media can support the other. Consequently, while there are many potential problems here, as there are in most instructional situations, they can be minimized or even averted by laying the groundwork. Some teachers succeed because they have a knack of turning possible liabilities into assets, so that the type of lesson becomes less important than how well it's given. So pay your phone bill, and let your son take those lessons.

OPENING REPERTOIRE

Q. Our state, Colorado, recently held its annual open scholastic championship tournament and I noticed that the elementary school section (K–3 and K–6) games featured the same openings. Almost every top game

began 1. e4 e5. The middle school (K–9 grades) and high school (10–12) sections, showed much more opening variety, but most of the top players' openings reflected their coaches' tastes, with several players repeating sometimes obscure lines as White and Black. At what age or ability level do you focus on specialized openings? Also, do you teach a specific opening repertoire to your students, or do you try to give students more freedom of choice, even at the possible expense, in the short run, of less practical success?
—*USA*

A. Generally, I don't focus on any particular opening variations. I tend to commence with discussions of opening principles. From the beginning I'd probably emphasize the center, development, the initiative, king safety, mobility, and several other important dos and don'ts. If I needed some opening lines to illustrate those concepts, I'd rely on king-pawn games, especially double king-pawn examples, simply because they're easier to understand and there are many more examples of a shorter nature from which to choose. Long variations are liable to eviscerate instructional value. Later on I'd likely move to asymmetrical king-pawn games before illustrating queen-pawn openings, since queen-pawn beginnings tend to be more subtle and therefore harder for newcomers to assimilate.

But there are no hard and fast rules here. If a coach truly believes in something else, that's okay if he or she can pull it off. Whatever works, works. Nonetheless, I do think a coach's task is less demanding in the straightforward double king-pawn lines, at least at first. Of course, there are always students who want to go their own way, trying everything new and unusual under the sun. I might advise them against such undertakings, and if I did, I'd give the reasons for my objections. Teachers should be willing to demonstrate that their thinking is not arbitrary.

If students remain resistant, however, I'd let them follow their personal choices. They will eventually learn the right or better way over the course of time, mostly by getting their chessic heads beaten in repeatedly. Few of us are going to continue traveling along a dismal path that goes nowhere if we find evidence of a hopeful path that goes somewhere. Besides, there are always some young people who will take a bad or wrong idea and eventually somehow show why it's good or right. Those are the people who change our world and enrich all of us. I don't think we should stop them.

STARTING A CLASS

Q. I am an elementary special education teacher in Indianapolis, Indiana, who also runs the chess club. I am a below average player who doesn't play in many USCF tournaments, but I love working with the children and seeing them grow to love chess. I was wondering if there are certain methods and/or materials that would increase my level of effectiveness in working with first through fifth graders. Thank you so much.
—USA

A. You're possibly already doing many things that work, but if you need a shot in the arm, you might start by building a small library of books that special education kids could actually use. You could begin the process by turning to an online chess catalog or a comparable service, purchasing a few items that seem to the point.

Remember that chess is highly visual, so you should emphasize acquiring children's books with large diagrams and minimal text, where the material is spaced proportionately and distinctly. Probably you should get one or two source books for yourself, with lots of clear tactics and tasks. You may also want to find software that lets you make your own diagrams to serve your instructional purposes. You might then prepare blocks of related illustrations, most likely with no more than four to a page, though two per page would be better and less confusing. You could then take many of these diagrams and create flash cards, possibly laminating them, with each one posing a problem on one side and its answer on the other—both diagrammed. And don't be afraid to draw arrows over the diagrams, like a football coach does with a playbook.

I would also procure a demonstration board and enough standard plastic chess sets to accommodate a full class. Maybe you should get two extra sets just to be safe. You might even want to obtain an unusual set, with bright colors, which you'll use at special moments to gain attention or shift focus. Furthermore, since chess is so graphic, you might put chess art on view and summary charts of key chess concepts as memory-jogs. Lastly, you could equip yourself with videos and films that teach chess and show it in positive light and dark.

TROPHY SIZE

Q. For many years I have been involved in all kinds of sports—hockey, baseball, swimming, chess, football, and so on—but I am always amazed and shocked about the size of chess trophies! They are huge! In fact some are taller than the kids who receive them! Chess trophies take the gold medal in size among any sport that I know. Why is this? If size matters, chess is the sport to get involved in!
—*Canada*

A. I'm not sure I agree with your premise. I don't think chess trophies are larger than trophies given in other activities. True, the larger ones are larger, but the smaller ones are smaller. And let's not overlook something (considering the size of some trophies, I'm not sure how anyone could). The wide world of sports bestows incredible awards—I mean bigger than people—including life size goalies and golden slam-dunkers as big as Shaquille O'Neal. Humongous objects are not just given out in sports, but for many activities having nothing to do with sporting competition.

I will grant, however, that the number of chess trophies presented in recent years has proliferated. When you ask top chess players from the past about their trophies, they think you're joking. They can't remember winning too many trophies, no matter how many tournaments they won.

What happened is this: chess teachers (if you ask them, among the smartest organizers going) got even wiser. They saw what their brother and sister coaches in baseball, soccer, football, basketball, hockey, tennis, golf, and punch ball were doing, and they realized chess was missing out on a gold mine. So they started using these baubles and gaudy trinkets of achievement to their own advantage. It's true that chess trophies tend to be flimsier, but the kids, although they're not unaware of the ersatz quality of what they're getting, want them anyway. But if you're asking me if I think there should be so much emphasis on winning trophies, I'd have to answer "no." It gives the wrong message, though I'm not sure what the message is, or should be. I have to find out more about these trophies. Let me talk to an organizer I know.

TOUCHING

Q. I teach chess in the public schools to elementary and middle school kids. Some of them are quite affectionate, and they are used to touching and being touched, the younger ones in particular. As a chess teacher, and a male chess teacher at that, I am concerned about touching students during lessons. I feel that often it is desirable to give the student a reassuring pat on the shoulder, yet in today's world such affection is often misunderstood. It also seems that women teachers are much freer to touch than men. I have had this conversation with many other teachers and each of us has our own thoughts on it. To what extent do you think it's all right for a chess teacher to touch students during class to show approbation?
—*USA*

A. Your question is one that's vital to all teachers, including those who teach chess. It brings to mind the story "Hands" from Sherwood Anderson's *Winesburg, Ohio*. The story, as I remember it, is about a teacher named Adolf Myers (also known as Wing Biddlebaum) who is best able to show his love for teaching and people by touching. The students adore him and his articulate hands. But one day a misguided youth spreads a false rumor about Adolf and the townspeople wind up driving him away and ruining him. He's never able to touch, or teach, again.

Touching is most definitely a type of communication, and young children often express themselves by feeling and holding. Many also view touching as a sign of acceptance. Furthermore, for some teachers, as with the Adolf Myers character in "Hands," touching and body language are an integral part of their teaching. It's their way of displaying the love and approval most students need.

Nevertheless, touching isn't the only way to convey empathy, or many other feelings. Think about the nature of chess itself. Other than to shake hands, chess players never touch while playing. Yet even though there's no physical contact, chess is an incredibly intimate game. In the process of sitting so close to our opponents we tend to learn a lot about them. In particular, after a few hours of tightly inhabiting the same space, we usually come to know if we like or dislike them, whether because of their facial expressions, their posture, the way they move the pieces, or from other forms of powerful, though indirect communication.

Of course, playing chess is not the same as teaching it. In the case of young children, some touching, such as a tap on the shoulder or a pat on the head, may possibly be permissible when trying to reassure or encourage. It's also true that society has traditionally been more tolerant of women who touch and less so of men. Not surprisingly, the thinking on this has changed slightly in recent years as more men have entered the profession and proved their worth as teachers, which could be reckoned pertinent to chess, where most of the teachers are men.

But whether male or female, teaching chess or other subjects, I don't think teachers should touch students if there's any chance the touching could be misconstrued or potentially injurious to the students. I think there are other ways to impart information or show support, and the experienced teacher knows them by training and nature. Smiling genuinely, using a certain tone of voice, saying suitably complimentary things, or any number of other skillfull responses can also get the point across, and they all avoid touching off a maelstrom of potential trouble.

BECOMING A COACH

Q. I am 23 years old and I live in the Caribbean. I am writing to you to find out about learning to be a coach. Do you give lessons on that? Thank you in advance.
—*Trinidad and Tobago*

A. I don't really give coaching lessons. I'm still learning how to be a coach myself. But you're right to ask me and other coaches for advice. Where possible, try to observe lessons in progress. You usually can discover far more from the actual thing than from its description. You might also take some chess lessons yourself, because when you spend time across from a teacher on a steady basis you tend to absorb the process almost by osmosis.

Indeed, some of the very best teachers learned their trade sitting on the other side of the table, as students. Another way to go would be to read the books of chess educators, especially those who provide copious insights into the art and science of teaching chess. And don't forget to contact official chess organizations, such as the U.S. Chess Federation and Chess-in-the-Schools as well as Trinidad's own national and junior chess organizations to see what they have to offer. But ultimately there's no substitute for experience, and there's no learning like learning on the job. So if you want to learn about teaching, just start doing it and don't stop.

BECOMING A JOURNALIST

Q. My question does not pertain to ratings, opening theory, or Ben Kingsley. I am quite curious to know how one becomes a chess journalist. Must one be an exceptional chess master, as certain Web sites would have us believe (by virtue of who they employ), or is background in writing and journalism satisfactory? I am sure in your career you have crossed paths with many sorts of reporters, photographers, and other sundry individuals. How did they achieve their opportunity? I am a playwriting student and chess player and I have tried to meld the two before (with minimal success). If there is any sort of step(s) or path you could recommend I take now, I would most appreciate it. But I am thankful for any sort of response, advice, anecdote, raspberries, etc. Keep up the good neo-Steinitzian-Nietzschean work!
—USA

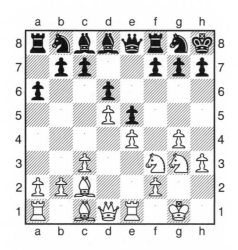

Lasker-Steinitz, Hastings 1895
A funny position. Black has just played 17. ... Ng8
and all eight pieces occupy the home rank.
White got the last laugh 23 moves later.

A. There's no single way to become anything, even a chess journalist. You can get there by being a good writer, a good chess player, both, or neither. There are no rules here, which can be very appealing.

Of course, you could attempt to cover yourself by working on both chess and writing. To improve your chess skills, play against good players every chance you get. To develop your writing talents, write as often as you can. Write about what interests you and about what doesn't. And if you're trying to get published, be willing to work for nothing at first, but only at first. Eventually you'll want to be paid for your efforts, which is why I recommend that you forget chess journalism completely. It pays nothing even when it pays, and the fringe benefits are truly on the fringe.

As far as developing a writing style, find yourself and go with that. Just be clear and direct. Chess players prefer clarity to subtlety, though they want that too. So don't be afraid to repeat things for emphasis, which is why I'm suggesting for a second time that you skip chess journalism and seek another career.

But if you must persist in your quest despite all my warnings, then it's clear that you're for real and you should continue your journey. As

James Joyce urges the budding artist at the end of the *Portrait of the Artist as a Young Man*, "Go to encounter for the millionth time the reality of experience." Forge ahead and give us some of the best chess writing the world has ever seen. Even chess people need a good read.

SLOWING DOWN

Q. I am the chess coach for the local elementary school chess club and I was wondering if you could give me some ideas on what to teach kids. I am a fairly good player, but I feel I have taught the kids all I know. They are good; as a matter of fact, they won the West Virginia State Elementary Chess Tournament last year, but I have a very difficult time to get them to slow down and think about their moves. I admit I am not well versed in the different openings and strategies, but I am the only person in the area who can play and is willing to try to coach them. In other words, HELP! Could you please give me some ideas on where I should be leading them? Thank you for your time.
—USA

A. You can get your students to slow down by making them record their moves. If they're playing practice games with clocks, be sure they have enough time both to think and keep a record. If they're not playing with clocks, then they have plenty of time to write comfortably.

Give them a procedure. For example, make them write down the opposing players' moves before starting to think about them. Otherwise, they may become so engrossed in play that they forget to record or scribble bizarre entries by mistake. In trying to correct their score sheets they'll wind up hanging pieces and getting mated. Some coaches take all this penning a step further, requiring their students to write down each intended move before playing it. It's a routine that helps provide a final check to avoid errors.

You can also insist that they analyze without moving the pieces. Make it a class rule: they have to tell you their thoughts, instead of demonstrating them on the board. Let them know that otherwise their answers will be considered wrong, even when they're right. Be consistent about this. They'll start to realize you mean business and it will be to their gain. Not only will explaining benefit their concentration and analysis, it will also give them practice at being patient. All young people can use a measure of that.

Focus on tactics, both in and out of class. Just be sure that, when they're in class, they say their variations instead of moving the pieces. Moreover, when they're doing homework, insist that they write out complete variations, not just the first moves. If they come back with skeletal solutions, have them take their work sheets back home and do them again. And if you think this may be too discouraging, you can align yourself with those educators who turn such things into positives, not by punishing the offenders, but by rewarding those who give fuller answers, even when the answers are dead wrong.

I wouldn't worry so much about openings. Simply let them study and play their own lines, however they acquire them. If you tried to show them variations, you might unintentionally mislead or persuade them to memorize moves without truly grasping content, and few things are more abhorrent to the chess mind than memory without understanding. But if you need to work with some book ideas, why don't you get a few different collections of short, well-annotated games, where important points are explained in words and variations. Then, if they want to learn more, you can direct them to other sources, to be investigated on their own. If you do anything else for them, get them to play often and against good competition. During these games, make sure they take their time and care less about simply winning and more for the thrill of experiencing a good fight. Help them to appreciate the uplift of mental battle and you'll be imparting something vital, extending beyond the chessboard, which teachers everywhere strive for and value. Better yet, get them to shake hands after losing and I'd really be impressed.

NOTATION AS A PLOY

Q. I'm an inquisitive USCF club level tournament director who is still learning and I have the following question. In a recent tournament my opponent would hide his notation from view until after his move was made. In one or two instances he would erase and change the hidden no-

tation before making the move. In lieu of the prohibited use of notation to assist memory, is the above an accepted practice?
—*USA*

A. There are sound reasons to get into the habit of writing the next intended move down before playing it. Noting your next move before you make it helps safeguard against blunders. If you see an appalling move written on the score sheet, it may trigger a reaction that tells you it's not right before you've made the mistake of playing it on the board. That reaction is your chance to save yourself.

Teachers also enjoin their students to write their next move down before playing it to ensure they don't forget to write them down at all. Scholastic players often fail to notate altogether, particularly if their opponents are responding quickly. Understandably, they focus on the action and let the recording of it go. Then, after the game, there's nothing to analyze but fragments. This is particularly troubling for the teacher, whose utility diminishes accordingly, having fewer specific moves to talk about.

Not all coaches bend every effort toward improving their students' play or making themselves more useful during postmortem analysis. Some, particularly those who like to tally up wins that translate to trophies for the school display case, encourage their students to wear out their pencils and erasers purely for psychological reasons. They assume that opposing players will feel unnerved (as you might have) by the sight of their adversaries intently scribbling, then erasing, then scribbling again. If you (or your students) feel irritated by this practice, fight fire with fire. Merely write down unflattering synonyms for your opponents' cranial matter at the spot you'd note your next move. Related words will do. Just make sure you're equipped with a suitable eraser, and bring your smile.

Psychology is part of any competition, and chess is no exception. Your opponents may not mind resorting to mind games, and so you might feel compelled to defend yourself accordingly. Indeed, it might help to observe what they're doing *off* the board, so long as you end up focusing on what's really happening *over* the board. Ultimately, that's the only place that has a right to command your attention.

CHESS CONSULTANTS

Q. I have read that you have worked on a few movie sets as a chess consultant. What does a chess consultant for a movie do? Do you set up the chess positions and make sure the games played are emotionally true to the scenes at hand, or has the screenwriter usually done that? (I think Vladimir Nabokov at least would have enjoyed that part of writing a script for *The Defense*.) Do you teach the actors to play chess? If so, does it depend on the actors' and/or directors' interest level in chess or rather in the authenticity of their performance (i.e., you could imagine a method actor needing to delve deeper into the mechanics of the game). Did the actors' actual ability to play chess affect their performance, in your opinion, or did it depend on the authority with which they handled the pieces regardless of whether they were making convincing moves? Was it your job to coach the actors on the psychological meaning of the moves they were making or did the moves usually have little to do with the look on the actors' faces?

Also, what did you think of *The Luzhin Defense*, both as a film on its own terms and in comparison to the book, including the changed ending? In general, are there any movies that are "truer" to the chess world and to the world of chess than others?

Don't worry, I'm not looking for a job as a movie chess consultant—I am just nosy about intersections of the chess and movie worlds.
—*USA*

A. The chess consultant's chief function is not to screw up the possibility of working as a chess consultant in the future. I've tried to do that by not getting in the way of anyone important while filming and by putting the chess pieces where the filmmakers say they should be even though I might say otherwise (I don't always know what I'm saying anyway). I don't really teach the actors how to play chess, and they don't really teach me how to act. In preparing a scene in which the actors have to make a series of moves, I often provide them with visual patterns rather than chess sequences, since many of them see a lot more than they think.

I've always told actors how I thought scenes should go, and some of them have told me where they thought I should go. And they've never really needed method acting to convey the message that in the world of film the chess player is very much only a pawn in the game. But don't get me wrong. I love every minute of it.

Moving to *The Luzhin Defense*, I liked its exquisite cinematography, and the performances of John Turturro and Emily Watson were truly luminous. But the second half of the film played a little too much on the queenside. I can only imagine how Nabokov would have reacted if he had still been alive. Surely he would have wanted to write the screenplay, and he might have insisted on being the film's chess consultant. But I don't think he would have planned on doing a cameo, appearing in the last scene and winning the big game. It could have ruined the plot.

CHAPTER 3

Chess Through the Ages

Do we grow older and wiser when the subject is chess? If you don't start young, should you bother starting at all? Many writers asked me about the effects of aging on their game. Some people felt they were too old to improve or learn. I tried to point out that the human spirit can overcome most setbacks, at any age.

But the bulk of the questions centered on children and their learning problems. Most of those queries came from parents and coaches, though a few emails were sent by the young people themselves. The writers asked about the best ages to learn, what should be accomplished by certain periods in their study, what to read, how to find suitable opponents, how often to play, and so on. Most parents and teachers demonstrated admirable sensitivity. There were a few who used their missives to proclaim how well their kids were doing, which meant something like how well *they* were doing. I wasn't so concerned about hurting their feelings as I was with stopping them from hurting the feelings of their charges.

Youthful writers effervesced with excitement and promise over the future. I tried my best to blend in a bit of the pragmatic, without getting in their way. Who wants to be run over?

BEST AGE

Q. At what age could lessons begin?
—*USA*

A. I find that the best age for kids to start learning chess is when they've reached the august age of five or six. I've introduced a number of students to the game at four, the same age that young people start grappling with other abstract concepts, complex ones in math and music. Supposedly, Capablanca, world chess champion from 1921–27, was four when he learned how to play the game merely by watching his father and uncle play. I've heard of a few kids learning earlier than that, not nearly as spectacularly, and one well-known chess teacher told me he began teaching his son at two. The teacher felt the lessons weren't very successful, though I should point out that his son went on to win several National Scholastic Championships.

I knew one parent who was a devotee of music teacher Dr. Sinichi Suzuki's teaching methods. The parent believed that he could instill receptivity to chess from the time of the child's birth. He argued, for example, that he could create an environment that would help develop a strong player by dangling mobiles of chess pieces above the crib, affixing large diagrams of chess positions on the walls and ceiling, displaying pictures of famous chess players and events in the child's room and throughout the living space, giving the child stuffed chess toys to play with and look at, singing songs and reading poems with chess themes, visiting tournaments and chess events just to be around the action, and simply by talking about chess at every opportunity. There may have been other stuff he did, like stock the kitchen cabinets with chocolate chess pieces and such, but I can't seem to remember everything he talked about doing.

Probably the best thing a parent could do to encourage a child to play chess early is simple enough: just demonstrate a personal interest in the game. Children naturally learn by wanting to imitate their parents, their first role models. Perhaps *that* is what happened to Capablanca, when he stood by the board to watch his father play his uncle.

But rather than starting at a particular age, it's perfectly acceptable for the parent to introduce chess whenever it seems appropriate. If the child gets excited, it makes sense to go on with playtime and short lessons. If the child shows very little or no interest, drop the matter and go on to something else.

Children learn best when the presentation is playful and fun. I'm reminded of an epigram from Martial about teaching:

> *Do the children crowd around your desk?*
> *That's the test. It's not in the text,*
> *since school should be like play.*
> *Put down the straps and paddles;*
> *Lessons aren't battles.*
> *We learn best in summer anyway.*

AGE THREE

Q. I have a daughter who will be three in March and I am trying to teach her to play chess. So far, she knows the names and setup of all the pieces except she has problems putting the queen on the right spot. Anyway, I would like to know if you could recommend any books for teaching chess to kids.
—*USA*

A. Let's be clear here. Do you mean books for your child to read on her own, books for you to read with her, or books for you to read for yourself so that you can learn how to teach her? Unless your daughter is John Stuart Mill come to life, I'm going to assume you're referring to books falling into the latter two categories. Any clear instructional book with large diagrams should do for the two of you working together. Why don't you take a look at the recent texts of David MacEnulty? He has put out some wonderful children's books, which also help parents learn how to teach the subject. And for tactics, Fred Wilson and Bruce Alberston have published some excellent collections. But why settle for my opinion? Go to a major bookstore, one with hundreds of chess titles, and spend an afternoon or evening looking at all the books. You're bound to find a bound volume you like.

FEWER PIECES

Q. My sons are four and two years old. I suggest the older one can start playing chess now. Indeed, we tried to play some games. But I cannot remember how I learnt chess and I am afraid of frustrating my son in using all the pieces. Do you have any hints for teaching little children? Or are there any good chess books for young beginners?
—Germany

A. I understand your concern about using all the pieces, and how that might be confusing. Judge the situation for yourself. There's nothing wrong with proceeding inchmeal, inventing quasi-chess activities and puzzles that use fewer pieces to introduce the real game gradually. You can always expand or correct the youngster's understanding over the course of time. There are rules for playing chess but not so much for teaching it.

However you do it, try to offer a totally pleasurable experience. Make the game seem both exciting and important. Avoid debilitating competitions. Build confidence, which is the secret of all good teaching. If you teach by playing (not a bad idea), don't play so much to win, but to have fun. You may feel this is not the way of the world, but there's plenty of time for your kids to check out the way this place works.

A child has a right to be a child, but if you insist on playing for real, you can still do it gently and compassionately. You can even be creative. For instance, when you're playing a youngster, and it comes to the point of winning, you might say:

"Here I can win in one move. If you can show me how, you win. If you can't, I win. Take your time and find the right answer. And if you tell me how to win, without moving the pieces, you win twice."

Such an approach, or some version of it, can keep a student involved to the very end of the session, and it encourages your youngster to analyze mentally. It also allows you to play an actual game without having to lose on purpose, while giving the young one a means to save face.

There are a number of good texts for kids, but I'm going to suggest one created for parents and teachers instead, George Francis Kane's *Chess and Children*. Published in 1974, this is a brilliant pathfinding work, written by one of the best chess teachers there ever was. It's worth making the effort to track it down.

A final piece of advice: If you can associate your child with a great teacher, no matter the discipline, whether it's chess or anything else, do so. It's always worth it. How will you recognize a great teacher? Don't worry. Your child will tell you.

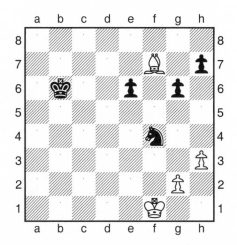

Fischer-Kane, San Francisco 1964
Black at age 15 draws with White
in a simultaneous exhibition.

CHESS FOR MY DAUGHTER?

Q. I think what you are doing is vital to the lifeblood of American chess and beyond! Keep it up! I enjoy chess, play online, and play one or two tournaments a year. I have a five-year-old daughter who is fascinated by my love of the game and we play once a week. She's very excited about chess, too, but I don't know how to teach her and keep it interesting (which is so important at this age). She enjoys playing on our Apple computer. Can you advise me on how to take her interest to a higher level? What about any good chess computer programs (for her age)?
—USA

A. There are many terrific chess books for children. Plenty of software products are also available, with specific features just for kids. It shouldn't be hard to find lesson material. But possibly the best thing you could do is simply to show your own love for chess. Your daughter will surely want to share those feelings with you, so continue to grant her easy access to the game, and encourage her to play fairly often. You might consider leaving out a chess set in a prominent area of your home. Such a display could provide abundant opportunities to talk about chess and its exponents in captivating ways.

Invite her to join you whenever you are looking at a game or puzzle. Sit at the table and make it seem as if you're on the same team, examining or solving together. And if you usually read together, there's no reason a few of the books couldn't be about chess. Then there are instructional videos and even movies, some of which have chess themes or chess in the background. You could sneak in a few of those and work chess into your discussion of the scenario.

Let's not forget computers. Since she's already starting to toy with her Apple machine, get her to be your partner in playing against it. Now your team might lose, and that could be discouraging, but you can lessen the hurt of such defeats by experiencing them together and laughing them off. She will learn a little chess while assimilating valuable life lessons from your carefree responses to those setbacks. And when your tandem manages to win, emphasize her contribution to the effort, pointing out real things she did to bring about the victory. Make her feel good by accentuating what she's done well. It's unlikely she'll ever get tired of hearing things she likes to hear.

KEEP IT FUN

Q. I have a six-year-old niece who seems interested in chess. She took an interest after playing a game against me. I've been playing for a little less than a year and during that time I've learnt a lot from books and experienced players. I'm rated somewhere around 1300. I'd like to know any tips you have for teaching a six-year-old the game. With a little coaxing she picks up obvious threats, such as when there is piece contact. She knows how most of the pieces move, but has trouble remembering how

knights move. I'd like to teach her more of the basics, but don't want to bore her. At the same time, making frequent recommendations and just letting her win games doesn't seem healthy either. Any advice?
—*USA*

A. The key is to make sure the activity stays fun, and there's an infinitude of ways to do that. Keep it light, offering advice in the spirit of play, while skillfully adapting to the changing moods of childhood. Whether or not this approach leads to mastery, it will promote the development of a healthy child. Naturally, that takes priority.

You can let her win all the time, but such an approach is certainly not required or recommended. There's nothing wrong with beating a student, as long as you know how to do so without causing pain or extinguishing passion for chess. For instance, playing more or less for real, you could offer her a cookie one move before implementing a task. Tell her she can save herself, saying that by finding your intended threat (let's say it's to win a piece), she gets to defend herself or to take her move back. If she doesn't find your threat, you're going to follow through on it and take her piece. (In all cases where the game hinges in the balance, try to put things in the positive or soften the blow. Instead of saying she "loses a piece," merely indicate that her intended move doesn't deal with your threat.) By constantly giving her chances to change her mind and make better decisions, she can stay in the game longer, to the very end, with all its instructional benefit.

Another idea is to allow her to change sides. At opportune moments during a game, ask her which side she'd rather have. If she prefers your side, turn the board around and let her play your position as her own. Later on, if you regain the advantage, you can make the same offer, turning the board around once again and letting her play from there (that's actually a technique used to develop defensive ability in more experienced players). You could do this as many times as you find useful, or you could limit the number of changes per game. Initially she might say "no," clinging to her own position, as children naturally do. But pose the possibility adeptly and consistently and in time you'll get her to play along. Perhaps you can combine the technique with an incentive, so she gets to associate one good thing with another. It's okay to experiment.

Of course, all this has to do with the art of instruction. The worst methods can flourish when employed by an experienced teacher, and the most proven ones can fail when not appreciated or handled properly. A good teacher can succeed even starting at the wrong place. So it's really not so much what you do but how you do it. Most of us know that. We just forget it now and then.

SAMPLING

Q. My son is six years old and has a rating of 960. He has never had formal lessons—he resists the idea fairly strongly and lectures bore him to tears. He just loves to play, including chess variants, mostly on the ICC (where his rating is around 1200). My questions are: How do you introduce the idea of lessons and still keep it fun? Do you feel that playing variants (losers chess, monster chess, etc.) impairs or assists chess development? I have been told that "it is criminal to not give such a talent lessons" but I am concerned that formal instruction can detract from what for him is fun at this age. (Along these lines, perhaps you know of an excellent teacher in the L.A. area who can walk this fine line.)
—*USA*

A. Instead of forming a relationship with a particular teacher right away—and there are plenty in the Los Angeles area who can satisfy your son's needs—why don't you let your son take individual lessons from a few different teachers, with you sitting in on each lesson. (Once the lessons start with a steady teacher, find a way to remove yourself naturally.) Make it clear to each teacher that your son does not yet want instruction per se, and that the teacher should keep this "one-time" lesson on a playful basis.

Most chess ideas a child needs to know can be integrated into instructionally fashioned games, and veteran teachers intuitively do that. Obviously, any teacher who objects to your concerns is not the right teacher. Later on, after the relationship is firmly established, the teacher can bridge into more formal coaching without making a big thing of it. Since the best lessons actually simulate real-game play, your son doesn't necessarily need a teacher if you can keep him nourished on a weekly diet of challenging games.

As far as playing chess on the Internet goes, that's fine, though you might try to steer him away from ridiculously fast time controls. Probably he should be playing games with limits between 10 and 20 minutes. With regard to chess variants, some teachers would prefer their students not to be exposed to them, for they can be addictive, and it's hard to stop kids once they've had a taste. Yet other teachers counter by saying it's best to let the student partake of those diversions anyhow, especially because they can be fun, and fun is what it's all about. Furthermore, a smattering of those variants may even have some value, particularly for stimulating imagination and heightening tactical invention.

Nevertheless, if you can, aim to regulate your son's participation in bughouse and its relatives. As similar as these variations may be, they're still not chess, and allotting too much time to them can distort one's approach to the main game. But it's clear you already appreciate the situation, and the issues you've raised show you to be a knowing and perceptive parent. I sense that together you and your son will soon find the right way, with or without the help of a suitable chess teacher.

LOSING

Q. I have been teaching chess to the youth of New York City for a few years now, and a problem that has never been easy for me is how to prepare a student for a "tournament slump." It is often the case that a student is truly growing as a player, but may encounter a few tournament losses in a row, and they sink into a significant despondency, sometimes wanting to quit chess altogether. While I let them know that losses may be seen as healthy learning experiences, I know that even nowadays, when I fall into a slump, all the consoling in the world doesn't help my wanting to stay in bed for a week. Maybe it's just a matter of maturity. Anyway, I'd greatly appreciate a response.
—USA

A. For everyone, though for children especially, some losses can be extremely painful. Losing at chess in particular has the power to leave us feeling outwitted and even humiliated.

I often hear parents and teachers saying how well their charges played right after a disheartening defeat. Obviously, they hope to placate their students, but unless the losers really did play well, they are likely to see through such artfulness and reject it.

For that reason, the most experienced teachers almost never tell their students that they've performed admirably when they clearly haven't. Concerned teachers tend to offer nothing in immediate aftermath, and when they do say anything, whether it's palliative remarks associated with a loss or compliments during a lesson, they aim to be specific, demonstrating with moves and reasons why the praise is appropriate. As a result, they have much more power to ameliorate at crucial times, when it really matters.

The best thing a teacher may be able to do after a student suffers an agonizing defeat is to wait for the right time to connect, saying something like: "I know how you feel." Sometimes alluding to his or her own losing experiences, and how painful they were, can help sneak in a laugh. Then, the student can join the teacher in stoic acceptance and humor, with the teacher suddenly becoming the conduit for the student's own hurt feelings. Don't be surprised if the laughter becomes a cathartic floodgate, with the kid crying his or her brains out. (It's not wrong to cry, but as you probably know, it's wrong to think it's wrong.) Once that release takes place, life generally moves on to getting some food, throwing and catching a ball, or participating in some other diverting activity. At the nationals, for instance, it's uncanny how often kids will wind up playing speed chess or bughouse for fun with the very players who beat them in the last round.

But you're right to try to cope with those problems before they happen. I wouldn't suggest telling students that it's okay to lose, however, since this might dull their competitive edge, triggering the very outcome to be avoided. Simply show students that they have options, whether winning or losing. If winning, they must opt for the most economical way to win. If losing, they must decide how to create problems for their opponents, which could possibly save the game at hand. The teacher's real aim should be to encourage students to be active participants in making their own decisions, for in chess few things are worse than feeling that you are under your opponent's thumb.

A student should be trained to assume the mindset of a dispassionate observer rather than falling into the role of the crestfallen victim in a losing game. When they focus on trying to optimize their opportunities to rescue a position in a tournament just as they would during analysis sessions in classrooms or privately, they can concentrate on looking for the best moves. Students who can be so objective are apt to achieve at least two things. They'll probably become more resourceful, capable of salvaging many potential losses, and they're likely to become more philosophical, better equipped to ameliorate their own pain and suffering. And teachers able to instill such wisdom are not only helping their own students play better chess, they're also serving the greater aims of humanity by encouraging the use of reason in everyday life.

MOVING TOO FAST

Q. My question is about a young student who plays too fast. We are trying to slow him down to play slower chess and think out his moves. Fast play leads to blunders and poor games. Can you give us some ideas to make this student play more slowly and more thoughtfully?
—*Canada*

A. Teachers and parents try everything here. They make kids sit on their hands, write their moves down beforehand, internalize certain procedures on each turn, and follow all sorts of mechanical routines to retard their impetuosity. Some of that may work, but nothing can beat constant practice at analyzing properly.

Decelerate things simply: stop them from moving pieces in analysis and training sessions without telling you their intentions. It might be difficult at first, but if you're consistent, and encourage them to explain their thoughts instead of demonstrating them, you will slow the kids down in a way that's bound to produce better play. Reward the procedure more than the right result. If they touch anything on the board, count it as wrong, even if they played the right move. But if they can explain their thinking, even when the scheme is wrong, they can be given the chance to save themselves by changing their minds. You can always balance things out later, making sure that those who get the correct answers, but who break form, receive credit as well—though not immediately, not until they've learned a lesson.

Much of real chess thinking has to do with discovering options and alternatives. Too often a young player will get a notion and play it without further thought, especially if it seems strong on the surface. Somehow you must ensure that they learn to mull over other options until they can settle on the one they think is best.

Let's say they have to respond to a particular threat from their opponent. And let's further say that they come up with a move that doesn't quite do it or even flops. If they suggest an inferior move, ask them if there's another move that meets the criteria of the situation and also "works." If they don't find another credible move, prod them until they do. Once they do, and the move is still inadequate, you must keep the interaction going until they unearth another possibility. If they finally determine a better move, ask them to compare the moves they've come up with to see which one they like most. If you do this consistently, and often enough, you will be instilling in them a very practicable technique that should certainly hold back their rashness and predispose them to use their time better in the search for logical moves and pertinent options. But these problems are typical and apparently eternal, and they bring to mind Lasker's insightful cogency: "If you see a good move, look for a better one." You see, they were making the same mistakes even then.

FREQUENCY

Q. I am the father of a fairly talented, eight-year-old chess player who just won the K–3 championship in Florida. He gets lessons from a master at our home every other Tuesday for 90 minutes per session, attends a chess club at school for 90 minutes once per week during the school year, attends a one week chess camp each summer, and plays quads at a mostly adult chess club for about three hours one evening per week. I also play him about three or four games per week, but quite frankly, while I can provide him decent competition, he usually beats me. He also studies annotated games for about 30 minutes per night, two or three nights per week, and spends about an hour or two per week teaching his six-year-old sister how to play. He prefers to study games from the top players in his age group (i.e., published board one and two games from later rounds of national or state championship tournaments) instead of historical games of masters. He also listens to and watches narrated games on a popular computer chess program from time to time. In the midst of all of this, he remains an excellent student and baseball player.

Two questions: Is it wise for him to be studying games of top kids, rather than games of masters? Is he getting enough or too much instruction? Note that we have allowed him to set his own chess schedule and he gives himself time off when he thinks he needs it. He had the opportunity to have the master every week, but decided that he wanted to have more "play time." I think he is making good decisions, and the results are showing it. He is still in love with the game. What do you think?
—*USA*

A. Your son surely is a promising young player, whose love and excitement for the game should take him quite far. I would not want to tamper with a program that appears to have worked so smoothly and effectively.

I do think, however, that much more might be gained from looking at instructive examples rather than the creations of his third-grade rivals. Scholastic productions are likely to be pockmarked with erroneous plans and gaping oversights. I'm amazed he's able to get his hands on enough legible score sheets to make his efforts worthwhile.

I would guess that the reason is that your son has been concentrating on beating specific players. Many young people play with such an aim, to defeat particular competitors. Most teachers are not comfortable with that approach. They feel it conveys the wrong message. Although it may not help him to beat the boy next door, studying examples selected for instructional or aesthetic reasons will generally teach him more about the game, and that should sustain his future development. But if he's happy doing what he's doing, let him go on being who he is. In the end, it's more important to be content, and that's usually the true path to success.

Finally, you ask if your son is getting too much instruction. Actually, he may be getting too little. He receives one private lesson every two weeks, while other top third-graders take as many as two and three lessons a week. But again, we all have different needs and tastes, and the regimen he's created for himself (I'm assuming the choices really are his) seems to be working very well. Be satisfied that you have such a talented and motivated child. Everyone should be so lucky.

LONG DISTANCE

Q. I have two nieces eight years of age. What is the first thing I should do to start introducing them to chess long distance? It should be noted that their parents do not play.
—*USA*

A. Start by telling them to get new parents, which you can do by correspondence, telephone, or email.

RESIGNING

Q. I have a number of questions about when to resign and when to play on. We teach our young chess players (rated under 1000) to play out a game and not resign when they are down pieces or believe that they have no way of winning. One reason for this is because there are numerous circumstances where young players can win a lost game when their opponent does not know how to win a won game (i.e., they do not know how to checkmate), and also playing on teaches a young player how to play when behind. First, do you agree with this, and second, at what point do you teach a child to resign a game? Related to this is the chess equivalent of "running up the score." Often I see players toying with an opponent, refusing to checkmate and just cleaning off their opponents' pieces or going after just one more queen. While I know this does not violate the rules of chess I feel it violates the spirit of the game. Are there any suggestion on how to handle this, other than praying to the gods of chess for a stalemate?
—*USA*

A. Your outlook is right on the money. Continue to embolden your students to resist even when the game is lost. Dissuade your students from giving up until they themselves are strong enough to win most won games by force. As a rule, students should be trained to fight tooth and nail. They must come to recognize that chess is a struggle. That approach develops resourcefulness and tough-mindedness, which are essential to top-level chess and all echelons of competitive society.

When it comes to running up the score, that is, making unneeded queens, the veteran teacher usually stresses the practical drawbacks. It might lead to stalemate, imprecise play, occasional time forfeiture, or at least an extension of the game, when anything might happen.

It's usually more effective to praise those who play sound chess rather than reproving players who consistently violate principles. Instead of overly criticizing those who pile up the score, give proper credit to those who win economically. Take the high road and keep things positive. That might not bring about immediate results for a particular individual, though over time it should influence the rest of the group, if not those students directly affected. You can't just remake the world. But constant reminders tend to add up, and the accumulation of small persuasions eventually matters, so think how much could be achieved if daily you reached out even to a single student. I like to begin each day thinking of Horace Mann's credo: "Be afraid to die before winning one small battle for humanity." I'm not resigned to it, but it seems like a pretty good philosophy to me.

TOURNAMENT DECISIONS

Q. I'm hoping you can offer me some advice. My ten-year-old daughter wants to compete in a big tournament coming up. This is notable because she has not competed in a tournament for about three years. At that time we left a tournament early because she got too upset after a loss. Since then her interest in chess has continued unabated; she plays online frequently and has a lesson every week. We had dropped the issue of tournaments completely, feeling it was more important to preserve her love of the game than to force her to confront its competitive aspect face-to-face. Here is the question: Should we convince her to compete in smaller tournaments before the big one? Her teacher thinks it might be poor planning to let her attend a stressful tournament without first building up her immunity to the pressures through practice at smaller tournaments. We don't want to be irresponsible, but we don't want her to burn out on the

smaller tournaments. Nor do we want to send her to the big tournament ill prepared. We also don't want to force her into the grind of frequent tournaments (which she has not expressed interest in) just so she can do well in the big tournament (which she has expressed interest in). We haven't talked to her about it at length because we don't want to create present anxiety by talking about past anxiety; we also think it might be possible that her added maturity will carry her through the competition with grace. Where do you come down on this issue?
—*England*

A. Why don't you give one of the lesser events a try, just to see how things go? If that experience turns out nicely, you can enter her in another tournament, making sure to get her approval on it first. If there's any lingering doubt, talk it out with her to see what her fears and reasons may be. If she agrees to play, enter her with the same provision, prepared to stop further entries if it turns out unsatisfactory. If she's still adamantly against playing, I would accept that as the way things are. You shouldn't impose your will on hers when to do so might inflict real damage—and over what, a chess tournament?

Nonetheless, I recognize your concerns. It's extremely difficult for a child to succeed in a competitive world without intelligent parental involvement and gentle pushing. There's always going to be some resistance to the threat of discomfit, even if the overall benefits might outweigh the slight difficulties. Still, you don't want to go too far and cause an emotional scar. But you sound like a sensitive and loving parent, so I don't imagine that will happen. You have already set priorities where they should be: maintaining her love of the game is paramount, embracing its competitive trappings is not.

INCENTIVES

Q. Do you think it's a good idea to give kids prizes as incentives to play?
—*USA*

A. This is one of those eternal questions, such as "Does the world consist of the one or the many?" or "Is there a meaning to life?" No matter how cogently you argue your position, the other side can construct a counter argument infuriatingly worthy of being heard. And that is practically the case here. Purists make a strong argument for playing the game for the game's sake, but chess teachers and organizers know a different reality. They realize that incentives are often needed to keep kids involved and motivated. And while this may be repugnant to hardcore chess players, educators contend that it's worth it to keep kids interested, almost no matter what it takes, because the benefits derived from chess are so great. That's the stronger logic for me, so I'm going to come down in favor of giving prizes and incentives. Getting kids to play chess at all outweighs the drawback of getting them to play for the wrong reasons.

TROPHIES

Q. What do you think is an appropriate prize level for an elementary school chess club? Trophies? Gift certificates? Books? Key chains for all entries? I'm getting ready to hold the school championship this spring and respect your opinion.
—*USA*

A. The trend these days is to give large trophies and plenty of them. There are events in which everyone garners a gargantuan trophy, with the trophies being bigger than the recipients. It also strikes many observers as curious how some contestants can win trophies even though they've failed to win a single game. Organizers are able to justify this superfluity of prizes by creating numerous awards in special categories, particularly for tournaments extending over an entire semester. Besides prizes for finishing at the top overall (such as Champion, 2nd place, etc.), awards are given for a range of achievements, including Most Improved Player, Most Outstanding Player, Most Valuable Player, Hardest Working Player, Rookie of the Year, Best Girl (certainly a controversial and dubious award in today's world), Best Attacker, Best Defender, Best Combination Player, Best Endgame Player, and so on.

It may sound as if I'm opposed to awarding so many prizes, and indeed I am, but I haven't been able to escape this phenomenon in my own teaching. I've felt constrained to give trophies, medals, books, ribbons, Beanie Babies, Pokémon cards, stickers, pencils, points (such as my master class points, as depicted in *Searching for Bobby Fischer*), and other trinkets to keep kids happy. Recently I've tried to get a handle on those excesses by finding an appropriate level of presentation. I'm not suggesting that you follow my approach, for it may not work in your circumstances, but what I aim to do now is give just one trophy for the overall champion (personalized, with the winner's name on it) and ribbons for 2nd and 3rd place. Anyone else worthy of being distinguished receives a certificate or possibly a book (okay, sometimes an extra pretzel).

It's natural for a student to react despondently if tons of trophies are awarded and he or she gets nothing. But it's hard for students and players to feel too badly for not receiving a trophy if only one trophy is presented, and it's just to the winner. Nevertheless, if a teacher or an organizer still feels compelled to satisfy the general need for a red badge of courage, he or she can provide certificates of participation to each student completing the course, tournament, or camp. That would be equitable without being materialistically ridiculous. It would also save money, which then could be used to run more tournaments, which eventually should produce more committed chess players (surely, some of us should be committed). That might seem a little unreal, but it's how I'd like to see things go. May your school championship proceed according to plan, wherever you purchase your trophies.

HOMEWORK

Q. I am wondering how much homework you expect your students to do. Since taking up chess teaching part time, I have been surprised to find bright youngsters in the nine- to 11-year range who seem to genuinely enjoy the game and their lessons, but show no interest in doing book work outside of lessons. The kind of homework I believe most useful at the 800–1000 rating level is the solution of combinations. A somewhat less conventional homework assignment I have used is the outright memorization of games such as those in Laszlo Polgar's *Chess* and Chernev's *Logical Chess Move by Move*. One motivational tool I have used when homework wasn't done was just to have the offender do it during lesson time. And on one occasion I just canceled the lesson. There is no haranguing or berating the students for these lapses; I just let them know what is expected. Getting back to the question I have for you: How much homework do you expect of your pre teen students, and how do you handle it when they don't do it?

—*USA*

A. I expect my students to do very little homework, so I almost never give any. Most of them play chess for sport and recreation. They're likely to abandon the game once it resembles school. When I do give homework it's in line with your approach. I give them tactical exercises, with problems offered in related blocks of two or four. Occasionally I ask them to familiarize themselves with games, opening traps, or useful endgame positions, though I keep such tasks to a minimum.

It really used to bother me when students didn't complete my homework assignments. It was terribly dispiriting to see work sheets left on the floor of the classroom, never to be taken home. To top it all off, the parents wondered why I never gave homework. I dealt with that by making students sign everything as soon as they got it. Then at least I could defend myself by presenting certain parents a packet of their son's or daughter's signed, stepped-on, unanswered homework sheets.

I became concerned with homework early in my career when I realized that I actually drove away some of my best and most promising students by trying to satisfy parental needs for drilling. When I give homework these days, it's usually to assign tactical books that my students can work through at their own pace. Their reward is finishing the book, not certificates or trophies.

You sound like a dedicated, intelligent teacher. Don't lose sight of one of the more valuable attributes of chess. By virtue of playing a game you can learn things about yourself and others that have lifelong value. Let's not kill these opportunities by turning play into a chore.

YOUNG GAMBITEERS

Q. I am a chess teacher that mostly teaches small children, 12-year-olds, etc., although I also teach some older children. I was wondering what openings you would advise small children to play. I know that they are supposed to play open attacking games but do you think that gambits are the way to go? I am afraid that I might overdo it by teaching them gambits since their attacking technique is not all that good and it might affect their results. Because I know that the choice of opening can have a major effect on your performance, I constantly worry that I am teaching them the wrong openings. Can you maybe outline a basic opening repertoire?

—*South Africa*

A. I don't think it's so important which openings you illustrate, as long as you choose examples that are lucid, certain, and short. That doesn't mean you have to offer games and lines from the 19th century or show artificial traps that never occur. You can find, for instance, plausible variations in the English Opening and King's Indian Defense that are crystal clear, definite, and not too long. And what's wrong with showing them gambits? By playing gambits, at least those backed by sound analysis, one naturally becomes more creative and resourceful. Besides, young gambiteers have a tendency to blitz through their opposition not only because aggression instills fear, but also because defensive skills generally take longer to acquire than attacking prowess. But why limit the scope of your presentation? Show them a little bit of everything so that they can sense the richness of the game. Show them all the sweets and they can choose their own candy.

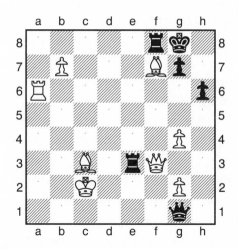

Capablanca-Marshall, New York 1918
Black resigns. White rebukes the Marshall Gambit
at the Manhattan Chess Club.

DYNAMIC OPENINGS

Q. Do you come across junior players who try to hasten their pace of learning chess openings by studying dynamic openings like the Sicilian when they have yet to grasp the concept of playing open games? How would you work with a student who does not put in time to learn and yet wishes to play theoretical openings? I've seen many kids play these openings like an expert from moves 1–15, then give away the advantage, owing to ignorance of the game plans and ideas. Many of these children take part in tournaments and most of them against adults. Is there a practical piece of advice you can give on how they can attain decent results minus a limited opening repertoire? What would be a good repertoire for a USCF 1400–1500 player from the age of 9 to 12 to learn? Your comments are most appreciated.
—Singapore

A. It's certainly easier and more customary to conduct classical openings before grappling with the subtleties of hypermodern and contemporary variants. But the same type of debate takes place over what phase to study first, the opening or the endgame. Most traditionalists favor starting with the endgame, as did Lasker, Tarrasch, and Capablanca, and they make very sound arguments in stating their judgment. But as other modern educators have come to realize, it doesn't matter how convincingly a position is affirmed if the student doesn't really believe it. You can't do your best if plagued by doubt.

For that reason, and because young people are usually excited by prospects of winning quickly and brilliantly, today's teachers often feed off this initial enthusiasm, delaying endgame study until a psychologically appropriate time. The same is comparably true for the study of classical openings. If students would rather immerse themselves in the celebrated games of their own time, let them do it. That's what playing chess for them is about—having fun and pretending to play like Kramnik and Kasparov.

If you want to create students who can make independent decisions, you can't tell them what to think and then expect them to do their own thinking. You can only try to guide them. The smart ones will want your help when it matters to them and when they can most benefit from it. And if they're not that smart, that's okay too. After all, this isn't math or language. It's chess, and they have the right to play it the way they want, even if it makes no sense to the rest of us.

I wouldn't worry about the suitability of their opening repertoires. Let them choose whatever variations they consider appealing, allowing them to make their own mistakes. Permit them to grow from the game's ups and downs gradually. Your job should primarily be to insure that chess remains a stimulating activity for them. Help them enjoy chess not merely to the level of their ability, but also to the degree of their interest. If things work out, your students might even let you inject a breath of classicism. Just think where that could lead.

DRAWISH OPENINGS

Q. My son, age eight, has started playing chess. His coach has taught him openings starting with e4, but is reluctant to teach him the English Opening, saying that it is very drawish. Is it true that games played with the English Opening are very drawish?
—*India*

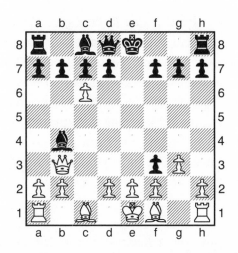

Petrosian-Ree, Wijk aan Zee 1971
White uses the English to win in 8 moves. Black resigns.

A. It depends. Sometimes the English is drawish and sometimes not. But that has nothing to do with why most coaches strenuously avoid showing their beginning eight-year-old students 1. c4. In order to play the English well it helps to have a sound grasp of rudiments, which are typically introduced by examining classical variations. Classical play relied on 1. e4, so naturally there's a plethora of examples stemming from king-pawn openings.

Moreover, newcomers are easily confused by the English, which seems to transgress against traditional principles. That's because it's characterized by the counterintuitive delay of central occupation and the apparent paradox of flank development. For those and other reasons, which I could detail but won't, teachers have tended to deter their students from playing it in the first place. But if your son really wants to learn the English, and the impulse definitely comes from him, not from you (who is irrelevant to the entire proceeding), that's wonderful too. Enthusiasm is the best asset in the quest for anything.

PLAYING UP

Q. Recently, my 12-year-old son played in a two-day tournament. The tournament included three divisions: Under 1400, Under 1800, and an

Open section. My son chose to play in the Open. His playing strength is around 1400 or so, and a few of the Expert and Master players there suggested that he should not have played in the Open. While playing "up" is generally regarded as a good idea, I was told that he should only play up by just one section. In other words, he should have played in the Under 1800 section. Is there any general rule of thumb for making these decisions? He played plenty of hard games, and though he lost pretty consistently, he also said he learned a lot playing very strong players. What do you say about this?

—*USA*

A. Usually I advise my students to play in their own section, whatever it is. On occasion, it's perfectly proper to play a section ahead to test the waters, but two sections ahead is another matter. If he or she wishes to play up so temerariously, and I deduce that's an improvident plan for the youngster, I'll say so and explain my thinking. But I will also indicate that the decision is his (or hers) and his (or her) parents' (gulp), and that everyone is the captain of his or her own ship. Since your son made the decision, the prudent thing would be to review the situation and assess its overall effect. Was it a valuable experience? Did he learn something important from it? Or did it tinge his chess with an unsuitable color? Only by discussing this with him and analyzing everything relevant can you decide if that's the kind of thing he should be doing. And if you can't evaluate it all conclusively, then maybe it's wise to let him learn how to seek his own future—in chess, and everything else.

COLLEGE

Q. I've been playing chess for two years and I've seen a relatively steady improvement. Of course, I started playing chess at the wrong time. I also began college two years ago and I go to a very challenging university. My rating now is about 1900 and my last four performance ratings have all been more than 2000 (some much higher) so I feel as though I'm still well on the rise. My main goal right now is to make Master. I don't know what a realistic time frame for this is. My guess is somewhere between three and four years, but obviously it could take longer. My question

really is, after getting serious at such a relatively old age, should I take advantage of any benefits or take care of any disadvantages of starting at a much older age? Also I'm curious to know have there been strong IMs or GMs that have started at such a late age (just for curiosity's sake)?
—*USA*

A. You're already a respectable player, and you're definitely young enough to still make significant advances in playing caliber, possibly even to the Master level. True, it may not be easy, and you're not six years old. But college age is not that old either, and that's when most of us acquire the knowledge we need to succeed in our respective professions. Are we saying here, that many professionals (doctors, lawyers, scientists, artists, businesspeople, and so on) are ill qualified because they've learned a good deal of their expertise as adults, not as children?

I'm reluctant to advise a player of your status without knowing a lot more about you, and you're not going to get anywhere with glib generalizations. Such things can work for beginners, inasmuch as most players can often profit much more from general concepts than particular ones when they're just starting out. But once you become fairly adept, you tend to need more pertinent solutions, applying particularly to who you are, instead of what you are.

I think the best course of action for you right now would be to have your games assessed by a strong and objective player, in your case, preferably of 2400 strength or better, who also has some experience at performing such analyses. It makes sense to get your play diagnosed before committing to any definite course of action.

Have there been strong players who reached the IM level or better in later life, who might serve as inspiring beacons? Of course there have been. Many of the game's strongest players learned in their teens. Akiba Rubinstein didn't learn how to play chess until he was 16. I think he did okay. Reuben Fine, for whom I worked as an assistant for two years, told me he learned the moves at eight yet didn't get really involved till his middle adolescence. And there are definitely others who became accomplished much later in their chess lives.

But I wouldn't look to them. I'd look to you, and based on your present level of rapid improvement, and who you appear to be, I'd say

99

you have an excellent opportunity to become a master in two to three years, playing and studying the game 20–30 hours a week. That doesn't mean you're categorically going to get there after following such a regimen. But you strike me as determined and possibly talented enough to have more than a bettor's chance. Good luck. You seem to know where you're going, and you're probably not going to stop there.

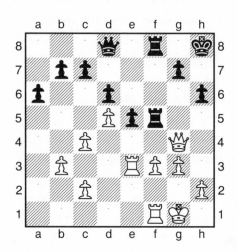

Janowski-Rubinstein, Karlsbad 1907
Black played the imaginative 1. ... Qb8!!,
with the idea of shifting the queen to the a7-g1 diagonal.
Does such wisdom come with age, or what?

AGE-OLD QUESTION

Q. I'm a young chess player, 20 years to be specific, and though I've known how to play chess for most of that time, I haven't taken it seriously until just recently. I find it difficult not to be discouraged by how the greatest players in the world seem to be very thoroughly exposed to the game at an early age. My questions are these: What players have achieved world-class play without beginning their training as a child? What can I do to help my odds of excelling, without the learning energies of a child?

—USA

A. I would be lying to you if I were to say learning chess at any early age doesn't generally help. I must also admit that I can't think of too many people who became world-class strength (I mean, really strong), who didn't learn before the age of 13. Sure, we could come up with a few names, as I have in the past, but that would only offer false hope.

Let me make another suggestion. Instead of aiming to become world class, why don't you strive for a more reasonable ambition, simply to get better? Isn't that why you play chess—to improve steadily while experiencing the pleasure of mental stimulation? That's easy enough to do. You can make progress by playing slightly superior opposition on a regular basis. You might very well lose a few more than you win, but you'll undoubtedly learn a lot more along the way.

At least learning from your losses is a more reasonable expectation than aiming to be the best there ever was. Not that I want to undermine anyone's hopes, but it's wise to be practical. You may fail with the first approach and still gain. Relying on the second plan for your future might set you up for failure without any profit. Just go out there and play chess. If improvement is to happen (and in your case I have no reason to doubt it will), it will take care of itself, as you're playing and being challenged. Nevertheless, whatever you do, don't be discouraged by not being able to play like Bobby Fischer used to. Not even he can do that on a regular basis, and look how much time and practice he's had at being Bobby Fischer.

LATE BLOOMERS

Q. What chance is there for older people, e.g., 40-something, to achieve a high level in chess? I read that an average of 10,000 hours is needed to achieve an expert level in music, math, or other professional fields (*Genius Explained*, Howard, Cambridge University Press). That is three hours a day for a decade. If someone, aged 40, has that amount of time and motivation, how high could he go? After all, there is no need for the physical development of, say, a concert violinist. Or should older people just settle for amateur status and be content with playing for fun? I personally wouldn't be happy with that, but I don't want to waste my time on wishful thinking.
—*United Kingdom*

A. I'd like to understand more about the older person in question before answering. It would help to know his or her present strength and experience. Let's say we're talking about you. If you're a rank beginner, your task could be demoralizing. But if you're a 1600 player, and you're willing to make the effort, you'd have a decent chance of getting somewhere. Some players have become experts well past the age of 40, so it can be done.

Of course there are difficulties, and no guarantees. Chess is a demanding game, and we have no right to expect excellence without toil and by virtue of some automatic formula. I can understand that you don't want to play chess merely for fun. But what makes you think that playing for pleasure excludes learning? You should always be able to play for both pleasure and steady improvement, even if you never reach the upper chess-playing classes. I have no expectation of getting any better, and I still love the game, even at my age.

THINKING BACK

Q. I have played chess since I was eight, more so since the introduction of computers. At present I am sitting around a rating of 1500–1600. I read books aplenty and study all my games where appropriate or just for fun. Can you recommend any books that might help me better myself this late down the learning road? I am now 43.
—*New Zealand*

A. I wouldn't say that there are any chess books in particular designed for the 43-year-old mind. Most of the better ones apply to good minds in general, without reference to age (with the exception of books for kids). It's also possible that you've read every book I could mention. But if I could go back to being 43, it would be a real pleasure to dabble through any of the outstanding game collections. To once again be moved by the greatness that is chess, I would eagerly plunge into the annotated gold of Capablanca, Nimzowitsch, Alekhine, Botvinnik, Keres, Fine, Euwe, Reshevsky, Smyslov, Tal, Petrosian, Geller, Polugaevsky, Larsen, Fischer, Karpov, and Kasparov. If you've never seriously looked at the play of these artists, now's the time to do it. And if you've already gone over the trails they've forged, it can't hurt to take those journeys one more time. Maybe it'll help you find your way back to your own right path, or even encourage you to explore woods you've never gone into before. But you never know, so you might want to take along a volume of Dante in case you get lost.

NEXT LEVEL

Q. I'm 50 years old and I am a 1900 USCF rated player from Sioux City, Iowa. I just never seem to improve. What reading material would you suggest for me that may help me get to the next level?

A. I'm not sure what you mean by getting to the next level. Are you talking about chess ability or age? Let's say you're talking about reaching the Expert class (2000) in chess. If so, there's no reading material in itself that will work, even this. Let's say you're talking about living long enough to reach a ripe old age. Then I'd say just about any reading material would work, even this.

OLDEST GRANDMASTERS

Q. I've been doing research regarding adult level improvement in chess. A recent interview by GM Baburin said he only became master (in the Soviet Union) when he was 21. In a book on the late Leonid Stein, it was stated that Stein became a master at the age of 24, but progressed quickly after that to a top GM. And if I remember correctly, IM John Shaw studied the game relatively late but is still improving. From online articles and other book sources, it is considered extremely difficult for much progress to take place for those studying chess in their late teens and early 20s. While I agree that those in this category have a nearly impossible time to make the top 100, what are some other examples of the levels achieved by players who studied the game late? For instance, can an expert 20-year-old still make IM or possibly GM with the right training in this day and age?
—USA

A. This is a sphere where very little is known. Ordinary experience tells us how hard it is for beginning adults to acquire real chess expertise, but there haven't been many scientific studies in this subject, if any important ones at all. For an unschooled man or woman to become a sophisticated player, it would really help if some of the groundwork had been laid when they were young children, rather than having to pick up the intricacies of the game from the beginning. But you can always find paradigmatic examples of extraordinary development after the teenage years. Leonid Stein, who became one of the world's greatest players, demonstrates that it's possible.

CONCENTRATION

Q. I have only been studying chess for a short time, although, I have been moving pieces for many years. I am retired from the Navy, where we "played" chess on board ship for years without getting deep into tactics, etc. My question is probably the dumbest question you have ever heard. I am 70 years old and find my biggest problem is concentration after about 15 moves. Is there a way to develop better concentration? I have been a pastor for more than 30 years and have no trouble memorizing Scripture and preaching with only an outline, so I must still have a good mind. I know it is not the love of the game because I truly love to play. I win my share of games against my equals, but never against stronger players. I play in the World Open each year in Philadelphia and local tournaments, when not on Sundays. Any help would be greatly appreciated.
—*USA*

A. Your question is by no means the dumbest question I've ever received (you should see some of them).

Obviously you have a good head, and playing chess is a terrific way to keep yourself sharp and productive. I wouldn't change your excellent program at all, so continue to play in the World Open and local tournaments. But clearly you've noticed that one of the first things to go as we start to get a little older is our ability to concentrate. Younger players are generally able to focus for longer periods.

You can help offset the disadvantage of aging by pacing yourself while playing. Take short respites when contesting longer games. Let your mind shut down for a minute or so, kind of like taking an afternoon nap. You might even help the process along by removing yourself from the board. Just walk away and find a comfortable place to sit. Close your eyes and try to relax. Do that a couple of times during each game and you'll be amazed how much stronger you feel and how much easier it is to call upon reserves when you really need them.

Will that solve the problem completely? There's no magic elixir for any ailment, but it's usually better to be proactive. It also helps to stay positive as you play the game for the best of reasons, for stimulating challenge and pure fun.

TRADING PIECES

Q. My father is going to be 80 years old and he loves to play chess. He has trouble with all the pieces on the board. Should his strategy be to trade pieces so that it becomes easier? I have been advising him to do this but he obstinately disagrees with me. What should I do?
—*USA*

A. Your father is right. One should trade when it makes sense and avoid trades when it doesn't.

Keep in mind that having fewer pieces on the board doesn't necessarily translate into a simpler game. Some trades can lead to positions of greater complexity, where all kinds of chess intangibles assume importance, such as space and unoccupied squares. So it would be a mistake to continue advocating that your dad exchange merely to simplify. You might as well tell your father that old chess players never die; they simply trade away.

Let your father think for himself. Fortunately, it's clear he already does.

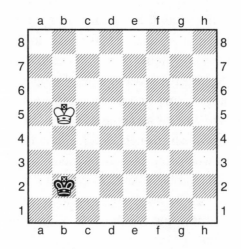

Lasker-Tarrasch, St. Petersburg 1914
Two men past 45 years of age trade down to a draw.

CHAPTER 4

Mind Play

How to visualize chess positions, how to calculate, how to analyze, what to think about, comprehending the nature of chess thinking: all of that and more are in this chapter. There are questions about blindfold play—there always are—and how to remember chess positions better. What to look for, when not to look at all, how to salvage hopeless situations, how to economize the thinking process, how to make a list of candidate moves, how to classify chess concepts: that's all here too.

Naturally, some answers compared different ways of thinking strategically and tactically. Clearly, emotions could get in the way of either type of thinking, so that particular problem had to be addressed as well. I also discovered that I had used the word "mindful" a ridiculous number of times. I never realized it had meant that much to me. But since many readers take note of such things (at least a chunky percentage of them), I did my best to remove all but one or two "mindful" references from the text. The chapter reads better and now I can look at myself in the mirror again (maybe I won't go that far).

VISUALIZATION

Q. Many books stress visualization and sight of the board in order to play well. Is this an innate skill or can it be developed? If it is something that can be developed, are there any drills or exercises that you could recommend? —*USA*

A. The faculty seems mainly to be innate, though capable of being sharpened and improved. Strengthen your cerebral muscles by exercising them regularly, making the effort to analyze mentally. If you want your visualization to improve, resist moving the pieces no matter how hard the situation appears or becomes. And if you give up on an example, continue to use your head when you look at the solution. That is, be sure to play the moves over in your mind before playing them on the board. Generally, try to solve all tactical situations by seeing ahead.

You can also develop your visualization skills by playing over entire games, stopping to check yourself every five moves or so. Simply start at the beginning of a game and try to play the first five moves in your mind. As you imagine the position after the fifth move (or every nth move), actually play the moves on the board for confirmation. Then, in the same way, proceed mentally onward to move ten. Now play those moves on the board to corroborate them as well. From there, forge ahead to move 15, following through with the same procedure right to the end of the game.

It might be easier doing this on a computer, where you can click around with relative ease. Certain books also serve nicely, such as those in the old Weltgeschichte Series. Published by a German company, those tomes presented hundreds of games played by a particular chess great, with diagrams interspersed every five moves. They were terrific sources of material, and very helpful to several generations of top players, since no real knowledge of German was needed

But there's no alchemy here. Regardless of how good you already are at visualizing ahead, you're probably not going to make much progress without putting in time and effort. For starters, that means always practicing the good habit of never moving the pieces when analyzing, no matter what, plain and simple.

HEAD TRIP

Q. I am a chess enthusiast from California and I play chess just for enjoyment. Many times, the fun that I would otherwise get is spoiled by my mistakes in calculations. I don't make beginner's blunders, but when I calculate I often miss a reply on the third or fourth move. I have read books on tactics and I am familiar with all the themes and motifs. It's not that I lose my queen to a fork, but I cannot adequately evaluate the position that would arise after the moves in my calculation, especially when the depth is more than three moves. I don't know what my rating is; due to lack of time, I haven't played in any tournaments. I sometimes play rapid chess on the Internet, and there my rating is around 1500. At this level, what should I do to improve my calculations?
—*USA*

A. Try to solve a couple of tactical problems in your mind every day, and resist the urge to become lazy. If you find you can't help moving the pieces when considering a puzzle, avoid temptation by working from diagrams rather than from positions set up on an actual board. You can find serviceable diagrams in practically any good combination book.

Give each problem at least five to ten minutes of focused thought before turning to the answer. Better yet, don't turn to the answer at all, at least not before you've invested a little piece of yourself. When you're not getting anywhere, simply close the book and come back to the problem refreshed at a subsequent point. You'd be surprised how often the answer suddenly materializes after an interim of unconscious contemplation. If you're still not making much progress, put the book down again and return to the challenge at a later time. Even if you never get the right answer, persist in using your head. Of course you'd like to get the solution, but it's even more important to cultivate the proper mindset for problem solving. For many, it's a sure road to winning chess.

SEEING POSITIONS

Q. In a recent column you wrote "How much math is needed to figure out the number of moves it takes to get somewhere on the board? The real

trick is keeping the picture of it in your head." I quite agree, but I find the "seeing ahead" part of the game to be quite difficult. Are there ways to develop this ability? Also, I would be very appreciative if you could provide a brief list of some useful books of chess puzzles (I'm fairly new to chess literature). Finally, with a view to choosing a couple of openings to concentrate on, I'm searching for a good current instructional book that would explain the Hows and Whys of the openings. I have Byron Jacob's book *Mastering the Opening*, and find that although it presents its information very well, it lacks depth and discussion of particular moves. (I enjoyed my dad's books by I. Horowitz, but I suspect they're quite dated.)
—*Canada*

A. You can improve your skill at "seeing" positions by analyzing in your head as often as possible. If you find that it's hard to resist touching the pieces once they're set up, never take them out in the first place. Better yet, hide the set or give it away, preferably to someone who isn't fixated on visualization.

Work with diagrams. When you're considering a puzzle, just focus on the puzzle. Consult the notes and answers only after you've spent some time with the chess picture. And don't be afraid to close your eyes and do some thinking and imagining without looking at anything. If you've ever seen Kasparov play a chess game, you can't miss how he occasionally looks away from the board, sometimes even at the ceiling, obviously trying to blot out the visual "noise" so that he can think without interference.

There is a ton of chess puzzle books. Even the ones universally despised have utility. They contain diagrams, which is what most sentient chess beings require. Rather than telling you the name of a volume that might work for you—an apparently nice person, but one whose chess needs are somewhat nebulous—why don't you check out any decent online chess catalogue? It will probably have sufficient information to help you make a discriminating selection. In the same catalogue you'll also encounter books that explain opening concepts. Some of these manuals, though not all, offer Horowitz's bold clarity in a contemporary setting.

DON'T LOOK NOW

Q. How does someone go about learning how to play blindfolded? I have a hard time studying books because I need a board in front of me or ChessMaster. I wish to study in my head for the convenience of it.
—*USA*

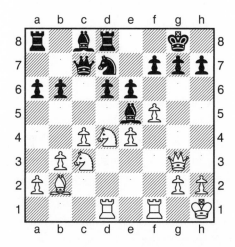

Alekhine-Sämisch, Berlin 1923
An amazing blindfold finish.
Black resigned after 1. fxe6!! Bxg3 2. exf7+ Kh8 3. Nd5.

A. Blindfold chess is a form of the game in which one or both of the players play without sight of the board. The blindfold player sits near the playing area, his back to the board or his eyes covered (so that he can't see the moves being played), and the moves are told to him by chess notation. The practice has a long history going back to the Middle Ages. It's often done as a public display, and the exhibitor sometimes contests multiple blindfold games simultaneously. The skill to conduct these séances, where as many as 50 sightless games or more are played at one time, is much admired and a source of constant inquiry.

If you really mean blindfold chess, you might start by wearing a blindfold. But perhaps you mean something else. Maybe you'd like to learn how to analyze in your mind, without moving the pieces. If that's what

111

you're after, the way to improve is quite simple. Just analyze in your head every chance you get, with no exceptions. It may be difficult at first, but if you force yourself to see variations and move sequences by imagining and visualizing on a regular basis, you'll get better at it eventually. Doing so may never quite become convenient, but surely practice should improve your facility for such calculations. There are no tricks to replace talent and hard work. If you already have the talent, fine. It will take you so far—but there's no escaping the work.

HOW TO THINK

Q. I am a chess enthusiast and beginning player. I always wanted to get this question cleared up. How do chess players think when playing a game? Of course, I have read all about analyzing a position and so on but still, is it a move-by-move thought process? When you have a plan and go about it, your opponent's move disrupts it and sometimes it fails. So it looks like you are constantly planning after every move but not achieving it because your opponent knows exactly what is going on in your mind. He defends against it well. My peers and I tend to have equal games. I want rather to have games where I develop an advantage and maintain it. Is there any advice you can give?
—*India*

A. How do good players think? They start by analyzing their opponent's last move for immediate pro-and-con tactics. They try to strengthen their own positions and spot possible weaknesses. They try to ward off danger ahead of time. They look for future possibilities and make plans, and they stay with their plans unless the situation requires a change or they see an opportunity, whereupon they alter their plans. Of course, they're not changing direction at all, because a good plan takes into account the possibility of unexpected or unforeseen possibilities. Good plans, like good planners, are flexible.

To learn more about planning, and also how good players think, turn to books containing well-annotated games, with notes in both words and variations. A balanced mixture is desirable if all the ideas are to be understood. Any thoroughly analyzed game collection should do, especially if the games are elucidated by the very player who played them. Generally, the more thoroughly the games are annotated by a top competitor, the better.

LITTLE THINKS

Q. I play a lot of online blitz (three or five minutes), averaging about 2100 on several chess sites. I find that when going back to slow chess at 35 moves in 75 minutes plus 15 minutes sudden death in my local league, I hardly feel that I play any better moves at the slow time limit than I do at the fast one. Can you suggest ways of making the maximum use of one's time at slower time limits?
—*England*

A. There's nothing wrong with playing both fast and slow chess. Just make sure one doesn't come right on the heels of the other. You wouldn't want to continue merrily along as if the conditions haven't changed, especially when they have. Playing fast chess is one thing. But if you're playing slower chess, try to utilize more of its defining characteristic—time. Take the time to consider possibilities, and you won't have to reply as instinctively as you might in online rapids.

In order to use time efficaciously it helps to have a routine, a set of steps you can follow when you don't know what to do. When you do know what to do, you'll just do it, dispensing with routine altogether. Not surprisingly, even players of the same skill level have different procedures, so you'll have to work out what's comfortable for you. But generally it's prudent to divide your thinking twofold: what you do on your move and what you do on your opponent's.

On your move, make sure you understand your opponent's last move, if it issues any threats, and whether or not it responds to your previous play. Since your clock is running, you shouldn't dither. You need to be specific and get on with it. Things are entirely different when your opponent's clock is ticking. That's when you can let your mind explore and wander.

On your opponent's turn, ask investigative questions about planning and evaluate future attacking possibilities. Consider potential enemy threats you must ward off before they become monstrous. If you partition your thinking accordingly, being specific and general at the appropriate times, while maintaining your concentration, you should squeeze a little more out of your play—and that's in a game where little thinks truly matter.

A CALCULATING MIND

Q. I have been reading that calculation comes only after clearly assessing the position and ruling out obviously flawed moves. Nevertheless, one eventually needs to calculate. Can you recommend books that specifically focus on training calculation? Also, I have been using Fritz 8 to go through my own games and those that have been annotated. With respect to annotated games, Fritz 8 allows one to open up another window to play through analysis variations. Some of those analyses are quite deep. Do you recommend that one should nevertheless play through each and every variation? And if not, how does someone follow those variations in one's head?
—USA

A. Plain old puzzle books will provide you the material for calculating lines of play. Don't even bother setting up the positions. Merely work with the diagrams. Allot yourself a certain amount of time, whatever you're comfortable with, and tackle a set number of problems each day. Practically any tactical book will suffice. Even if it's a bad book, how bad could it be? Who cares what the "writer" says about the positions? It's the positions that matter, as long as they come from, or could have come from, real games. Just make sure the diagrams are clear.

To be sure, if you're looking for the right book, you're already going wrong. It's not only text that matters, it's also process. You'll want to develop the wherewithal to stay with a position, even when the course gets tough. It's easy to give up as we start losing our way, but that's where proper practice comes in. And that means analyzing in your head, without moving the pieces.

But let me add this: There's no need to calculate extensively all the time. In most situations the real knack is to determine what to look at.

Work at assessing what's generally important in order to find the right path without too much calculation. Don't waste your time playing out every variation in detail.

Much of chess has to do with developing your intuitive sense, and that's not going to be enhanced by raw computation exercises. To improve intuition, it would almost be better to play over the games of people similar to Capablanca, not that there are thousands of players like him. If you insist on a mechanical approach, play through Capa's games, or the games of a stand-in, hardly stopping to consider the comments, unless a move has surprised you. Over time this should heighten your awareness of when to calculate in the first place, and that's probably the best starting point when it comes to the art of analysis, of which calculation is only a part.

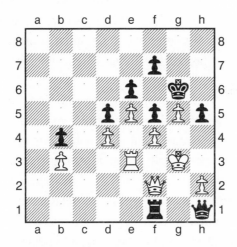

Nimzowitsch-Capablanca, New York 1927
Black forces White to resign without much calculation.

ANALYZE THIS

Q. Currently, in most positions, I consciously look at three things after the opponent has moved: 1. What new squares or pieces are attacked by the piece that moved? 2. Which enemy pieces are given protection by the move, either where they are or on another possible square? 3. Have any significant lines or squares been cleared or blocked by the move?

Next I usually consider every legal move I have, even if only for a split second, picking a few candidate moves. Then I try to analyze each candidate move one at a time without any redundant thinking (which I am not completely convinced is ideal, since calculating a variation a second time sometimes gives me a fresh perspective). After I have selected my final move, I ask three questions before I move the piece: 1. What are the different ways the piece can be attacked? 2. Are there any pieces or significant squares that my move takes protection away from? 3. Are there any significant lines or squares that are cleared or blocked by my move? What are your thoughts on sticking to a strict regimen for calculating as opposed to letting one's intuition guide the analysis?
—*Japan*

A. Your approach is certainly well informed, but you may be giving yourself too many tasks. You can fall into a crevice trying to scale a mountain. Let's approach this as if you're playing against someone in a real game. You can apply similar procedures for solving problems and for using software alike.

It's your turn. The first thing you should do is to look at your opponent's move. If you're being threatened, make a mental note of it. Whatever move you choose must deal with your opponent's threat or threats. If you're not being threatened, you're free to proceed to your next step.

Here it is: After you've ascertained whether or not you're being threatened, decide whether your opponent's move responds to your last move. That gets you back to your own play, and keeps you focused on the game and the process of playing logically. Good chess isn't conducted as if it's a collection of independent moves with no relation to each other. It can come to that, especially the way some of us play, but that's not the ideal approach. It's much better to play with a plan.

You shouldn't alter your plan without definite reason—say, for example, because your opponent's move rebuffs or challenges your presuppositions, or simply because you've missed something you hadn't considered. If your opponent did fail to reply to your move, make another mental note to come back to that circumstance. That way, you can either follow through on what your opponent failed to counter or exploit your opponent's breakdown in logic.

Now for your third step: If you don't have to answer any threats or capitalize on your opponent's letdowns, look for moves that foster your aims, based on your previous planning. If you didn't have a plan earlier, now would be a good time to develop one, though you should have had one earlier, from the beginning. You might be better able to explore these questions on your opponent's time, when your mind is freer to roam and you're not pressed by the exigencies of the clock.

Whatever you're doing, whether it's answering threats, taking advantage of unresponsive opposing moves, or furthering your own general ends, the trick is to come up with intelligent alternatives. You don't want to consider everything, just everything that matters. That's where the so-called list of candidate moves comes in. Let's say that you've gone through your initial period of asking internalized questions, however you ask or phrase them, and regardless of the order you've followed. Let's also say that you've found a move that seems to satisfy your needs. Try to find another move that does virtually the same things. If you find such a move, you suddenly have two moves to evaluate and compare. Which one do you like better?

A third or fourth possibility may recommend itself. At that point, hit your mental brakes. If you don't, the whole thing is likely to become unwieldy, and your entire analytic edifice may start to collapse. Try to work with no more than four possibilities, and winnow your list down to the point where you find the move you like best.

Obviously, it doesn't have to be done this precise way. But if you're looking for procedure, this is manageable and efficient. A good chunk of chess thinking has to do with comparing reasonable options. To do this effectively you'll want to reduce what you have to look at, not increase it to overwhelming proportions, with more steps entailed than the human mind can process (having too many choices can be equivalent to having no choice at all, and you wind up lost in confusion). Clearly, you're a dedicated student, and that means a great deal. Step back, now, and look at the big picture. It's time to rid yourself of all the unnecessary toil and to start enjoying the game for what it really is: not work, but play, pure and simple. It's simple, right?

BUT DON'T ANALYZE THIS

Q. In all answers you give when you are referring to solving problems you insist on solving the problem without moving the pieces. I even saw a movie some time ago with Ben Kingsley as the instructor and a prodigy boy. Kingsley set up the pieces for the boy to look at. Then he threw them on the floor. Is this just a Hollywood trick? Can you please explain what is the gain when you solve a problem without moving the pieces?
—*Greece*

A. In chess we try to look ahead to see the consequences of our actions. In order to improve that skill we have to train by analyzing and calculating moves in our minds. To practice visualizing, you have to rely on your synapses, neurons, and self-discipline.

If you don't move the pieces, you force yourself to foresee what might happen. Practicing using your imaging abilities leads to immediate chessic gain: you get, with rigorous application, the ability to predetermine and hopefully control the future (of the game). Let's face it. During play, nobody is going to let you check out a variation on the board to fathom if it allows you to win. So you're going to have to see your way to the truth. If you don't prepare for such envisioning ahead of time, how will you ever be secure enough to do this in direct competition? By magic? Those kinds of tricks should be left for editing rooms and Hollywood's special effects. That's where they seem to work best (but they do work).

UNDERSTANDING BEATS MEMORY

Q. Hello. I'm 41 years old. My rating is more than 1750. I love the game very much and have a good memory for numbers, but for chess, it's hopeless. Even to memorize sometimes the main line of an opening that I saw one week ago. Is it first of all a lack of understanding of the positions, and is there a certain method to improve on my problem?
—*Belgium*

A. There are things you can do to memorize more effectively, but to my knowledge nothing can be done to better your memory. You have what you have, though your memory might not be the problem.

Maybe you're not remembering because you're not understanding. So the next time you're engrossed in an opening line, don't just try to commit the move order to memory. This is a dead end, for chess is a game of reason, not rote. Instead try to appreciate why each move is played, what the aims of the opening are, how your opponent can thwart you, and so on. If you can't get these ideas on your own, become a pest and ask others who know what they're doing why certain moves are played. You could also have your play analyzed by a master or teacher and see what he or she recommends. You'll probably go further digesting their suggestions than you would by memorizing the main line of a randomly chosen attack or defense.

Q&A METHOD

Q. In your book *Chess Complete* you say that you prefer to encourage your students to learn how to think rather than structure their chess lessons. While I have some idea of what you mean, could you please elaborate?
—*England*

A. At the start of my teaching career I noticed that most of my students played perfunctorily, without much consideration of their opponents' moves or their own. Students seemed to strive for those rote setups without real comprehension, and even after their opponents veered far from their track. Sometimes they got away with it because their opponents operated in similar universes, but not always. To prosper as a teacher it was clear that I'd have to serve as more than a mere database. I'd have to show students how to think when I wasn't so sure myself.

I began to question every move and suggestion, even the good ones. I decided that this procedure could furnish instructional insights while necessarily slowing down my students so that they'd have more time to think. It would also invite them to look ahead to anticipate problems before they materialized. I reasoned that if my questions were consistent, and I asked typical ones repeatedly, students would gradually internalize those types of cues, as well as the analytical approach we were using. They might start to ask themselves comparable questions in their own games. At some point all that questioning would result in better move selection and superior chess. Beyond that I believed it would impart what I considered to be a powerful truism: By asking a good question one practically has the answer. In chess, that often translates to the right move.

Accordingly, I resisted giving structured lessons. I wanted to be free to muse at the board, in front of the student, to illustrate how I analyzed unfamiliar positions. I encouraged my students to join me as analytic equals. That, I thought, would build their confidence, and our lessons would equilibrate into friendly conversations, where I sometimes learned as much as I taught. The real advantage would pass to the student.

That's about it. I could fill a book with all the other methods and special exercises I've essayed to help students think while playing chess, but none have proved more valuable than the art of asking exploratory questions. And there's nothing profound, remarkable, or new about it. You can find it in the dialectics of Talmudic scholars, and you can see it in the Socratic dialogues. But it's also a technique that teachers ordinarily employ in the performance of their everyday duties. By questioning a student's thoughts, using the answers to ask further questions, a teacher lays groundwork for the student's eventual adoption of what many us have come to call the analytic method. The process succeeds when it culminates in a realization: that the teacher is no longer needed.

CANDIDATE LIST

Q. I'm an intermediate player, but whenever I'm calculating variations or candidate moves, I keep forgetting about them and I'll have to think all over again. What should I do to fix this problem?
—*Malaysia*

A. You could fix it by giving up chess. You could fix it by becoming a character in *Star Trek* and aligning yourself with the Borg. Or you could try to fix it by structuring your approach.

Let's focus on the last of these three. Maybe you're already doing this, but if you're not, you should concentrate at first on your form. As you're exploring a position for candidate moves, you should make sure to construct a short mental list of worthy possibilities before analyzing any of them in depth. This is critical, for the mere act of creating a list gives you something definite to refer back to, in case you forget, and it also makes it possible to compare the ideas better so that you could establish a proper pecking order to the candidate moves. By grouping and arranging them together you'll sense which ones should be looked at first and which can be eliminated altogether. To be sure, one of the main analytic tasks chess players perform is to compare reasonable alternatives. Regardless how we fashion it, we're constantly seeing how several different moves deal with a specific problem to see which moves we prefer.

Making sure you have proper form is one thing that might help, and really keeping your focus while analyzing is another. If you're letting your attention go astray, if you don't fix your thoughts in place to begin with, and if your ideas lack defining concreteness, it's very unlikely you'll remember much at all. Of course I don't know you, and there might be something personal that should be factored into the equation. But if I had to offer general advice, I'd suggest that you get back to basics and reconsider your starting approach. Get that right, and other helpful things may follow.

THINKING ABOUT THINKING

Q. I've heard that studying the games of masters can help one improve his or her play. And I've recently heard that a certain grandmaster stated that a player should "annotate his own games" in order to improve. Therefore, I ask, in your opinion, which is a better way for a player to improve—studying the games of the masters or his own games (maybe they are equally as beneficial)? Also, exactly how should one "annotate" his or her own games in order to get the most out of it?
—USA

A. Perusing the games of grandmasters and masters might very well improve one's play. Maybe. If you're a total newcomer, you might gain much more from working with basic texts than with books of esoteric moves and complex analyses well beyond your experience and present level of understanding. If you labor too often over unreadable material you might become so discouraged that you wind up abandoning ship. I'm also willing to bet that the grandmaster you're paraphrasing was referring to players of significant skill and experience. His suggestion might help players of lesser stature, of course, but it probably wouldn't be as effective or meaningful.

Actually, the best games for you to study are not those between two grandmasters, nor between two players of your own strength. By far the best games to study, if you can get your hands on them, would be games between players of mixed abilities: that is, between grandmasters and players of your own class. The players of your strength would likely make the errors typical of your class, and the grandmasters would undoubtedly take advantage of those mistakes. That's powerful instruction.

But you're not going to find many of those mixed contests, so I'm going to suggest that you place greater emphasis on the analysis of your own games, preferably with the aid of a strong and sympathetic player. But I don't think you have to annotate your games so much as simply figure out where you erred and what you could have done better. If possible, you might consider taking some instruction to assist you in analyzing your games and tendencies. Naturally, you can use software, friends, and your mind to get the job done, but having a knowledgeable and considerate adviser in your corner couldn't hurt.

Learn how to analyze chess positions in the first place, whether you write down your ideas or not. If you want some sense of what the analytic process is like, and thereby better your calculations and evaluations, you might want to check out several of the works of Alexander Kotov, including *Think Like a Grandmaster* and *Play Like a Grandmaster*. Both books have many practical ideas on the art of analysis, and they're both quite entertaining. So was Kotov, but that may not be as relevant as his admirers thought.

DEFENSE

Q. It's been a year since I took on chess studying with a more serious approach; I've been playing a lot on the Internet and on every site my rating is around 1400 (we all know that Internet ratings are quite a bit higher than the real ones), but I'm just not satisfied with it. I would like to have at least a 2000 rating on the Internet, and then I will be able to

say that I'm on the right track. Right now I've been solving hundreds of puzzles of varying difficulties, but that doesn't seem to be getting me anywhere. My biggest problem is still that I make too many tactical mistakes in my games. Usually I can see some crushing move, but fail to see the crushing move my opponent has already begun to play on me. Am I missing out on something when I solve the puzzles or is there something that I must pay special attention to? What else can I do to correct this weakness of mine? Thank you very much for your help.
—*Mexico*

A. Studying tactics may not have solved your problem yet, but it's still a sensible recourse. If you've been having trouble with tactics, you should be working on tactics. And how do you know it hasn't gotten you anywhere? That kind of thing takes time. You may well be on the way toward improvement, possibly getting stronger every day, and still don't see gains because pieces of the puzzle are yet to be put in their proper places.

Perhaps you need to concentrate more on defensive play, and there are a few excellent books dealing with that part of the game. *The Art of Defense* by Soltis and *The Art of Defense in Chess* by Polugaevsky and Damsky come to mind. There's also a very good chapter entitled "How to Defend Difficult Positions" in *The Art of the Middle Game* by Kotov and Keres.

One aspect of defense is perspective—that is, how the board is perceived. You can cultivate a better defensive attitude if you practice trying to imagine yourself as being your opponent. Try to picture yourself in his or her place (not necessarily wearing the same clothes).

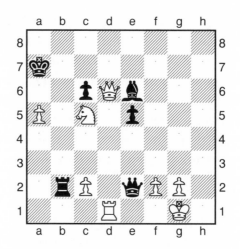

Soltis-Biyasis, Norristown 1973
White forces a quick mate with 1. Qc7+.

RULES OF COUNTER-ENGAGEMENT

Q. When is a counterattack effective and when it is a mistake? I know from my little experience that counterattacks might be very dangerous if you don't take care of all the possibilities that might arise from your opponent's reply to your counterattack. I have managed to find some basic "counterattack rules," such as: Don't counterattack if your opponent can move his attacked piece and check you (unless you can capture the checking piece). I have come to some more rules, but I found that there are too many complications to set up clear, useful rules. Can you help me to state those rules clearly? Is that possible at all?
—Israel

A. You have to be careful about such general rules. You can consult them but you shouldn't rely on them. All your decisions should be based on what's really taking place over the board, not on some wide-ranging encapsulation that's supposed to explain everything (you're not going to find a unified field theory here). For that reason I am hesitant to restate your counterattack principles. Besides, I doubt whether any reformulations would prove enlightening or very beneficial.

I am also a little unsure of what you mean exactly by "counterattack." It could be you're suggesting that a counterattack is a pure attack that takes no notice of your opponent's move. If you do mean that, you may be misunderstanding the nature of most counterattacks.

In all instances, you should look at your opponent's last move and figure out what it does. If it threatens you (undoubtedly one of the possibilities), you should make sure that you respond. Ideally, with your next move, you should do at least two things. You should cope with your opponent's threat, intention, or plan (unless your opponent's move is ridiculous or irrelevant). And you should also try to foster your own ends. A good counterattack doesn't integrally have to be stronger than your opponent's move, or come first (though those are valuable attributes). Whatever good things stem from your counterattack, nonetheless, you should make certain it nullifies your opponent's threats—if there are any. I suppose one rule might be that you can play a counterattack if it succeeds regardless what your opponent played on the last move, and no matter what he plays on the next moves. But what kind of rule is that? You don't need a rule to give pedigree to a counterattack, or for most chess moves. You need concrete analysis to determine if your counterattack (or move) actually works. If the counterattack (or move) works, the rule works—for that occasion.

The best time to resort to general advice is when specific analysis doesn't seem to be getting anywhere. This may be helpful at different times, one being when you're losing. For example, if it seems that you're under heavy attack and are likely to lose if you do nothing, and if you can't seem to find moves that contend with your opponent's impending threats and aggressive possibilities—that is, if you have nothing to lose— then you might think of trying to divert your opponent, hoping to get him focused more on your imaginary or empty threats than on his own aims. By deflecting your adversary, you may lure him off track, and that might give you opportunities to come back. But that is more a piece of advice and less a rule or principle. And even in the situation where you might consider following such counsel, you're still going to calculate and judge in explicit moves as much as reasonably useful, and not in broad generalizations. Think too generally, or not at all, and you're bound to hang something or get mated. What fun is that?

THE BOARD IS GREENER ON THE OTHER SIDE

Q. I've read and enjoyed some of your work, while playing chess on and off for about 10 years, but every now and again the passion for the game flares up and I get really involved in it. My question is probably stupid, but I'll make it anyway: When I analyze my games I often see moves that I could have made, better ones than those I actually played, and I enter these better moves in my comments of the game. My problem is that I can see my new moves, but I'm never sure of the moves my opponent would play in response. Is there any method I should follow in trying to determine his moves?
—*Brazil*

A. I'd tell you to try to see more of his moves and less of your own, but I'm afraid that strategy might work and throw off my whole approach.

The world is an uncertain place. We can seldom be sure of anything, which is why we often resort to strategies, probabilities, rules of thumb, and plain old intuition. You might get a better feel for the opposition's thinking if you practice trying to put yourself on the other player's side of the board, envisioning the game from your opponent's vantage point. That is, actually pretend you're sitting across from yourself, preparing to attack your own forces. That should give you a contrasting take on things, while unveiling some of your adversary's potential aims and hoped-for tricks.

In your training sessions you can facilitate such perspective extrapolations by physically turning the board around, but in your real games you simply have to apply some spatial conceptualizing, making believe you're the other player.

That kind of imagining can especially help improve direct defense and its partner, the prophylactic skill of warding off future attacks to your position. For example, instead of just trying to figure out the best move from your own active point of view, you should also attempt to assume the mindset and stationing of your opponent so that you can determine your adversary's best move—what devious plans he or she is trying to unleash on you. Armed with such bilateral awareness, you have a much better opportunity to find moves that thwart your opponent's schemes while fostering your own intentions. That in itself doesn't guarantee you'll always be able to devise your opponent's likely moves. But it should make you at least a tad more receptive to discovering his or her prospects, which must mean something in a game where anticipation, the minimizing of weaknesses, and the accumulation of small advantages combine to make all the difference.

SACRIFICES

Q. I think I have a common problem that you may be able to help with. I'm rated around 1850. I seem to have stopped improving, and I've taken a hard look at my games to see what I'm doing wrong. One thing I noticed is that unless there is a forcing continuation I can see the end of, I will never sacrifice material. When I have a weak pawn, I will keep defending it until my position is totally cramped and falls apart, and later I'll find out that I could have just sacrificed it and all my pieces would be active. I don't even think about that during the game—I have to defend my pawn! Generally, I have no idea when a pawn sacrifice is worth it, when it gives good compensation and when it's just a loss of material. Let alone things like exchange sacrifices. Any hints on how I can work on this?
—*Netherlands*

A. By far the most overriding element in chess is material. We should never give it away lightly, because there's only a certain amount of it. A pawn is a pawn in any country in the world. For the most part, we don't want to sacrifice our men. We want to sacrifice the other guy's men. That's why most sacrifices are not really sacrifices at all. They're only expedient sacrifices, leading by force to at least a clear improvement in the position. What kind of sacrifice is it when you know ahead of time that the story has to have a happy ending?

But you raise a good point about defending weak material foolishly. It's often wiser to surrender it for nonmaterial compensation or to create useful complications. You can become better at exploiting these situations if you get more practice with them.

Why don't you try playing on the Internet, perhaps going on as a guest if you're worried about losing rating points? Attempt to sacrifice material meaningfully to gain relevant experience. Constantly immerse yourself in sacrificial circumstances, and you'll become more at ease with them. You can fuel these attempts at sacrificial orgies by working with a few of the books devoted to the subject (there are many). Other than those things, it can't hurt to stay alert to your situation, as indeed you seem to be. By being aware of a problem, we have a much better chance to do something about it.

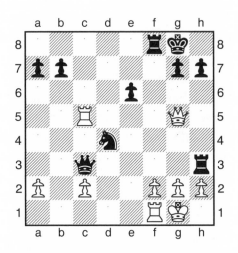

Levitsky-Marshall, Breslau 1912
A famous queen sacrifice. White resigned after 1. ... Qg3!!.

STYLE

Q. I am a class B player in my 20s. Recently I had the opportunity to take about a dozen chess lessons from an FM who was visiting my province for an extended stay. Most of the lessons consisted of going over my games from previous tournaments and having him point out where I went wrong (even if I won!) and what choices I made were good ones. In addition, he helped me develop a "style" of play and an opening repertoire that was consistent. One comment that he made struck me. He said "as you develop as a player you will be more likely, in a given position, to choose a move that suits you stylistically than one that leads to objective equality." What do think of the chess teacher who stresses to the student the need for finding a style of play over playing moves that are believed to be absolutely correct?

—*Canada*

A. I agree with your chess teacher. That is, as you continue developing as a player, it's likely that you'll choose moves consistent with a style. That doesn't mean you should ignore a strong move when you see it, especially if the move is clearly best. Probably your teacher was referring to murky situations, where the right move is better for intangible reasons, and where playing certain alternatives might not necessarily be deleterious. In those instances choosing innocuous moves suitable to a style may lead to positions in which you feel more comfortable. If you're an attacking wizard, you don't necessarily want to play the "correct" move if it leaves you a lifeless middlegame. If you're a positional player, you don't automatically want to play the "correct" move if it immerses you in a jungle of loose pieces and complicated lines.

So play the right move, if you know what it is and where to go with it, but not if you know what it is but don't like where you're headed. As you develop your own style, make sure you understand its limitations. Try to be aware of its presence and affect. The truly complete player factors in everything pertinent, from the analysis of opening specialists to keeping subjective tendencies in mind. You can try to be a better player, but you can't stop being yourself. What do I think of a chess teacher who understands the importance of style in selecting moves? I think he knows what he's talking about.

BLINDFOLD CHESS

Q. I have heard about people playing blindfold chess (without view of the board). My question is are some people born with this ability or is there a way to train to do it?

—*Canada*

A. Some people do seem to be born with an innate propensity for visualization, which can help them master blindfold chess. There are techniques you can use to sharpen and somewhat develop blindfold skills, but those in no way can replace real talent. They can only supplement it. Here's what I do with my own students, some of whom are young children, just to make them more at ease with doing things in their heads.

First, I encourage them to become familiar with the board, including its lines, colors, connection points, and key squares. I insist they analyze without moving the pieces, no matter how hard the position. After awhile they become more comfortable visualizing possible moves in their minds. They enjoy realizing that it's not as hard as their friends might think.

Our practice sessions include visualizing the move being played. They must say the move in algebraic notation, and sometimes additionally in descriptive notation, which has its place as well. (Descriptive notation can help with classification; in endgames, for instance, it's more inclusive and elegant to say "the problems of the rook-pawn" rather than "the problems of the a- and h-pawns.") Moreover, I won't let them say things like "now I want to go here," and they point to a square— that's unacceptable. My students generally identify supportive pieces, relations among pieces and squares, future possibilities, and any other germane information. They also point out potential tactics or themes that seem to be relevant to the developing situation. Finally, they must give a very definite reason for playing the candidate move and to explain it in context of the entire game. By visualizing the move, saying it, describing it, with lots of classification, and explaining it, especially by creating a storyline, they gradually develop a number of different safety mechanisms to fall back on in order to play through a game without sight of the board.

During the process, my students are creating a narrative, a storyline, where all the story's facts are connected by logic. Have you ever noticed how often chess concepts and classic games are taught by narrative, where the presenter tries to convince us that the contest was won by virtue of a grand design? The reality may be nothing like this, of course, but chess writers and teachers often illustrate the material precisely that way—with logic—so that students can remember it better. Anyhow, blindfold players also rely on a similar kind of narrative to bring together all the elements needed to recall and visualize a chess position.

Doing these things will not, in themselves, produce a great blindfold player. But if you have no particular visual skill to start with, or if you do and simply want to arm yourself to the teeth with memory tools, using this method will lend structure to the procedure and augment whatever native aptitude one has. Just because you have talent doesn't mean you shouldn't also have technique. Perhaps the greatest blindfold player the world has ever seen doesn't rely on associative tricks, but there's only one of him, or is it her?

VISUALIZATION, NOT BLINDFOLD

Q. I've heard that learning to play blindfold chess is a good way to improve your game. Do you agree? What is the best way to learn how to do this?
—USA

A. Do you mean analyzing positions in your head, or actually playing a game without sight of the board? Regularly analyzing in your head has great value to your overall play. Strong players are almost always good analysts. There's no getting away from it.

Blindfold chess, where you play an entire game without sight of the board, is not quite the same thing, however. Surprisingly, the main talent exercised here is not seeing ahead so much as it is remembering what you've already played, which is somewhat antithetical—and frankly, un-necessary—to what's needed during standard over-the-board chess. Imagine putting all that effort into memorizing, when the chief labor should be concerned with thinking.

If you want to get the most out of an hour's work, you'll gain far more from using the time to analyze positions and tactics without moving the pieces than you would from straining to play a blindfold game. Much of that game might consist of mechanically played opening moves, while the rest is likely to be pockmarked with blunders, obvious oversights, and plans based on Alice-in-Wonderland logic. Is this really the stuff you want to commit to memory? Stay with solving tactics in your head, and leave the exhibitionism to those who need to feel they're being looked at and admired.

131

BOARD OR SCREEN

Q. I am a medium-strength club player who enjoys the study of chess, both from written sources (books, magazines) and computer sources (Internet games and CDs). I am curious about whether it is best to analyze positions on the board or to look at the computer screen. I find it more pleasurable and easier to analyze from a board, but with so many computer sources, I find myself looking at a screen a lot and where the temptation to click away and move the pieces is great. Is there any experience or research that suggests people analyze better (without moving the pieces) from a board than from a computer monitor, and what is your general advice about the correct training technique when being confronted with a position on a computer—analyze from the screen or print it out and set up the position on the board?
—*Denmark*

A. I'm not aware of any relevant studies, though obviously positions set up on a board have greater dimension. The pieces and the squares they occupy are palpable things. Chess, however, is a game of ideas, and its terrain and figures are concepts needing no physical reality. The computer screen therefore is more than adequate to represent such abstractions, assuming the interface is sufficiently clear. Moreover, by virtue of being on screen, it becomes much easier to sample variations, regardless how intricate, without losing your starting place. Setting up situations by hand, on the other hand, can be tiring, confusing, error-prone, and, therefore, discouraging. So it seems much more can be achieved over a shorter span by using the marvels of modern technology. If you want to take more time on any given position, you can do so on screen just as well as you can on board.

I realize there are detractors of computer chess, many from outside the game's domain, who tend to put it down as superficial, especially because things can go by so quickly it seems hardly possible to give them serious thought. But thinking time is not the sole factor. Intensity can play a role, and often a truer picture doesn't begin to emerge until many examples are considered, albeit if only tangentially. The trick is to sense when to invest greater effort in one thing than disperse energy over many things. It's doubtful that anyone—even non-playing critics of chess—can appreciate either approach properly if they haven't explored both.

BARBARIAN CHESS

Q. My fiancé and I love to play games, including backgammon, Monopoly, cards, Go, Scrabble, and other word games. We are very competitive, and I am almost as good as he is, especially at chess, though he does not think I am that good, claiming that I am too defensive. He also thinks that chess is the least intelligent game we play, and he does not like chess players, referring to some of them as "barbarians" who can only play chess. Recently I bought a book on how to play chess better and my fiancé criticized me. He is not really a reader, and I certainly cannot get him to read anything that I read, and sometimes it hurts my feelings. He says that truly talented people do not have to read a book to master a game anyway. They do it with natural ability, and it is only those without intelligence who turn to books. Do you think he is right?
—*USA*

A. Not only do I think he's wrong, I suspect he can't read, even though he supposedly plays Scrabble. But that is something you'll find out soon enough. Right now go on reading and trying to improve. It can't hurt to arm yourself before the barbarians get to the gate.

A FAMILY AFFAIR

Q. I am a 38-year-old woman who just recently started studying chess in a more serious manner. I've enjoyed playing all sorts of games, but have been fascinated with chess for a long time. My brother-in-law has played a lot of chess with friends and considers studying chess a waste of time. He thinks the most important thing is to play as much as possible to improve your game. I feel that my game and perspective have improved with books and videos, yet I still haven't been able to beat my brother-in-law in chess. Do you consider that just playing a lot is a better technique than studying?
—*USA*

A. I'm not sure where to start, so let's begin with your brother-in-law. Even if he continues to beat you, that doesn't mean that studying chess has no value. He may be an excellent player (it's possible), and whether you pursue the game his way, merely by playing, or your way, by combining study and play, he may still continue to beat you in head-to-head competition. So you shouldn't base your chess plans merely on the results of those contests.

It's also unclear what he means by saying that studying chess is a waste of time. Does he mean that studying chess for you is a waste of time, because he understands your nature and knows what's best for you? Or does he mean that it's a waste of time to study chess in general, for anyone under any conditions? The latter assertion is, naturally, preposterous, so I'm going to assume he means something like the former. That is, he believes you and those similar to you stand to gain more from playing and less from studying. While this is debatable, it's entirely reasonable, and may even be true in your individual case, though I'd have to know more about you to say for sure.

I know of one grandmaster who believes chess can't be taught. And there are other strong players who share that opinion, or a version of it, though they are in the minority. But most chess authorities believe that chess is teachable, and that to become really adept at the game you should engross yourself in both play and study.

But what are we talking about here? By your own words it's clear you've gained a lot from your efforts. It's also evident that you take considerable pleasure in studying the game, whether by reading books or watching videos. Shouldn't those positive feelings and experiences take precedence over everything else? You enjoy doing what you're doing, so why do you care what your brother-in-law thinks? Nevertheless, if you're really concerned, and still have doubts, do some reconnaissance. Send me a few of his recorded games and I'll tell you what I think about what he thinks.

NOTATIONAL ASSESSMENTS

Q. When playing through a game or analysis, I am often frustrated by a terse string of moves, with insufficient explanation, if any, often ending with notation implying a nebulous advantage to one side. Often I have no idea why this is the case. What techniques can a club player employ to better understand some of these assessments?

—*Australia*

A. I can understand your frustration with clipped commentary. Not only does it seem cold and impersonal, but it often leaves out the connective tissue that ties ideas together. We usually need words for that, but because chess is played so widely, chess writers have sought ways to make their ideas universally intelligible to get beyond language barriers (and to save space and time). So they have resorted to symbols that can be understood regardless of one's native tongue. You can learn more about those symbols, and what they stand for, by looking in the front part of any Chess Informant. You can also find very good explanations on the Internet.

But if I interpret you correctly, symbols aren't the real problem. It seems that you're unclear why analysts come to certain conclusions in the first place, and you're looking for ways to help you understand those assessments better. This reminds me of one Capablanca comment. He notes that his opponent resigned, but states unequivocally that it didn't matter because the game would have ended in 16 moves anyway. He concludes his commentary by saying something like: "I leave it to the reader to work out."

You may be able to interpret some of the unexplained thinking by asking a few probing questions. For example, try asking questions about elements pertinent to that position. While not automatically providing the answers you want, such an investigation could point out differences in material, pawn structure, space, time, king safety, and other factors which may give you a better take on the position. Or you could ask another set of internalized questions, this group focusing on plans and future possibilities. Some of these might suggest tactical ideas that suddenly explain the analyst's original symbolic appraisals. And who knows what other questions the position may trigger to lead you to a fuller understanding.

If you still have doubts, you could show the position to others to see what they think. It's surprising how often another player, even one not so strong, might have an insight. Then there are computers. With a chess software tool, you could search for related positions. A review of those search-generated examples might inform or clarify the analysis under contention, even without any helpful commentary, by virtue of merely supplying additional illustrations (the more times you see an idea, the more likely it will eventually click). You could also set up the position on a chess program and play it out a number of times. That might illuminate the annotator's judgments even further, especially if the computer takes both sides of the bet, playing against you first from one side, then the other. If all that fails, I suppose you could turn to a different kind of chess literature completely, one relying more on words and less on exclamation points. You know, like I am doing here.

SKIPPING NOTES

Q. I don't mind playing over annotated games, but sometimes the annotations are so complicated that it becomes a problem to constantly go back to where the position used to be. I get tired and I lose interest. Do I have to read every note to get something out of it?
—*USA*

A. Supposedly, the serious competitor wants to know it all. But you can pass over certain comments, especially complicated ones that diminish the pleasure of the activity. Most players just want to see the game anyway, and too many side variations tend to break the flow. So instead of laboring through every note, especially lengthy concatenations of moves given with little or no explanation, you might just skip over the tedious stuff and move on. Players don't have to grasp everything a game has to offer to derive benefit from following the moves. Besides, too much work might dissuade the student from studying chess at all, which would be far worse.

The amateur can usually make chess capital by assimilating typical strategies and positions. That absorbing process gradually makes one more intuitive and less reliant on nuts-and-bolts analysis, not that there's anything wrong with being a calculator, inasmuch as complete gamesters also need to be analytical and reductive. So if you want to disregard a specific note to cut to a general idea, or find that it's more fun to ignore a why to get to a what, go right ahead. It's what many people do anyway, even if they don't admit it.

FEAR

Q. I find myself sometimes incapable of playing, sometimes even training, for fear of making a stupid move ("stupid" as in contrast with a "less good" or "bad" move). As soon as I get unintentionally behind in material or position, I more or less freeze, panic, and quit the game. Computers, of course, don't mind that. But it can be a bit frustrating for real people. Of course, one could say, "so, find another game," but apart from liking chess, I don't like running away from myself this way. Since I'm not unique, others must have had such experiences as well. Do you have any suggestions on how to proceed to overcome this rather difficult handicap? —*France*

A. There are no easy answers here, and what answers there may be are possibly better sought in the world of psychotherapy. But I have certainly encountered this problem in my work. If you were one of my own students I'd try to impress upon you the importance of starting with a certain outlook. I'd want you to accept what you probably already know to be so. No one's perfect, and losing is part of living.

I'd point out the obvious: no one ever won a game by resigning. I'd add that successful players often get into hopeless positions, yet somehow they fight to the very end, sometimes becoming most dangerous when verging on defeat. In all cases, I'd want my students to assess particular situations objectively before proceeding.

Once they've determined that the position before them is losing, I'd urge them to accept that dispassionately, without getting too emotionally involved. Of course it's hard to be so coldly analytic (we're not machines), but such an approach provides the best hope. I'd try to encourage them to treat their losing positions as mere exercises. Then, they might start to feel unfettered, free to pursue the situation scientifically and rationally. It's a matter of removing fear so they can jump-start the thinking process.

It would help, when plagued with doubt, if students had the self-awareness to pose a directive type of question. I'd want them to ask themselves something like: What can I do to make this position as hard as possible for my opponent to win?

Start with a fundamental truth: opponents want their winning games to finish quickly. They don't want to fight anymore. They want their adversaries to resign. Frustrating that by putting up stiff resistance is the wisest course of action. To be sure, it might save the game. But even if it doesn't it gives us an opportunity to hold our heads high. No matter the result of an individual chess game, we should want our opponents to imagine they've been through a war. There should be another aim too: to earn respect, not only from our opponents, but also from people we care about and who care about us.

We're not going to inspire much respect, outwardly or inwardly, if we give up without a fight. Perhaps that's incentive not to willfully abandon your next chess game?

EMOTIONS—PART ONE

Q. My question concerns the psychology of the game. I have played tournament chess for four years at a local club in Allentown, PA. Upon reflection of my games, I notice that there is a tremendous roller coaster effect on my emotions during the game. High points occur as you win a piece or imagine a mating net being built, and low points happen after you did not correctly analyze the position and your opponent springs a "surprise" move on the board. These high and low points detract from clear reasoning about the true game position. I am trying to keep the internal highs from becoming too high before the end of the game, and I am trying to keep the internal lows from becoming too low during the game so that I do not mentally concede the game too early. What recommendations do you have for smoothing out the roller coaster effects so that I can play my best chess or improve the quality of my play?
—*USA*

A. It's not so easy, I know, but strive to think less about results and more about the intellectual challenges the game offers. Try treating each position as a problem-solving venture or scientific investigation, where winning is secondary to excavating the truth. This should help you become more dispassionate in your analysis and selection of moves.

Much of this objectivity can be preconditioned by how you treat losing positions in your own play. Recognize that you have a losing game, making sure you understand why, instead of letting your emotions run rampant. Remember that recognition doesn't imply acceptance. Rather it announces your intention to get on top of the situation so that your mind can devote all of its energy to finding resources and ways to make your opponent's aims difficult to achieve.

After impartially analyzing and assessing, your internal monologue might go something like this: I have a losing game. How can I proceed to create counter-chances and make my opponent's job as hard as possible? A question like this heralds your determination to defy like Botvinnik would, while putting you in just the proper frame of mind to fight back and possibly turn things around.

Accordingly, if you have promising moves, get into the habit of not playing them right away. Instead, ask questions about your plans. That approach tends to remove you from the emotional realm (though emotions have their place too) while putting you more in an investigative framework. Such demeanor is needed to judge the true worth of your ideas, so that you can find practical opportunities and muster resistance.

It all gets back to what Lasker said (I think it was Lasker): "If you see a good move, look for a better one." In other words, take your time, and realize that your first thoughts may not quite be on the dollar. By asking questions and slowing down, you may find other answers that work better. So that's my advice. Take the reins, pace yourself, ask questions, and try as best you can to be more objective. Over time, the constant implementation of this approach may become part of your procedure, and naturally you'll discover that your emotions interfere far less with the logic that sound chess play requires.

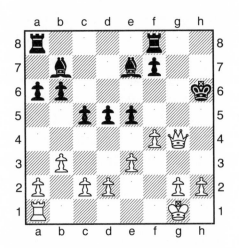

Lasker-Bauer, Amsterdam 1889
White didn't need to look for a better move than 1. Qd7!

WINNING ISN'T EVERYTHING

Q. From some experience of teaching chess over the Internet, as well as from reading your column, I have noticed that many players are extremely performance-oriented. Most complain about not being able to break a rating limit. So they set concrete goals of reaching a certain rating within a given time period. I am a little perplexed about the reasons why chess students would willingly put themselves under such pressure. Unless we go into discussion of the professional chess world, individual ratings have no practical significance in terms of individual standards of living or even opportunities open to them in the chess world. Anyone can go into the open section of the World Open and have an excellent chance of playing with a grandmaster in the first round. And with the development of Internet chess anyone can play with a GM online for a few bucks. Meanwhile, under the pressure of getting rating points, students try to find some reliable laws and guidelines in chess that would help them win. This leads to over-simplification of chess, standardization of ideas, which, in itself, in my opinion, is the strongest retarding force for chess improvement.

It seems to me that some players undertake chess study not so much to improve their play, but to ease the burden of having to think for themselves! This completely annihilates the very idea behind playing chess. Instead the game is entirely turned into a means of achieving nothing but gratification of one's ego (unless of course that is the point!). I am wondering to what extent you consider these observations correct. And if so, do you believe that this extreme performance orientation among weak players is due to ignorance of the game or just overall spirit of competitiveness that permeates American society (or any society for that matter)?

—*USA*

A. We do tend to place too much emphasis on arbitrary achievements and too little on real gains in ability and comprehension. We do place too much urgency on immediate success rather than giving ourselves enough time to mature naturally. We do wind up doing things for the wrong reasons, such as for status, instead of for positive ones, such as for enjoyment and personal growth.

We're also particularly obsessed with numbers and ratings, as if ratings were an exact measure of intelligence. Clearly many chess players seek an easy way out, trying to get to specific rating levels quickly, hoping to circumvent the exertion it takes to understand the game properly, let alone master it. That partly explains why we try to apply rules of thumb instead of investing the effort needed to calculate concrete variations. To be sure, unschooled players are more prone to place undo weight on superficial considerations. Often, that's because they don't yet know enough about the game to appreciate its subtle art. But the truth is strong players have their own false gods. They, too, mislead themselves, albeit at a more sophisticated level of deception, thinking that their narrow expertise confers truth and understanding when in reality they have neither. They simply play chess better than the rest of us.

You suggest that the quest for shallow attainments may have much to do with society and the pressure it exerts. Surely, there's some merit to that contention. American society is very competitive. But people are people, and competition is a way of life everywhere. Deep down we all have the same primitive needs and urges, and we're all trying to stay alive.

That is what Thomas Hobbes laid the groundwork for in the *Leviathan* when he portrayed life as being "nasty, solitary, brutish and short." That is what Herbert Spencer and Charles Darwin meant when they talked about "survival of the fittest." That is what Emanuel Lasker gave a chessic turn to when he described the game as "a struggle." And maybe that explains why people seek chess improvement for its own sake. They can't help themselves because they're always competing. It's a rook-eat-rook world.

CHAPTER 5

Tech Games

New technologies are affecting everything, and chess is no exception. Computers, software, the Internet, and state-of-the-art literature make their presence felt in this section. People wanted to know which teaching and playing programs were best. They were curious about online sites for playing. And of course they wanted to know about books, periodicals, and other specialized literature. I provided assistance where I could, but I shied away from comparing products I knew little about. There are simply too many of them out there, and new ones are appearing daily.

But I did my best to answer questions about how moves are evaluated algorithmically, what speeds to play at, how to use the new technologies to learn better and faster, and generally how to get more out of modern-day chess materials. I emphasized making use of accessible things, from libraries to free software and Web sites. I figured we pay for enough things in this world. Why add chess to the budget?

Finally, whether there's rational thought behind it or not, I've included in this section questions about speed chess (which makes use of the new clocks), correspondence chess (which makes use of the new stamps), and bughouse chess (which seems to make use of everything on the planet).

POSTAL CHESS

Q. Do you think correspondence chess has pedagogical value for a beginning or intermediate player? I find it enjoyable because there's time to think through the moves and even research the positions (say, in the opening). I don't know if one would want to play correspondence chess exclusively until the player has a fair amount of experience with a clock (quick-thinking does seem to be an important part of the game and the learning process), but it seems correspondence chess is useful because it allows one to think through the position more deeply.
—USA

A. Obviously, any form of chess that affords time to think is preferable to most kinds of fast chess games, though speed chess has its place and value too, since it presents many ideas over the course of a session and forces you to stay focused. Let your mind wander in speed chess and you're lost. Either you'll leave something unprotected or lose on time.

The nice thing about correspondence chess is that it provides so much extra time between moves that you can really sink your teeth into variations and positions. You can look up lines in different books to compare evaluations, and you can spend your own time weighing the alternatives and analyzing. Furthermore, you can test out certain ideas against computer chess programs for further back up and reinforcement. With your opponent's knowledge and approval, you can even use the games chiefly for training, showing the positions to strong players to get their feedback, if this can be done without an unfair advantage over your opponent.

But I wouldn't spend all my time (or all my postage) on correspondence chess either. For most players, it's not real chess, because you lose the immediacy and impact of sitting across from a live opponent. Certainly one of the reasons we play chess is to experience face-to-face, stimulating, intellectual contact with other people. Of course, you can find social attraction in correspondence chess (and online); some of the ex-

144

change between players can be quite invigorating. (You might want to read Woody Allen's short piece, "The Gossage-Vardabedian Papers," in his book *Getting Even*. It captures much of the flavor of what we're talking about, and it's very funny.) Still, unless you simply have no choice, try to spend most of your available chess time at an actual chessboard, sitting directly across from the opposition you're hoping to outwit and throttle. As a way to improve, it simply can't be beat.

TIME TO TAKE TIME

Q. I am 32 years old, and I have once again come back to competitive chess after yet another leave of absence. I have recently discovered the joys of web-based correspondence chess. Playing this way is particularly convenient for me as I am the father of a 21-month-old child. Correspondence chess offers me full flexibility as to when and where I can play. My question is the following: Would you recommend correspondence chess to intermediate chess players as a tool for improving their play? Obviously, time management is very different than in over-the-board games, but I hope I am right in expecting correspondence chess to help me think deeper (rather than faster). Indeed, for the first time in my chess life, I find myself double-checking my moves and thinking one last time about my opponent's potential threats and replies before moving.
— *USA*

A. I advocate virtually all forms of chess as a way to develop one's game, including correspondence chess and its sister on the Web. Of course, a lot goes on in the universe, so if you're asking whether correspondence chess could help a player advance more than other forms of chess, I'd have to qualify my answer. If you tend to take too long to move and incessantly find yourself in time trouble, I wouldn't recommend correspondence chess as a way to surmount the problem. If you ordinarily move too quickly, however, and don't seem to invest enough time in weighing options and reasonable possibilities, then correspondence chess might prove to be beneficial. Undoubtedly, if you habitually play too fast, you'll want to place yourself in circumstances where you have more time to ponder prospects.

145

Correspondence chess does afford ample time for deliberate thought. But it couldn't hurt to play with slower time controls in general, nor would it detract from the quality of your play if you take more time when practicing.

TEACHING TECHNIQUES

Q. To what extent do you use computer-based instruction in your lessons? Also, what teaching techniques do you employ when using computers?
—*USA*

A. I first started using computers to aid in instructing chess around 1980, when I was a spokesperson for Mattel Electronics. The company had come out with several handheld computer games, including one that played chess. But that particular series of products was fairly primitive, and as the technology became more advanced and accessible, it offered more and more opportunities for teachers and students alike.

One thing I like to do is play with the student in tandem against the computer. There's an immediacy to it that can't be gotten from looking at a game after it's been played, when some of the thinking behind the moves has become muddled or lost. By virtue of being there as the game is conceived, the teacher can ask particularly relevant questions to derive insights into how and what the student is thinking.

This method also avoids the problem of incorrect scores, where moves have been recorded inaccurately or not all. Every teacher knows how frustrating it can be to reconstruct a game from mysterious jottings and blank spaces.

But there's yet another factor that makes this form of instruction, playing with the student against the computer, especially helpful. Discussion between teacher and student can be revealing and direct without affecting the opponent's response. Think how absurd it would be to discuss strategy and tactics with a student in front of a live opponent.

Fortunately for us, computers are still too dumb to react to what the teacher and student are considering. The machine plays on as if in a vacuum, oblivious to such consultations. So the teacher can state a plan openly and the student can actually see ideas implemented, practically with no interference. The result is powerful instruction, for the student sees the value of the teacher's thinking immediately and successfully, rather than having to comprehend it in the lingering doubt of analytic afterthought.

Post-game suggestions are seldom as effective as instant explanations. That's true even when the teacher's on-site suggestions are off the mark, for the computer allows moves to be taken back. So if a plan doesn't work, the teacher-student pair can see why, and that, too, becomes a valuable learning experience. Sometimes the student overrides the teacher's guidance and insists on following through with his or her own reasoning. But once it becomes clear that the journey has gone awry, the game can be taken back to the point of dispute and replayed using the teacher's idea. The likely difference in outcome should speak for itself. The student learns the hard way, and the hard way is usually memorable.

That technique, though, is not the only means by which computers can be used to assist chess study. For example, with regard to opening work, you could take the last known theoretical position and play numerous games from there to generate new ideas and to extend the length of your pet lines. Or you could use various software products to search for related situations to see how they were handled by leading players, hoping to find useful analogies and contrasts. Such a strategy aims to amass a stockpile of corresponding positions so that selected patterns and concepts can be assimilated by sheer force and in all their totality. While we never want to stop thinking, there is something to be said for some repetitive learning until certain useful reactions become automatic and therefore "intuitive." That frees energy for creativity and productive thinking, as well as for inspirational awareness of when principles should be violated.

One of the most instructive things a student can use a computer for is to compile his or her own games. Keeping a record enables the material to be referenced quickly, easily, and in distinctive ways that highlight key ideas. The process also tends to reduce mistakes and save time. A mere click will take you back to the branching point without having to move pieces or check for incorrect placements. Finally, if the program allows it, you can then print out positions from your games for visual reinforcement.

Those are just a few of the things you can do with computers. Surely much more will be learned as chess teachers continue to equip themselves with new technology. Who knows what can be done with I-Pods?

ROBOTS

Q. What do you think about robots who play chess?
—*USA*

A. Start by getting a robot. Command the robot to play against you in a way that helps develop your opening repertoire. Specifically, play short games against it, stopping at move 15 or so. See how the robot evaluates the final position. It's likely to assess your position with a negative number. That means you may be losing.

Follow the game backward until you arrive at a point where the robot thinks you're doing well, in that it assigns a positive number to your position. That means you might be winning. Then try to play from there, this time playing a move different from the one that gave you a minus sign.

Keep repeating that process, playing and retracting, in each case going back to when you had a positive number (assuming there is such a place to go back to), until you achieve move 15 with at least an equal position or better. Count how many times you must begin again until you finally reach move 15 with at least an equal position. That number, averaged out to include all your attempts, is your "takeback index." Optimally, you'll want to get your takeback index down as low as possible. You know, like golf. The robot, undoubtedly, will be pleased to help.

FUTURE OF CHESS

Q. I am a young student of chess who has improved steadily over the last four years after taking up the game. My question is whether or not chess is really worth pursuing, or am I wasting my time? Recently, with the in-

creasing strength of computers, and the decline in the amount of over-the-board tournaments and turnout, will chess still be around in 30 years? Or will some supercomputer have solved chess by then, and will it then become nothing more than a mathematical curiosity, not worthy of playing? I would like chess to be a companion for life, as it has been for so many other generations, but I'm scared that it may be dying, and that this great pastime will be forgotten. Can you give your opinion and some guidance? Thank you for your time.
—*USA*

A. You're asking the wrong person about the worth of chess. I'm prejudiced. I think it's the greatest game there is, and I believe finding challenging and stimulating leisure time is absolutely cardinal to civilization. But just for the sake of argument, let's presume that computers will eventually solve the game. Why should that stop people from playing? Most of us continue to pursue, long after learning how they're done, ridiculously trivial tasks that require little or no expertise at all. Do you have any idea how many people, for hours on end, mindlessly play solitaire or other jejune games (such as bullet chess)? Computers haven't halted those activities in the slightest. In fact, they've actually fueled their proliferation.

I don't see that the rise of artificial intelligence will put an end to chess. Millions of people already play the game even though they have no chance whatsoever of beating the world champion. For them, he is just as good as a perfect machine. What difference does it make if the best player in the world is called Garry Kasparov, Vladimir Kramnik or Deep Blue? If anything, the success of computers might actually increase our own development, probably far beyond the level naturally achieved without them. Most of us are pleased by improving our ability regardless how we do it.

So do I think chess eventually will be ignored or forgotten because the computer can suddenly do it better than any person? The camera can capture the human face far more accurately than Rembrandt, but that hasn't stopped the world from continuing to appreciate his portraits. The music of Bach and Mozart can be recorded and duplicated perfectly in the studio, but that hasn't stopped people from continuing to attend live performances of their compositions. Perhaps computers will eventually play mistake-proof chess, reducing the game to a tautology. Would that stop true fans from continuing to admire the classic confrontations, those vicissitudinary battles between Alekhine and Capablanca, Fischer and Spassky, and Karpov and Kasparov? In truth it's the subtle imperfections that skilled humans give to things that make them interesting, that give them character.

Will our great pastime eventually be abandoned or forgotten? Not by you, not if you love it, and not by me, because I'm going to get many more questions just like yours.

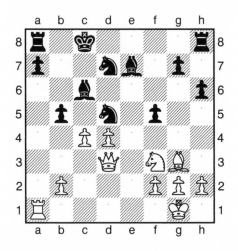

Deep Blue-Kasparov, New York 1997
Black resigns the sixth game. White wins the match.

INTUITIVELY PLAYED

Q. I have used what I considered a unique method (that I'm sure would be of special interest to you), to improve my chess intuition. Many years ago I watched two masters play speed chess. While watching I would try to guess, "feel," the best move, or rather the move that each master would make. Somehow I'm sure that this method improved my chess intuition. There being little time to consider the position logically I would consider the "feel" of the moves made. Incidentally, the names of the two players were Ionel Ronn and Bruce Pandolfini. Not much is written in

150

chess literature about improving chess intuition other than that intuition is really developed from reading, watching, and playing lots of games over the years. That it is really, in a sense, subconscious knowledge acquired.
—*USA*

A. Speed chess tends to be more intuitive in that we have to make decisions without being able to analyze exhaustively, as we could with more time at our disposal. (If you want to read a good book on chess intuition, I suggest you pick up Beliavsky's *Secrets of Chess Intuition*). Indeed, after slight consideration in most fast chess games, we often have to go with what feels right, if we don't want to risk overstepping the time limit. But there's an upside to speed chess, which is that it compels us to be more focused. We can't afford to let our minds wander, and that forces us to work harder and to experience a peculiar kind of learning—though only if we take the enterprise seriously. If we're just fooling around, the intensity won't be there, but the superficial analysis will be.

I remember the Romanian-Israeli-French Chess Master Ionel Ronn very well and with great affection. He was a true intellectual, who cared about ideas as if they were precious jewels. I also recall those speed sessions at his Greenwich Village Chess Shop vividly, and some of the games indelibly burned their moves into my resource bank. They were truly impassioned encounters, especially because I was afraid he was going to beat my brains in, with some of my loyal charges nearby. And sometimes he did, whereupon he'd lecture me on deconstruction and postmodern interpretation, and though defeated, I'd sit there and love every moment of it. Thanks for bringing back all those wonderful memories.

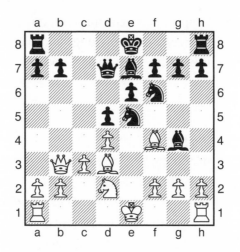

Pandolfini-Ronn, New York 1976
White retakes on e5 with the pawn and wins a piece.
The same blunder by Black occurred twice in the
same speed session (the players had had a few).

SPEEDY BOBBY

Q. I think your endgame book is one of the great five or six books all chess players should have. I read that blitz can do a lot for your game (Mark Buckley's *Chess Analysis*) and that it is fast food leading nowhere (Yermolinsky). What do you think? Did fast blitz play help Bobby Fischer as Buckley says?
—Ireland

A. Both positions could be defended adequately. When you play blitz you get to see more games and positions. After you've seen a lot of situations you can place particular emphasis on the most appealing ideas and follow-up with further study. Speed chess also tends to develop tactical awareness, though not necessarily for the deep stuff, and that's perhaps the chief argument against it. Too much blitz instills superficiality, where the tendency is to play for shallow tactics and coffee house traps.

But it doesn't have to be that way, especially if you're aware of the potential problems and consciously try to balance your program, with an emphasis on more serious chess pursuits. Certainly you shouldn't play an abundance of speed chess just prior to entering a tournament with slower time controls. Yet speed chess can be fun, and the attainment of pleasure is one reason we play at all. So if you suddenly feel an urge to play some blitz, go right ahead, but do it with an overview of who you are and where you want to be. Did speed chess help Bobby Fischer? I don't know. He did play remarkably well, fast or slow.

CRUISE CONTROL

Q. I am just beginning to take up chess seriously. My opponents on both the Internet and in person often complain my moves are too time-consuming. I want to think the position out. I want to contemplate what my opponents' reactions may be to the moves I am considering and, after that, what my response will be. I usually spend about 1.5 to five minutes in games with no time limits. I get such comments as, "The more time you spend on a game, the fewer games you play and the slower you'll improve. The more games the better." So I ask what is an acceptable length of time in casual games? Am I spending too much time?
—*USA*

A. If you'd like time to think, 10-20 minutes per side is a typical time limit for casual play. Of course you can take longer than that, but then the games are no longer casual. Moreover, less time than that doesn't really give you enough time to mull things over.

The "advice" you've been getting from opponents is questionable. True, the more games you play, the more different situations you'll experience. But that doesn't mean you'll learn anything under those conditions. Some things are counterintuitive, and need time to be investigated. Other ideas only come out through analysis. How are you to discover them unless you have the opportunity to think? So while your opponents may have a point, I suspect it would be to their advantage for you to move quickly. My suggestion when playing them: Slow it down even more. They will find that unbearable, move impatiently, and throw away games left and right. It's all about control, and that could be the way for you to seize it.

MATCH GAME

Q. I have been playing chess since I was eight (I am now 32), but have only taken it "seriously" for the past few years, playing in one or two tournaments a year as my schedule allows. One way I have been able to play more often is through various Internet chess servers. My question concerns the large gap between my over-the-board rating (around 1030) and my online rating (around 1430 for quick games and over 1500 for standard games on USChessLive). What causes this kind of difference in performance? What can I do to improve my over-the-board game so that it matches my online game?
—*USA*

A. I'm not sure it's possible to match the two, since the conditions under which the ratings are achieved are radically dissimilar. Playing with a mouse or keyboard could never be the same as seizing and moving an actual chess piece. Competing directly against a live opponent, with his or her attendant expressions and body language movements directly impinging on us, could never quite equate to facing a two-dimensional screen in our pajamas.

Furthermore, when the playing pools aren't comparable, as is likely the case, beating a 1200 player online doesn't necessarily mean you'd beat a 1200 player over the board. One set of 1200 players is different from the other. They're similar terms (each type of 1200 player), related words if you will, but not exact synonyms.

And there are still other factors. An online rating is likely to have been achieved at faster speeds, with its concomitant hazards. Faster games are usually (though not always) played more carelessly. It doesn't have to be that way, but that's often the way it goes. What's more, since we can afford to lose online without exposing our identity, many of us are willing to take risks we might not take when sitting across the board from a person who hasn't showered all weekend. Factor in the fact that some people are particularly good at speed play. If they naturally move more quickly, they tend to turn speed play itself into a winning strategy by keeping the game going as long as possible. For them, the real fun is being down the king's army but winning purely because they can survive a few seconds longer. There are even differences between speed ratings realized online and speed ratings earned, often to one's discredit, over the board.

So many things can account for numerical disparities. I'm not even sure we should bother trying to make the two ratings parallel. Just accept the truth that they can be (and often are) different, like apples and oranges.

CDS OR BOOKS

Q. With the proliferation of chess CDs—some of which are prior books— I read somewhere that content from the CD is retained up to 80 percent better than from the same book. I am now thinking that maybe I will purchase the CD rather than the book of the same content to further my retention of the material. I realize the drawbacks—a book being more portable—but it may be worth a try. What do you think of the CD vs. the book?
—*Canada*

A. Chess is a visual game. It doesn't require words as much as it does clear and distinct pictures. On screen the images can jump out at you, and there are all kinds of things you can do with them, aside from the illegal or immoral. You can enlarge them, highlight them, draw on them, and even write on them. Within the program, you can find them quickly, going back and forth among them at will and caprice. You can print them out for transport and affixation to a page, or for transported rapture and unadulterated fixation. You have the added benefit of not having to work with a board. That means you can save scads of time you would have wasted setting and resetting the positions. By having the ability to go light-speed ahead or backward, you can hone your art of analysis to unexpected levels of insight, without ever having to fear loss of position or just getting lost. A simple stimulus from the mouse will get you back to where you were, if that's the place you suddenly want to be.

Since you can click your way from example to example, you can do so much more in the course of a keyboard session than you could in the checkered confines of light-and-dark squares. Boards and pieces have dimension, but, in the domain of conception, that's flatland. I'm not even sure books will be more portable in the future. We can already carry around small devices that offer hundreds of tomes. So there's really no comparison. Software is most definitely the better way to go.

ONLINE VS. OVER-THE-BOARD

Q. Which type of chess is stronger: email chess or chess over the board?
—*Puerto Rico*

A. By email chess I presume you mean online chess, though I'm not sure what you're asking. Are you curious which form of chess is better, especially for you? Are you wondering which manner of playing chess produces higher quality contests in general? Or are you really asking something else and I haven't figured it out yet? My answers to each of these questions might be different, if I could satisfy them at all. But let's pretend I can and continue the charade.

I can't say which means of playing chess would be more appropriate for you as an individual because I know nothing about you. But perhaps you wonder which method leads to superior play? Alas, it appears that the scientific world, ever in search of new research topics that may win funding and influence people through publication in prestigious journals, has yet to discover this particular field of study. I don't think they know if there's a correspondence, and I know I don't.

It seems to me that playing superb chess is more likely to be a variable of time than how you move the pieces. I'm not sure that it matters whether you grasp them or click them, as long as you spend a sufficient period analyzing the position. The more time you invest, the more likely you'll produce exceptional results. Now if you're actually concerned with something else, and I've missed the point, perhaps some of the confusion stems from the electronic medium used to pose the question. If you could ask the same query in person, without the filtering effect of an interface, it's possible I might come up with the brilliant response you certainly deserve. For now, you'll have to settle for a mundane one.

BACK TO THE BOARD

Q. I've been playing non blitz computer chess over the Internet for a number of years, to the point of not even seeing how high the dust had accumulated on my wooden board and pieces. Now I have joined a chess club, am playing people over the board in rated tournaments, and have found that my Internet exploits have in many ways been more of a hindrance than a help. I do not see the whole board as I would if looking at a chess diagram on a computer screen. So oftentimes I miss obvious opportunities or just make dumb mistakes. I have to force myself to write down my moves, something that the computer automatically did for me. I have to remember to start my opponent's clock after I make my move; I have on more than one occasion lost a game due to time trouble just because I forgot until it was too late to start the other guy's clock. And I have to deal with staring onlookers—albeit, mostly quiet ones—and the idiosyncrasies of different players; one fellow continuously cracks his knuckles when it's not his turn, another moans, groans, and contorts his face like he is in pain when he is thinking, and the list goes on. I am sure that I am not the only one who has experienced these things, and in time, they should not be as problematic as they are now. Nonetheless, I have not read of the dangers of playing 100 percent of the time over the Internet, even in USCF rated real-time Internet games. Do you have any thoughts on the subject?
—USA

A. Almost all the grumblings I hear concern the dangers of Internet speed chess. For many people it's played at too fast a clip for their satisfaction and benefit. I've rarely heard anyone tout its superiority vis-à-vis over-the-board chess. That's almost what you seem to be doing, and that's probably what you should continue to do, since it's been so comfortable for you.

Maybe you shouldn't go to the club as much. Perhaps they could even refund a portion of your fee, before it's too late. There must be some excuse that could move them. Otherwise, you might be able to persuade the management to get some computer terminals for the club premises. That way you could combine the best of both worlds, playing at the club but with an interface that keeps score and time. Still, I must admit that particular solution wouldn't eliminate the idiosyncratic behavior of your fellow club members. Their peculiarities tend to be beyond the control of reasonable people, nor are Caissa's eccentric children known for their spirit of compromise. So it's hard to say how to proceed. Where's Bobby Fischer when you really need him? Iceland?

FUN SPEED

Q. I was just reading through your Q&A column. I have never heard anyone say that there was a gainful way to play speed chess. My children love speed chess (by speed chess I am referring to anything G/10 and under). But as a father and a coach, I am in the practice of putting a halt to any speed chess two to three weeks before a tournament—not to mention the negative comments I make about speed chess only creating bad habits. It would be helpful if you could tell me how to get some real milk out of the speed chess cow.
—*USA*

A. We have to be careful about following maxims, principles, and general assertions and stipulations blindly. Such oversimplifications usually fail to factor into account limitations, exceptions, subtle differences, and, for that matter, anything like a specific condition.

Take for example the principle "knights before bishops." Obviously, if players followed such a guideline exclusively the chessboard would be populated mainly by openings that resembled the Four Knights' Game. That would be a version of chess Hades, and none of us need experience it to know we don't want to be there. Furthermore, that particular advice (knights before bishops) is clearly unreliable, and sometimes downright wrong.

Some of the same kinds of objections can be made against the injunction not to play speed chess. Truly, too much speed chess just prior to serious competition can be deleterious, especially for young people, when the carry-over effect incites them to conduct what should be two hours of play in a meager ten minutes. It's likely your apprehension has been stoked by analogously disheartening experience.

So I join you in recognizing the potential ill consequences of too much, untimely, or imprudently conducted speed chess. I wonder, though, if not allowing them to play for two to three weeks before a tournament might be an overreaction. Of course, most coaches want their students to be prepared to win. But many of the most successful ones emphasize playing chess for fun, reasoning that children perform better (don't we all?) when the enterprise is joyful. As a coach and parent you naturally have a critically directed eye, and you certainly know your children best. But I'd be careful about denying them moments that, if properly reined, could increase their zest for play.

Can speed chess have prospective value? We all know the possible drawbacks, which include promoting superficiality and emphasizing the clock over the actual play. But just as obvious are some of its positive features. It can offer more opportunities to play tactically and aggressively. It can force us to play more relevantly, because we can't afford to lose our focus with the time ticking away. It's not that fast games encourage us to abandon analysis. It's that fast games constrain us to analyze more efficiently. So we lose something (thoroughness), and we gain something (intensity). In fact, some productive kinds of ratiocination are not based on how much time you put in but on the application of focused concentration. Unless a certain threshold is reached you might never find the answer. Speed chess can give us training at being so attentive.

Furthermore, even the best trained young players will find themselves unexpectedly running out of time here and there. If they haven't had sufficient experience at moving quickly in practice sessions, where they can acquire helpful routines with careful monitoring, how can they be expected to navigate the treacherous waters of time pressure when they need to in meaningful games? I can't tell you how many strong players I've seen undone by weaker ones because they were unable to cope with a shortage of time in grossly winning positions.

Speed chess can also help us test-drive several ideas in a single session, and those ideas can be examined later. If a player has had trouble with a particular variation during a bunch of rapid games, answers can be sought in times of contemplative reflection. Moreover, if you work with a partner such as a coach or father, you can tap speed chess to generate information. Say, for instance, that opening theory takes you only so far on a definite line. You can then play 50-100 fast games (or some suitable number) from the last known or evaluated position and thereby produce at least some moves worthy of further investigation. Those notions can then be analyzed dispassionately in your mental laboratory to assess their true worth. And such scrutiny doesn't have to be confined to the opening. One can employ the same technique for exploring the nuances of any curious position.

So you're right to be concerned. Uncontrolled, unsupervised speed chess can have disastrous results on one's serious play. But I wouldn't dismiss blitz chess altogether. Chess, thank goodness, isn't the army, even when preparing for battle conditions. All we are saying is let's give fun a chance.

TABLE GAMES

Q. I am a 20-year-old player with the rating of around 1750–1800. I play almost all of my chess on the Internet and as a result I only play games with time controls like G/15 and 5 seconds per move, G/25 with no increment, or even blitz sometimes. I never sense the need for more time, but my question is: Is my chess "missing something" because I never sit down for a four-hour game at the table? Can this habit stop me from advancing beyond my current level? Thank you very much in advance.
—*Israel*

A. Because you're only 20 years old you'll probably improve by virtue of playing a lot of chess, no matter how you do it. But your chess games would be different and probably superior if you invested more time in them. And unless you're not human, your play should also be affected by sitting directly across from real beings, not that modern interfaces don't have character. Why don't you give slower, face-to-face tournament play a try? You may find it fulfilling in ways you've never expected. If you wind up hating it, you can continue blitzing ahead on the Internet, without giving it another thought. So stop tabling those four-hour games.

INTERNET SPEEDS

Q. I am an average intermediate player, rated perhaps about USCF 1600, who until now has mostly played against one or two keen chess friends but never joined a club. I have a limited amount of time available for chess but enjoy reading chess books, love playing the game, and would like to become a strong intermediate player over time. I was pleased to recently discover the Internet chess servers, and I am ready to start playing lots of practice games online and later study them to see how I might improve.

My question is: What would you suggest as a good time-control to use for an intermediate player for his or her regular practice games? I find I need a reasonable amount of time to look at the board, come up with a strategic plan, test it in my mind, and then execute it by making a move. I find it easy to do this when there is one hour per player available, but most opponents on the Internet are interested in playing shorter games. So I am thinking it is probably more practical to make my regular practice games limited to only 20 or 30 minutes per player, but given the bewildering array of time-controls available, Fischer time increments and ordinary, it is hard for the average player like me to know exactly which to choose! Does the developing player have to be wary of choosing the wrong time-control? Thank you for your informative column.
—*Australia*

A. It's hard to say what's right for an individual. I suggest that you assay different time controls of 20 minutes or more, say at five-minute intervals. You could also try increments, where a certain number of seconds are added for every move made. After a trial period you can decide for yourself which of those circumstances work well for you. It's usually best to experience a set of conditions firsthand.

I'd suggest, however, that you stick to your guns and avoid the mindless rapidity of typical Internet games. Maybe it's true that many players seek breakneck controls, and after issuing some challenges you might have to wait a bit before getting an opponent. But you shouldn't really have trouble meeting opponents who prefer more time. Eventually you'll make contacts and find friendly adversaries who tend to go online

161

at specific slots. You might even be able to schedule playing sessions with them as you get to know their habits.

Do you have to be wary of choosing the wrong time control? Not if you approach the matter experimentally and objectively. Be a scientist. Maybe you won't be able to prove what works, but you'll often be able to sense what doesn't work, and nothing teaches like failed experience.

BULLET CHESS

Q. Since I don't really have time, I play mainly on the Internet, especially very fast time controls, like bullet chess. I don't think my play is improving as fast as I would like, and sometimes I think my game would be stronger at slower time controls. What do you think of two-minute chess?
—*USA*

A. I think it's better than one-minute chess and worse than three-minute chess. Even better would be 30-minute chess, though I'm not saying your play would then be 30 times stronger. But let me ask you something. Other than inducing carpal tunnel syndrome, do you really think you're gaining much from bullet chess?

BUGHOUSE CHESS

Q. Do you see any benefits that a chess player can obtain by playing bughouse? In general, how do you feel about your students playing in bughouse and/or blitz competition on the day(s) prior to competing in the main event at the National Scholastic Championships?
—*USA*

A. Bughouse is a variation of chess played between two teams, with two players per side. There are two boards, one game played on one board, and a second game played on the other board. Team members sit on the same side of the table, with one team member having White and the other Black. The key features of the game are twofold: captured pieces are given to one's teammate to be used on the adjacent board, and the presence of two clocks, one for each game, with time taking precedence over many other considerations. To my knowledge, the game was invented in the 1960s and popularized at the Marshall Chess Club in New York City by a group of the club's juniors (I know because I took part in those fantastic early games, along with Andy Soltis, Robin Spital, Peter Sepulveda, Russ Garber, Marc Yoffie, Doug Ginsberg, David Daniels, Morgan Ellin, Tony Deutsch, Harry Ploss, and the rest of the crew—some of the same people who play-tested the games of Allan B. Calhamer, the inventor of Diplomacy, an intriguing strategy game. Bughouse is a wild version of chess, where practically anything can happen.

Bughouse chess is controversial for teachers and parents. They worry that the unusual rules and tactics of bughouse will mess up young tournament players. Because bughouse is usually contested at a fast time control, they feel that too much of it will be a bad thing, inducing superficiality. The same argument is made against playing a lot of speed chess.

Critics of bughouse point out other issues. The positions can become downright fantastic, what with the early presence of multiple pieces of the same kind (three knights, nine pawns, and so on); the strange placement of forces, which occurs because units can be positioned without the usual preparation; the ability to take the king, since time can't be sacrificed to replay illegal moves; and the fact that the game is played with a partner, as if real chess games could be salvaged by sudden cooperation or magical intervention.

Those are all valid concerns, and most supporters of bughouse acknowledge such potential problems. But they are apt to place greater emphasis on what they believe to be the beneficial aspects of bughouse.

Advocates admit that bughouse (like speed chess) tends to be overly tactical. They don't view that as a negative. They feel bughouse gives young chess players abundant opportunities to hone their attacking weapons. While some of those attacks are unlikely to arise in standard chess, exponents contend that the unusual situations produced in bughouse actually stimulate imagination and creativity. Bughouse players also claim that playing their game affords youngsters chances to develop their defensive skills. The continual nature of the onslaught in bughouse forces its practitioners to stay on red alert.

Bughouse is usually played at a fast time control, and like most rapid play, bughouse compels greater intensity and concentration. If you let your attention wander in fast sessions, they argue, you'll probably overlook winning moves or worse, miss threats and lose. Those in favor of bughouse and speed chess say they allow players to engage in numerous games during the time it otherwise takes to play just one. Participants thus encounter in a typical series many more ideas than they ordinarily do in a single chess game, even if such a contest is more thoughtful and lasts much longer than the entire group of faster games. Of course, critics of bughouse could counter those contentions reasonably, but probably not with enough certainty and finality to settle the debate.

Teachers and parents frequently argue in favor of bughouse from a nonchess perspective. Bughouse enthusiasts suggest, for instance, that the game promotes cooperation and gives kids practice at socialization. They point out that team play can minimize the sting of losing, a deterrent for many young chess players. Chess purists understandably might cringe at these arguments, but such considerations are important to parents and teachers concerned with a young person's well-rounded development.

Bughouse can be a lot of fun, and it may enable indifferent players to keep their hand in standard chess. Some chess teachers discourage bughouse altogether. I don't go that far, but I do try to distance young players from excessive bughouse or speed chess just prior to serious competition, such as National Scholastic Championships, where impulsiveness, a likely carry-over, can be disastrous. But computers, the Internet, bughouse, speed chess, and related activities, offered in proper proportions, can, in my opinion, supplement the play and study of standard chess while helping to create an effective and fulfilling instructional environment.

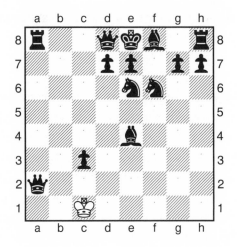

White has a bughouse mate in three. He has a knight and two pawns available to be placed on the board. White puts a pawn on f7, check. Black's king takes it. Then White puts his knight on e5, check. Regardless where Black moves his king, to e8 or g8, White mates by placing his remaining pawn on f7.

EVALUATION FUNCTION

Q. I'd like your opinion of my recent idea for chess training, head-to-head against the computer. I refer to it as "20-20 chess." My premise is based upon the belief that a "class" player is going to be busted by move 40 against a Fritz 7 or 8. But if he has played a credible game, he will still be in the fight at, say, move 20, with probably a slight positional disadvantage—or at worst, close to a pawn down in the evaluation (whether he realizes it or not, since all hints and evaluation windows would be turned off). My newest notion is that at move 20, the class player switches sides and plays out the balance of the game, striving to win or hold what should be a slightly better position by then. In this way you're "rewarded" twice for having played well. (One gets the satisfaction of holding Fritz to a low +/= evaluation in the first half, and then getting in some

practical experience at trying to win a superior position, and therefore not being "sent to the showers early.")
—*USA*

A. On paper, I like your suggestion, though it may not always work out so well practically. Most players, even truly good ones, would be busted far earlier than around move 40 against today's chess software, particularly Fritz. Nonetheless, assuming you haven't been mated by move 20, your idea seems to have considerable value as a training technique, especially for garnering experience in winning won games. Actually, I've known players to experiment in similar ways, attempting to play out dominant positions achieved from the computer's side, only to see their advantage slip away after a move or two. But then they usually switch sides once more, or as often as necessary, until they can savor the thrill of making the decisive move. Regardless, win or lose, they don't usually take a shower. That's just not their way.

EVALUATIONS ASSESSED

Q. I have been playing chess regularly for a little more than a year now. I mainly play computer opponents (various chess engines and ChessMaster 9000 personalities) as there is no local club (though I'm working on changing that) and for various reasons I have a disdain for playing on the Internet. While I have no real rating, I currently seem to have about an even record with ChessMaster personalities that are put at about 1400–1500.

My question concerns the computer analysis I put most of my games through in ChessMaster. How useful is this and can I get more benefit out of it than I currently am? Specifically, when the program gives the main line of a move it didn't like with the recommended move, it compares the material exchanged in each circumstance. I have always had the impression that I was getting a tactical analysis with little or no weight given to positional considerations. Though I realize the importance of studying tactics at my level, when I play I'm not always playing for material. This was underscored with a game I just analyzed. I had just promoted a pawn and aside from the new queen and the kings, there were only a couple of pawns for each side on the far end of the board that had no chance to promote before the ax fell. As my king moved in for the standard king and queen versus king mate, not only did the computer not note the inevitable until three moves from the end, but it was still considering triflings like pawns gained or lost with the move. Deck chairs on the Titanic and all, and this from a program that never fails to note the forced mate in ten that I missed.

So how should I take this analysis? How do the benefits of going over the game on my own or with a stronger human player compare? To be sure, it finds a great many errors, explaining why my game fell apart several moves later and the like. Can I expect much more?
—*Canada*

A. For most chess software, move evaluations are based almost exclusively on concrete elements, with overwhelming emphasis placed on material and forcing variations. Intangible factors, such as positional pluses and minuses, are very hard to quantify meaningfully. As good as they've become, algorithmic move-generators like ChessMaster 9000 simply don't appreciate fine points and immaterial considerations adequately. Of course, chess-playing programs usually don't have to. Even with their simplistic methods of assessment, computers typically play in the 2500 realm or better. That's good enough to flatten most of us who think we play this game at a decent level.

I applaud the efforts of code writers busily trying to create diagnostics to help you understand your play, but they have a long way to go. You can usually get a much more pertinent and nuanced investigation of your game from a qualified teacher or coach. Nonetheless, computers do have great value, and routinely perform certain operations with greater reliance than humans.

For that reason you might try employing both methods. Use the computer at the outset. It will spell out obvious things and calculations probably better than most human observers. It's also apt to weigh certain moves and possibly criteria, which could be important, that the human mind might dismiss. But then follow up with a second analysis from a recognized expert. He or she will probably point out things the computer didn't appreciate. By using both tools—the computer and the human expert—

you'll wind up getting a fuller slice of reality. That's the way I think I'd go, shooting for the big picture with every possible weapon in the arsenal.

TEST RESULTS

Q. Recently I sought advice on how to improve my game. More specifically, I used a sample study program. The advice I received was to study one- and two-move mates and combinations along with the more positional aspects of the game. The time specified was a couple of years! Really? One- and two-move mates and combinations for a couple of years?! Would this be an example of just generic advice? I don't doubt the recommender's qualifications, nor his wisdom, but if I'm to study such simple combinations for years on end, I *might* be a good player in ten years! Perhaps I am just an impatient American! Please comment, console, and/or quell my impatient fears. I guess the real question is how badly do I wish to improve?
—*USA*

A. There is nothing inherently wrong with the advice the sample study program provided. Solving one- and two-move mates is surely not an inefficacious idea, though I wouldn't automatically equate the number of moves you must find to the level of difficulty you face. Less may be more, and often is. Moreover, if you want to develop your tactical skill, it's generally desirable to rely on actual positions rather than composed problems with circumstances not naturally applying to typical chess games.

Though finding mating tactics can be fun and is usually profitable, you may have other immediate needs that should be tackled first. Perhaps you should be concentrating your efforts on openings, principles, planning, pawn play, the endgame, or something else. Nor is there any reason that you have to work on a particular course for a specific period, such as two years, two-and-a-quarter years, 1.56 years, or some other irrational figure (perhaps pi or an uplifting transcendental number) pulled from the abyss of some deviser's mind without any inherent logic for the program it's supposed to support.

Every one of these lamebrain notions has virtually no didactic value when applied to real people. But somehow it's been ingrained into us that unless the instruction is rigorously laid out, with precise steps in sequence — as if it were a scientifically determined regimen—it can't possibly work. I'd like to inflict great mental pain on some of the espousers of these sophomorically contrived and tortuous systems, but society has its rules, too. (I was thinking maybe they could be tied to a chair in front of a computer terminal and forced to fend for their nourishment by passing their own tests for a period of no less than one year.) It's because every one is unique that I don't like giving advice before I've had a chance to analyze who I'm giving advice to. Accordingly, you might consider turning to a strong player or teacher to evaluate your game before locking yourself into a programmer's bemused agenda for the next couple of eons.

As a rule, don't trust anyone who doesn't want to know who you are. Teachers who care about you ask questions about you. They might want to know your age, when you first learned to play, how you learned, how long you've been playing, how often you play, which chess books you've read, which chess books you have but haven't read, who you play, the time controls you typically play under, how much time you have to study (daily and weekly), if you have a rating, how good you think you are, how good you really are, how you feel about tournament play, what your occupation is or what grade you're in, what things you turn to for fun, what nonchess books you've read recently, what your hobbies are, what you think you need to work on the most to improve your chess, how you're affected by competition, if you like playing on the Internet, if you enjoy regular assignments, what you think your strong and weak points are, whether or not you can hack being questioned and scrutinized in the first place. I don't know of any programmed chess instruction that assesses all that.

The teacher should also test-and-check you a bit (okay, computer chess programs do attempt to do that, but usually without satisfying resolution, often because they can't appreciate intangibles), to see how you analyze, cope with certain situations, and frankly what things you know and don't know. Only after all this analysis and questioning and testing, and possibly much more, should a teacher begin to make suggestions to help you. Then and only then are you being treated as an individual with

169

personalized requirements. Of course, as a student, you don't have to seek and even demand such an effort from the teacher or program. You could just accept "generic" advice and see where that gets you. It will probably get you to the place most people get to, but I suspect you'd rather be somewhere else. It's possible to pass "Go" and get there right now.

WHAT THEY CAN'T DO

Q. First of all, I must admit that I'm unfamiliar with how chess computers are programmed, but I was curious. Often one is presented a situation in which a choice of two moves seems to be entirely equal, and it isn't until later in the game that you realize that you could have saved a tempo or gained a positional advantage by choosing one move over the other. Are computers capable of such in-depth analysis now, or will they play flawlessly in the future?
—*USA*

A. Chess is a very complex game. As good as computers are at calculating forced variations, they're programmed to compute only so far in unclear conditions. They'll go as far as their event horizon will take them. People only look so far as well, especially when they can't find their way. In those instances the human mind is more likely to rely on a sophisticated generalization, which may indeed receive the largest part of its vigor from intuition.

Regardless of who is playing the moves, or analyzing them, whether the impulses are electronic or anthropomorphic, it's not atypical for certain determinants to become evident later on, far beyond the analytic stopping point. That feature of the game adds to its peculiar charm. Suddenly we can be hit with something unexpectedly startling that reveals an underlying truth. Computers are not omniscient or omnipotent. They can't see everything, and they certainly can't do everything. So far.

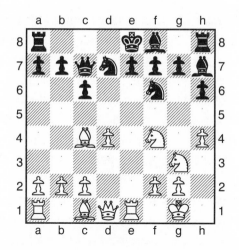

Porreca-Bronstein, Belgrade 1954
Let's see a computer find 1. ... Bg8.

TECH STUDY

Q. Hi, I'm a chess amateur from Hong Kong, China. Let me first describe how dull the chess atmosphere is here in Hong Kong. Chess is not popular. Here in Hong Kong people play xiangqi, the Chinese version of chess. The Hong Kong Chess Federation organizes very few tournaments for juniors each year, and they charge very expensively. The chess books in the public library are not really enough. The worst thing is, the only chess club here is the Hong Kong Chess Club run by the HKCF, which is very inconvenient for people who live very far away like me.

My question is how can I improve my chess in such a city? I have thought about correspondence chess, but I cannot find a suitable opponent. I have tried playing with computers but those silicones cannot explain anything except tactics. Playing endgame studies or tactical puzzles are useless unless you can employ them in a real battle. I hope to find more resources from the Internet. Do you have any suggestions? If possible, I hope you can offer something like a "training program" for me. I am about 1800, and may spare an hour to study chess every day.
—*China*

A. I think the Internet offers the perfect solution for you. The amount of available information out there seems inexhaustible and much of it is free. In addition to Chesscafe.com, you might check out what Chessville.com, Pgnmentor.com, Chesscorner.com, Chessopolis.com, and Uschess.org/scholastic/sc-research.html have to say about instructional chess software. Those addresses should provide some useful information, though it's easy enough to do your own searches and discover all kinds of interesting sites. The other tack you can pursue is to play chess online. You should be playing regularly and following up by examining the critical parts of those games. If you don't have access to a strong player, for whatever reason, you may want to make a onetime purchase of a program such as Fritz. Whenever you're not sure how to judge a position, simply input it in the Fritz analysis engine and see how it evaluates the situation and what it recommends. You don't need verbal language. The moves are your words and they tell you what to do better than Shakespeare ever could.

ENLIGHTENING

Q. Is a high lightning (speed) rating more than just an indication of a player's ability to memorize opening moves? Sometimes I wonder.
—USA

A. I don't wonder about that at all. Knowing opening variations is certainly a key ingredient in successful blitz play, but hardly the only one. Your speed play is definitely enhanced by factors such as aggressiveness, tactical facility, confidence, resourcefulness, mental toughness, concentration, alertness, awareness of the clock, coolness under fire, and even pure reflexes. I'm sure I'm leaving some things out, so you may want to be careful not to deceive yourself into thinking it's solely a matter of opening knowledge. It's best to save deceptions for the chessboard and unsuspecting opponents.

DRAW YOUR CONCLUSIONS

Q. I recently watched an old episode of *Star Trek: The Next Generation*. I believe the episode was called "Peek Performance." The subplot of the story involves Data, the android, who loses his confidence after losing a high tech strategy game to a high-ranking Star Fleet official, who happens to be an alien. Anyways, Data believed that his programming was flawed because he lost the game. Jumping to the end of the show, Data has a rematch with the alien and is able to frustrate his opponent's every move by not playing to win but rather for a draw. The alien walks away in frustration and, in a sense, even though there was no winner, the victory was Data's. The reason I bring this up is because of the way that computers have been beating the human grandmasters lately (somewhat depressing). Maybe the way to win against the machine is to not let the machine win at all. Finally, the question: If a grandmaster wanted to, can he or she force the machine to a draw at will and not give up a victory to the old nuts and bolts opponent?

A. When we play for a draw from the get-go, we often increase our chances of losing. We tend to compete too passively and our opponents sense they can attack us without fear of reprisal. A better way to play is to push for the advantage, trying to get a winning game without incurring unnecessary risk. Playing actively, we can hope either to win or cow our opponent into accepting a draw. Adversaries will stubbornly resist agreeing to anything if they think they have a draw in hand, with carte blanche to attempt all kinds of active things without retaliatory consequence.

I must inject a word of caution, however. If you want to draw against a machine, play to win, but make sure you don't sacrifice any pawns. Otherwise, the artificially gifted one will munch on your stuff and laugh all the way to the computer bank, perhaps gloating with a programmed joke or two.

Can a grandmaster force a draw against a computer at will? Some of them might have trouble forcing a draw against mere anthropoids, let alone software wonders such as the impudent Fritz. But they surely know what they have to do to obtain the best chance for a draw. And that's to play for the edge—without going over it.

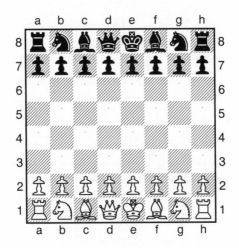

Marshall-Tartakover, Hamburg 1930
Final position.The quintessential grandmaster draw.

CHAPTER 6

Culture, Place, & Time

In this chapter, questions are posed, and not necessarily answered, about the history of the game, both modern-day and ancient. Much suggests more myth than history. This is also the chapter of comparisons. Chess is compared to math, music, language, philosophy, literature, film, and other games—in other words, all those things I know nothing about. But that's where I did my best to fool the writers, by looking up things and taking the time to think about what I was going to look up. Fortunately, many of the questions themselves are entertaining, so maybe a good time will be had just by reading them.

There was even one question about whether chess had any value. That was a tough one, but after a few days of coming up with nothing, I managed to slip in a bevy of ideas I had always proclaimed about chess in my lectures and teaching, and no one was the wiser, least of all me. Who knew they would take the contrivances of that answer and offer them as wisdom all over the place?

ORIGINS

Q. Who were the first people to play chess and where were they from?
—USA

A. Unless new information has been unearthed recently, the game of chess can be traced at least to the sixth century A.D. and the Indus Valley, between India and ancient Persia. Presumably, those living there and others passing through played it. We don't really know how the game was invented, though there are suspicions. As soon as we discover the culprits we'll let you know.

CHATURANGA'S CRUSADE

Q. I have read that several of the chess pieces have changed since its introduction into Europe during The Crusades. Originally the bishop was a ship (which would explain its diagonal move) and the castle was originally an elephant. Is this true? If so, I would like to get a chess set that uses the original pieces. Do you know of a source?
—USA

A. You have it backward. In Chaturanga, the earliest form of Indian chess, predating The Crusades by more than 500 years, the bishop started as an elephant (which could explain its diagonal move), and the rook began as a ship. Actually, it might have been a chariot. There are advocates for both possibilities, and you can learn about the controversy by reading Henry Davidson's *A Short History of Chess*. You may indeed be able to find a chess set that uses reproductions of the original pieces, but I'm not aware of anyone selling them. If I see anything informative on this, I shall note it in Hindi or Urdu.

HISTORY DECONSTRUCTED

Q. I am about an 1800 player, who is often discouraged when I look at chess analysis. They make it seem that these guys are perfect and that they see everything, and I haven't seen any of these things. Do they really see everything they say they do during the real games? How come these games always seem to work out logically, right down to the end? At least that is how the annotators make it seem. Isn't this what teachers do when they try to teach chess? They distort the truth, it seems to me. (I have had more than a few lessons.) Sometimes I wonder if some of these things are made up. Then I read these stories about Morphy and Capablanca, and how they never studied the game. This blows my mind. Is some of this made up? If it is, can any of this help my understanding of the game of chess anyway? On the other hand, maybe it's true, and some of us do play more clearly than the rest of us, with a clear style that everyone can understand. It's almost as if they're not human, the players or the analysts, and I need to understand at the 1800 level. Is this what they feel they need to do to reach me? If it's not true, and they don't play as clearly as the chess writers say they do, how come they don't play more clearly? What is the theory on this? I'm really perplexed and could use some guidance.

—*USA*

A. I'm also perplexed, and in need of guidance, but I will try to answer your questions, assuming I can figure out what they are. As a human teacher I realize that education often takes liberties with the truth. Competitive chess can be full of ups and downs, with the results in question until the very end. Even the best players doubt themselves and veer off course. But since unity and purpose are easier to study than the disarray and welter of bona fide battle, analysts tend to impose logical progressions that might possibly have eluded the combatants during the course of actual play. In other words, hindsight can explain anything.

Since players are concerned with surviving, not teaching, it's unreasonable to expect them to play with so much clarity that their ideas become obvious. That would be the surest way to lose, to play moves that anyone could understand. So it's no wonder that annotations are often skewed and a little unreal. They don't truly describe what went on between the two players. Nonetheless, creative retelling can sometimes be an acceptable teaching method, as long as the student is reminded that the perfect world of chess elucidation does not correlate well with the uncertainty of over-the-board play.

Chess history, like the history of any sport, is sometimes deconstructed or plain distorted to make individuals seem more incredible than they actually were. Too many of us have come to believe that some of the most outstanding players never studied chess, and that they got as far as they did on "natural talent," whatever that means. Not only is this terribly dissuasive to ordinary chess students, but to foist and perpetuate such fables is insulting to all the other hardworking standouts in the chess pantheon. No one—not even Morphy or Capablanca—ever rose to the top of this stellar game without total commitment. But to say otherwise can make for a good story. Perhaps some of these fairy tales, when spun by expert fashioners, may actually broaden one's understanding of the game. But I can't help thinking how much better off many of us might be if writers, analysts, teachers, and especially players, used their skills to tell the simple truth.

NATURE VERSUS NURTURE

Q. It seems odd to me that with all the information that is available to the chess enthusiast today through books, videos, DVDs, Web sites, software and computers, we are still asking the same questions. How can I play chess well? How can I improve significantly? A quick look at the USCF Web site indicates a rating history of my fellow tournament players that hasn't changed much in ten years! It appears to me that most players improve initially somewhat, and then plateau at a level that won't improve much, despite their efforts in studying the game with the vast material available. This may explain why many low-rated players think there must be some "secrets" that only grandmasters know. All this brings me to question whether having private lessons from an instructor is one of these "secrets" for significant improvement. The other possibility is that chess is something where most people just don't "get it." You either have what it takes, or you don't. You can only improve on something that is already there. If you don't agree (and I figure you won't), then how do you explain the situation?
—*USA*

A. I think it could be helpful to pin down what you mean by playing chess "well" and improving "significantly." Some of us, for instance, might conclude that we're getting nowhere unless we're verging on mastery. Others may be happy merely with winning an under-1300 tournament. Some of us seek at least a gain of a couple of rating classes as a sign of improvement. Others may be content with a surge of a paltry 50 points.

Let's say you define a significant improvement as the latter, a gain of 50 points. Even then you have to make distinctions. Advancing from 750 to 800 is not the same thing as going from 2150 to 2200. Were gains achieved in almost no time or over a period of years? What about the age of the subject and the type of opposition he or she normally faces? There's a big difference between gaining those points as a child of eight or as a 25-year-old adult. Acquiring 50 rating points in classroom play against unschooled novices is incredibly easier than doing it in weekend contests at the Marshall Chess Club against veteran tournament competitors. And let's remember—we're all individuals (I love saying that). A suitable answer should also take into account a student's persona and peculiar needs.

So if your concerns are to be addressed satisfactorily, it makes sense to define our premises more precisely. Most of us simply are not going to eat an apple in the same way we'd consume an orange.

You make a good point when you suggest that most players eventually tend to hit a plateau. No matter how innately endowed one might be, obstacles of some sort are apt to slow down development or bring it to a sudden halt. Knowledge and experience should begin to play an increasingly pivotal role. Suddenly, it's not just about talent, unless of course one defines talent only by some ultimate success, quite apart from how it's achieved.

It's often possible to get beyond transitory impasses to advance toward higher levels of performance, and there may be a variety of ways to do it. Some of us need the aid of teachers and strong players. Others do it on our own. Some of us do it by purposeful reading and use of software. Some of us make our gains by playing more challenging opposition as often as we can. Others don't play at all, at least for a while, until interest has once again piqued. Then we seem to improve just like that, without apparently doing anything definite whatsoever. Who knows why some of us who do virtually nothing manage to get to the same or better place as those who do practically everything? The point is that there aren't any formulas to nail down our goals. If there were, we all would achieve our ends applying them purely by rote.

If chess teaches us anything, it's that each one of us is unique, and not just in trivial ways. Despite our common humanity, we still function differently enough to require tailored solutions.

There are no secrets to success. To be sure, having a great teacher or state-of-the-art tools might help. And some of us just seem to "have it" while some of us don't. But why is it that many of those with apparently everything on their side falter and those who enter the Valley of Death unarmed conquer? How come some of the most talented bomb out spectacularly and some of the supposedly least talented seem to fly straight to the top?

I can only ask those questions. I can't answer them. But I can say this. Nothing, not even a carefully protected grandmaster secret, can replace good health, an objective frame of mind, an upbeat disposition to adversity tempered by a degree of equanimity, a reasonably based practicality and philosophic attitude, a resolutely incorporated tough-mindedness, a holistically integrated approach, a true passion for the enterprise, and the ability and wherewithal to think for oneself—the latter, more than anything. If you can offer another set of generalities to bring about success, it wouldn't surprise me and they might work just as well.

CHESS, MATH, AND MUSIC

Q. I have read that math, piano, and chess all connect together. I am curious to know how true this statement is. I have spoken to a few chess players and some say there is no math correlation whatsoever. Other chess players have a strong interest in playing the piano. I am interested to read your comments on the matter. When one plays the piano and takes math lessons as extra activities will it help improve their game of chess?
—USA

A. There's no certified correlation between mathematics and chess, though some qualities may be useful in the performance of both disciplines. Part of the confusion on this comes about by misuse of the term mathematics. Is it particularly mathematical to count pieces and pawns? No, this is common sense arithmetic, nothing more. By the same token, how much math is needed to figure out the number of moves it takes to get somewhere on the board? The real trick is keeping the picture of it in your head. Something similar could be said for recognizing a pattern by the arrangement of pieces. Sure, it has somewhat to do with geometry, but is such perception predominantly mathematical or simply spatial? Can we really say that the mental exercise of proving a theorem exactly corresponds to analyzing a chess position?

Nor is there evidence to confirm that mathematicians excel in chess or that chess players necessarily succeed in math. Of course, there are examples blending the two fields. Emanuel Lasker and Max Euwe, two world chess champions, were professional mathematicians. Math genius Carl Friedrich Gauss discovered that it takes five queens to attack every square on the entire chessboard. But he wasn't interested in how this could be done chessically. He simply wanted to prove it mathematically, without any regard to specific positions whatsoever. And while Hungarian math whiz John von Neumann loved chess, his good friend Albert Einstein hated it.

Much the same kind of thinking applies to the comparison of music and chess, both of which are commonly understood as artistic endeavors. While many musical artists enjoy chess, and many chess players love music, very few individuals (such as Grandmaster Mark Taimanov, who is also a concert pianist) have developed real expertise in both and surely no direct relation between chess and music has ever been established. Nonetheless, there's much general talk that suggests more intimate relationships among the three practices.

Actually, most of the scientific research has focused on just two of the three: music and math. Current studies suggest that simply listening to music won't turn you into Einstein. Listening to music analytically is another matter, and that sort of training does seem to correlate with better mathematical skills and musical expertise. Math and music get circuited close together, in the brain's left hemisphere. Interestingly, this is only a short distance away from one of the several locations for processing language. As for chess, we just don't know enough to say, although one recent study suggests that grandmasters input and manipulate the same chess information differently than young learners. But maybe we surmised that already.

The only nexus I know of for sure concerns prodigies. Psychologists have found that these three areas spawn prodigies in great number for some reason. The thinking is that each of these disciplines requires a special language. Some children are able to intuit these wordless tongues and go quite far, sometimes before they have acquired advanced language skills. But true masters in any field aren't made so intuitively. They still need great practice, experience, and even the use of many words.

Does this nebulous association mean that taking math or music lessons is likely to improve your chess in itself? Perhaps, though if you really wanted to take lessons in math or music, you should do so because you wish to improve in either of these fields and accordingly would enjoy the challenge. To better my chess, however, I wouldn't go to a musician or mathematician. I'd go to a chess player, the very best one I could find.

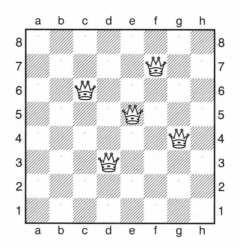

One of Gauss's 638 fundamental solutions to the five-queen problem. Every square is guarded or occupied.

CHESS AND LANGUAGE

Q. Are you aware of any studies that have been conducted on the relationship between the ability to play chess and the ability to learn to speak languages other than one's native tongue? Alternatively, might there be studies showing that bilingual (or multilingual) people are better chess players?

—*USA*

A. Your questions are fascinating, though I'm not aware of any studies done on the possible relation of chess and linguistics. It has been shown, I believe at least in a study conducted by Dr. Stuart Margulies, that children who play chess read better, but this seems more likely because kids studying chess turn to chess books, not because chess inherently improves reading skills.

Howard Gardner, in his theory of multiple intelligences, does point out that talented people are usually gifted in at least two areas, and that on some level those areas may be related. For example, strong chess players tend to have at least two strengths, usually in the logical-mathematical realm and in that of spatial relations. To my knowledge, however, no correlation has been established between chess and verbal language or chess and multilingual abilities.

Each of these areas (chess, music, and math) seem to rely on specialized nonverbal languages that children sometimes intuit, and they can do this without knowing much about their own native language. That might explain somewhat the existence of prodigies in those disciplines. I believe Professor David Feldman, based on his work at Tufts, explored that correspondence in his book *Nature's Gambit*.

But as good as kids can become in those recondite fields, they never quite reach the loftier echelons of mastery without first maturing. For instance, Mozart was incredibly prodigious at a tender age, but his early creations were by no means equal to the majesty of his later productions. And as good as Capablanca and Reshevsky were at eight, it took years of growth and development before they assumed the mantle of world-class grandmasters. Even so, though most authorities think that language may aid abstract comprehension, we can't say for sure to what extent the acquisition of language impacts on the attainment of true mastery.

What we do realize is that smart people are smart for numerous reasons. In the current scheme there's room for the inclusion of various expressions of aptitude, including those needed for verbalizing and those helpful for playing chess. Maybe one day some ingenious person will connect those talents and chess players will derive new insights into how both games (chess and language) are played. For now, what we cannot speak about we must play over in silence.

VALUE OF CHESS

Q. As a public school teacher who tries to teach chess, I am constantly trying to explain the value of chess to other teachers, administrators, parents, and people in general. It's not always such an easy task. I figure you, with your many years of experience, have had to justify the value of the game many times. What kinds of reasons do you give for playing chess when trying to sell it? In other words, what do you tell people that chess players do when playing chess? (What talents do they need to play the game, etc.) I respect your opinion on this question maybe more than anyone else's.
—*USA*

A. In some ways I feel the game sells itself. Just watch kids playing chess and you'll be left with little doubt. But I wouldn't echo the former position of the U.S. Chess Federation, which used to claim that "chess makes kids smart." I found that educators were almost always repelled by those words.

I'd argue that playing chess gives kids practice at doing things that some smart people do, though some dumb people play chess, too. I'm not a cognitive scientist, so instead of stating what chess does for the human brain, I'd rather focus on the mental skills chess players enlist, as I see it from my unscientific, anecdotal, teacher's point of view.

Chess players draw analogies between things. They're constantly comparing and contrasting, investigating how situations are alike and how they differ. Moreover, chess players typically adapt the solution of one problem to solve another, and another, and another.

Chess players also tend to chunk concepts together, in Gestalt, holistic fashion, so that one thing stands for many. This explains how they can look at a small portion of the board and, by inference, reliably assume where most of the other units are, as well as where some aren't. Accordingly, chess players often try to classify what they see. They'll wonder which opening generated a particular position. When they encounter a tactic or stratagem, they'll try to name it. They do this for a simple reason: when something appears in a category, it usually takes on a whole bunch of characteristics associated with that group, so that suddenly many other things can be assumed by implication.

Chess players also naturally arrange facts in series, making sure everything follows logically. They learn fairly early on that many problems are solved by changing the sequence—that is, by reversing the move order, or by playing the second idea first. Furthermore, chess players are receptive to the notion that reorganizing the elements is a vital aspect of creativity. (Scrabble players typically experience these creative afflatuses when they rearrange the tiles on their racks.)

Then there's the way chess players refocus their lenses. They are cognizant that sometimes it helps to change perspective, to look at circumstances from the other player's vantage point or simply from a different angle. So, when trying to figure out how to defend, chess players often pretend it's the opponent's move. Occasionally, chess players actually get up and change their line of sight, even to the extent of standing behind the other player, though here it might be sagacious to consider the size of the opponent before shifting anywhere.

That brings us to perhaps the most important thing chess players do, and this is visualizing moves and positions in their heads. Chess players not only try to envision the future, they try to control it to their own ends. Even here chess players rely on different approaches. Sometimes they must make sophisticated generalizations about the way things might go. That is an aspect of strategy. But most typically doing headwork implies calculating variations: you know, figuring out where to reply if he or she moves somewhere. You can't avoid that concrete give-and-take if you want to play chess. And still other solutions are achieved without seeing very much at all, where suddenly a player gets an insight that seems to come from the ethereal plane. That brings us back to creativity and intuition, to which most players are hardly attentive, yet its value is undeniable to the spirit of play. It's surprising how many important decisions are made for purely emotional reasons, just like real life.

Chess players are also inclined to be target-oriented. Once they imagine their aim, they naturally look homeward, toward the starting point of the quest, similar to the way many of us try to solve mazes. That is, some chess players look backward, from the goal to the middle. Then they look forward, again toward the middle, hoping to bring the two lines of thought together, or close enough to link. The difference is that in chess the maze is more conceptual than actual.

Whoever you talk to, whether parent, teacher, or administrator, I'd tell them that chess players are fond of step-by-step procedures, and they appreciate a good algorithm. Moreover, they are prone to break complex ideas down into simpler ones. At the same time, they typically build elaborate structures of ideas, such as comprehensive opening systems and intricate middlegame strategies. Furthermore, though chess players love precise variations and clear reasons, they are not unfamiliar with the principles of generalizing. Still, they know that the most beautiful generalization can be destroyed by a single hostile fact, as in the case of an unexpected move that defies a theory or proves to be a valuable exception to it.

Then there's beauty. Chess players seek it. They value solutions that rely on aesthetic principles, such as simplicity, economy, proportion, and so on. They are usually repulsed by an idea that goes against the grain. But they also grasp that true beauty may contain a dash of the ugly, in that the real world naturally contains imperfections, irregularities, and unexpected chaos. It may be their integrity, however, that leads them to resign once the point has been made. But at the same time, their resourcefulness and practicality keeps them involved until the last chance to salvage a position has finally disappeared, for they know no one ever won by resigning.

On the human level, chess players appreciate psychology. They understand the importance of one's constitution, and how the stronger tends to wear down the weaker. Chess players are idealistic. They naturally strive for truth, but they can be awfully realistic when the situation calls for it. They are aware that sometimes errors have to be admitted and plans changed. They will do whatever works in the situation at hand. They can be superbly optimistic, and they have great passions. They love beautiful combinations, resourceful defenses, grand strategies, precision, ingenious tactics, finesses, nuances, sudden turns and twists, and many more things, perfect and imperfect. They also want to feel part of a community.

They recognize the value of participating in an intellectual environment, with its own universal language, that bridges many cultural differences. They learn to believe in themselves, and chess offers them a chance to stand on their own two feet. The game tells them that they must accept the consequences of their actions. Ultimately, it gives them focus and purpose, and once they succeed at chess they feel they can do anything.

I could say much more. Others could say it much better. But I'm also sure you don't really need anyone's advice to help you promote the game. As I said up front, the game sells itself. And if some of us won't buy it, maybe chess isn't quite right for them. Some people love saying "no," and some will vote for the other guy no matter what. Funny thing is, in chess, there's room for them, too.

FOUR-FOLD ROOT OF INSUFFICIENT REASON

Q. Is it true that the pointy-headed guy is worth one-half more points than the horsey?
—*USA*

A. That depends what you mean by the colorful term "horsey," the actual value you have in mind with the concept "one-half more points," the nature of the thing you refer to as the "pointy-headed guy," and what you really intend to signify by using the word "true."

RAND-SPASSKY LIAISON

Q. I read that you are a philosophy buff and I am curious as to your reactions and hopefully some comments on an open letter written by Ayn Rand to Boris Spassky in 1972. The letter appears in her book, *Philosophy: Who Needs It*. Of particular interest is her comment that the reason many Russians "fled into the world of chess," was an escape from their totalitarian culture. Also, I would like your reaction to her comment, "Chess removes the motor of intellectual effort—the question 'What for?'—and leaves a somewhat frightening phenomenon: 'intellectual effort devoid of purpose.'"
—*USA*

A. I read that I am a philosophy buff, too, though I never saw Ayn Rand's letter to Boris Spassky. I did read her *Fountainhead*, however, all 700 pages of it (or is it 800?). It did nothing for my chess, but left me terribly sympathetic to Boris Spassky. Actually, I agree with her contention. Chess does provide an escape, so it's easy to see why the game could provide some respite from a totalitarian culture. Yet I suggest there are other reasons the Russians have done so well at chess, not least of all being that they love it. Maybe that explains their success more than anything else.

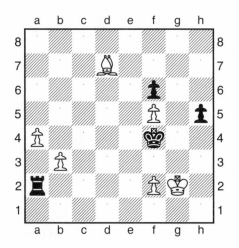

Spassky-Fischer, Reykjavik 1972
White resigns the 21st game and the World Championship.
He also had to cope with Ayn Rand's letter.

EITHER/OR

Q. I notice that some of your answers are very long, and many of them could be turned into columns or books. There are many chess columns and many chess books. It seems like there are hundreds of books on many bookshelves in the stores, like Barnes & Noble and dozens of big chains. I wondered why you don't turn some of your answers into other columns and books, and why you haven't written any chess books yourself, like Fred Reinfeld and du Mont? Maybe you think it would be too

hard to do, or maybe you haven't thought of it. Does this seem reasonable or am I missing something?
—*USA*

A. You're missing something.

CHESS BOOKS

Q. I enjoy reading your answers to chess questions, particularly those about books. Can you tell me which two books have most influenced your thinking, how old you were when you read them, and if they explain the motivation behind the fashioning of your column?
—*USA*

A. Your question is provocative and practically impossible to answer, so I'm going to try. At 16 I read Bertrand Russell's *Religion and Science*, and his clarity and logic inspired me. The other work that comes to mind is Freud's *A General Introduction to Psychoanalysis*, which I read at 17. I especially loved his manner of presentation. The chess in both books, or lack thereof, helped shape this column.

MY BOOKS

Q. Supposedly, you have written 30 books. I am a collector, but I don't have that many of them. Where can I see the list? Besides, I like your style.
—*Bermuda*

A. I think the only one with a complete list is my mother. Maybe she can be induced to copy it out, especially since she also seems to like my style.

THIS BOOK

Q. I'm a long-time reader, first-time writer. Your column has been like a beacon shining in the wilderness for me. I live in what has charitably been described as the middle of nowhere, where chess fanaticism is somewhat scarce. I own all of your books that I have been able to find (don't worry, I own books by other chess luminaries as well), but I have found that reading your columns, answering specific and random (the writers' fault, not yours) chess questions has added immeasurably to my chess education.

Do you plan to do a book in this format? If not, would reader response encourage you to do so? I think there is something about this format, knowing that other people have questions similar to mine and are learning right along with me at different levels that makes the material more approachable. And of course your answers are always informative and chessically invaluable (and often quite funny).
—*USA*

A. Thank you for your kind words, but no, I do not plan to do a book in this format. I doubt that you would either, not if you got some of the responses I get now and then. But overall it's been fun, and I suspect I've learned as much or more than I've dispensed. For the most part the readers have been really great, even those who hate my guts. Besides, maybe they know something. Perhaps *they* should do the book.

DO BOTH

Q. Are classic books better than new ones? I'm a Brazilian chess player with a FIDE rating of 2150. I have a bothersome question that nobody, including very strong players, ever explains: Should I put aside the classic books and only study modern chess writings (this is the opinion of GM John Nunn)? Or, must I first study the classical texts? I have many, many books, classic and modern, but which group would best help me to improve? I'm working, I don't have much free time, and I am 40 years old. My dream is to play in a Brazilian Championship, so I know that hard work is necessary if I'm to survive in that tournament. I don't like opening study and am not sure what would give me the best return on the study hours I put into chess.
—*Brazil*

A. There are intelligent arguments for both sides on this question. Some authorities contend that older books lack immediate relevance and may even include outmoded concepts and refuted strategies that could lead students down an erroneous trail. Others advocate a thorough grounding in fundamental ideas, developed in more seminal works, so players can understand the rationale behind contemporary views.

Clearly, when we study traditional texts, we're scrutinizing openings and variations that are played less often, and therefore seldom encountered in the competitive world of 2005. On the other hand, by excluding the classics, we may wind up being ill-prepared to react to moves we hadn't anticipated, regardless how unsound they are, whatever the year.

Recently, Garry Kasparov was in New York City and several gifted young players had the opportunity to have him analyze their play. Kasparov pointed out that some of the players were completely unschooled in the classic literature. He was surprised that their emphasis had been on current opening books to the exclusion of the famous texts of Alekhine, Botvinnik, Bronstein, and so on. Apparently, he was appalled at how little was known about chess history, including the AVRO 1938 and Zurich 1953 events. So it's easy enough to understand Nunn's reasoning, but it's not hard to grasp Kasparov's either.

A clash of outstanding intellects implies that there may not be a definitive answer to your question. Perhaps there is a categorically proper way to handle the situation, or maybe resolution is to be found in some more relative manner, by following the method that works best for the individual. Then there's Aristotle. No, he didn't play chess, even though some people mistakenly suppose that the invention of the game can be ascribed to him. But he did believe in some applicable things, like balance and striving for a golden mean. If he were a chess teacher alive today, he might suggest that you do both. That is, spend some time learning about chess history and theory through the original treatises. And then take care of present-era thinking by regular contact with printed and online periodicals.

To guide you from the past to the present with an essentially omniscient and latter-day standard, you might turn to Kasparov's new series *My Great Predecessors*. Using that as your home base, you can veer off and study more singular things, knowing safety can always be found by turning back to this virtuoso's superbly comprehensive overview. So for instance, if you've just read his section on Capablanca, you could then play over all the games in *My Chess Career*, for example, to reinforce what you've been studying. Thereafter, you might turn to ChessBase or some other piece of software to see how today's players are grappling with the lines played by and against Capablanca. But it's okay to aspire to success in some utterly different fashion, too, creatively using a variety of tools in personalized ways you find satisfying. As in most pursuits of excellence, real gains can be made while actually having fun and on your own terms—somewhat.

RIVALRIES

Q. Thank you for your column, books, and everything else you have done to help chess enthusiasts enjoy the game even more. Enjoying the game for its experience, and *not* for the ratings or even wins, seems to be one of the underlying themes of your column, so I thought I should ask this (perhaps rhetorical) question: Why is it that the world of chess is so riddled with lack of respect for opponents and petty bickering between grandmasters rather than the sportsman-like conduct that fits this truly noble game? Throughout its history, it seems that the world of professional players has been full of conflict, petty intrigue, disdain for the opponent, and prima donna behavior. Alekhine, Capablanca, Bogoljubov, Keres, Botvinnik, Fischer, Karpov, Kasparov, and Kramnik all seem to have, at one point or another, engaged in deriding their opponents publicly, blaming each other for whatnot, refuting the score of games as the result of political interference or something else, avoiding each other, and generally behaving like an intellectual heavyweight version of the World Wrestling Federation. Even worse, the same behavior of contempt and feeling of intellectual superiority seem to even be expressed in chess books and courses. Jeremy Silman does it throughout his books and even you are depicted to espouse that philosophy in the film *Searching for Bobby Fischer* (this does not seem to fit the statement you make in your column but perhaps you've changed your point of view or the film was seeking more drama). Any other game, it seems to me, seeks to relate itself to its fans and promote likable personalities of its stars, while chess has accumulated a long record of contempt and ridicule of its amateurs and has produced some of the most unlikable characters as its

192

champions. Could this be a natural behavior for a game that is so devoid of chance and circumstance that any win or loss is treated like an automatic statement about the relative value of the players' intellect, or is it just a plain case of poor behavior? I used to play competitive rugby, a game where you literally inflict and receive pain, and yet I have never seen such lack of respect for the opponent on the rugby field that I have seen reading chess books and magazines. Perhaps the intellectual comparisons are something that is more difficult to bear than pain? Or am I just bestowing a poor judgment on the world of chess based on insufficient knowledge and a few extreme examples?
—*Bulgaria*

A. I don't know that what you state about chess is true, and if it's true, I don't know that it especially applies to chess. Granted, leading chess players have been known not to get along with specific rivals, and there have been infamous feuds. Alekhine and Capablanca, Botvinnik and Keres, and even Kasparov and Karpov come to mind. But at the heart of such rivalries usually there's a core of adversarial respect. Alekhine might have avoided a return match with Capablanca, but it wasn't because he thought Capablanca was an inferior player. He admired Capa's play and studied it in great depth. Botvinnik probably disliked Keres, and he did criticize his match play, but at the same time, he praised Keres as an outstanding tournament competitor, second to none in his time. Kasparov and Karpov may not be on the best of terms, but each has admitted that the other was the other great player in the world during their classic confrontations.

But let's say you're right, and chess players tend to say nasty things about their competitors. Is this unique to chess? Are chess players any more flagrant in their criticisms than scientists, philosophers, and artists? Isaac Newton went out of his way to crush anyone who might have detracted from his theories. Schopenhauer thought Hegel was a lower life form. Freud despised Adler. Picasso had no respect for other artists. Hemingway repeatedly put down Fitzgerald. And just recently, the hatred between Popper and Wittgenstein was made public in *Wittgenstein's Poker*. The list goes on and on. Maybe leading intellectuals in any field tend to loathe rival intellectuals.

Perhaps athletes and other physical competitors seem better natured. You indeed may have experienced good sportsmanship in rugby. If so, it could be because athletics offer a chance to release tensions denied in more confined competitions. But I wonder if this is really true. Joe DiMaggio and Ted Williams definitely didn't like each other. Each thought the other was not as good of a hitter, got too much attention, and was paid more than he was worth. Hall-of-Fame Football Coach Vince Lombardi strongly put down his American Football League opponent in the 1967 Super Bowl. After the game was over, and Lombardi could afford to be magnanimous, he dismissed the Kansas City Chiefs as second-rate. Muhammad Ali often described his opponents in ungenerous terms to psyche them out. What about the incessant trash-talking and show-boating in much of today's big-time sports?

I'm not saying chess players are beyond reproach. The game is fiercely competitive, and tense conflict can bring out the worst in people. To be sure, some chess authorities can be unkind in their public responses, but so are many of our greatest scientists, artists, writers, philosophers, statesmen, and even our most cherished athletic heroes. Maybe there's more to this, but let's just leave it at that.

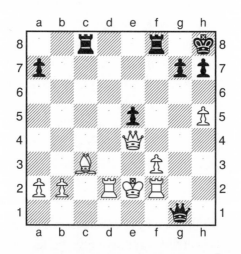

Capablanca-Euwe, Holland 1938
White having fun at the AVRO tournament.
He played 1. h6 and Black resigned.

THE TOP FIVE

Q. I am an avid pusher of pawns, and love chess history of the game's greats. In your well-informed opinion, who are the top five greatest world champions? (I realize this question is very difficult to answer because of different eras, difficulty gauging strength of opponents, and many past champions didn't have access to Pentium 3 and 4 computers.)
—*USA*

A. Finally, an easy question. But I need to clarify some things. Are we talking about now, or in the future? Are we including computers? Are we basing our answer on ratings, or results in certain types of competitions? Ought we to consider duration at the top, or number of games played as champion? Is superiority over rivals more meaningful than all-time numerical ranking? Do we take notice of the amount of textbook examples and analytic references drawn from their play? Are we to pay attention to published opinions? Does chronological appearance play a role? What about factoring in their writings? Should we compare people who've never played each other, and had no common opponents? So you see, it's a fairly easy inquiry to satisfy, once we've answered a number of preliminary questions first.

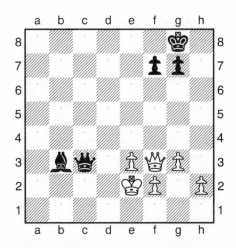

Reshevsky-Fischer, New York 1963
Black forces mate in four.

STRONGEST PLAYERS

Q. I was just reading the interview with Garry Kasparov about his new book and in the second interview he implies Bobby Fischer was afraid of Karpov. Kasparov also implies that Karpov would have beaten Fischer convincingly. I heard, although I'm unsure, that Fischer was voted Chess Player of the Century, and I'm assuming that this vote was by a great deal of chess professionals. So, do you think Kasparov may be a little biased? What do you think? By the way, I always thought Spassky was the strongest Russian chess player until he faded away shortly after Fischer defeated him for the world championship.
—USA

A. How could Fischer not have been afraid of Karpov? The 12th world champion was an overwhelming force, who had an uncanny knack of luring the world's best players into voids of chessic abyss. Kasparov himself found this out in head-to-head confrontation something like several hundred times. Might Karpov have actually beaten Fischer in 1975? That was a very real possibility, but not a certainty. Fischer's genius and will to win might well have found a way to triumph. But the same arguments could be made for Karpov and Kasparov. Both of them also have genius and a will to win. So it may be a truly unanswerable question.

Boris Spassky, by the way, was a formidable over-the-board opponent, especially during the mid-1960s. But Fischer did beat him straight up, and Spassky didn't fare that well against either Karpov or Kasparov in their respective conflicts. Though to be fair to Boris, the match against Bobby was a circus, and he didn't confront either of the two "Ks" at his best. Such fantasy matches simply aren't in the pawns.

Okay, Bobby Fischer may have been voted the Chess Player of the Century, but isn't it likely that this had a lot to do with what he did for the stature of the game in the eyes of the public around 1972 in addition to his actual ability? (Meanwhile, he's done other things for the stature of the game, but you can read about that everywhere.)

Kasparov has attained the highest rating in history. But if Fischer had realized that soon after his early retirement someone else would exceed his top rating, he might very well have piled on the rating points while he still could, so that no one would ever have a chance to surpass him. This doesn't mean that Kasparov isn't the greatest chess player ever. The opinion of most authorities says that he is. Nevertheless, there's just no way to verify which champion is the greatest unless all of them had confronted each other at the top of their games, and up to now that's never been possible.

I think Kasparov is to be applauded for trying to be objective when objectivity is so difficult to achieve. After all, can you imagine any reigning king in any endeavor whatsoever conceding higher status to another member of the royal house? It goes against the conceptual grain of being best. So it's to be expected that people think him biased and his opinions one-sided. But if he had come out the other way, in effect claiming that Fischer was stronger, would that have been believed either? Or would we slyly reason, as chess players are wont to do, that by appearing to take the higher road he was really trying to mislead us into thinking he was safe in his own superiority and merely being magnanimous? That's a no-win situation, where any statement puts Kasparov in the passenger's seat.

If only Fischer had been the one to analyze the situation publicly. Perhaps then we'd wind up concluding that Kasparov at his best was the stronger player, regardless of what Bobby thinks (whatever he thinks that can be printed in algebraic notation). Now, if we could only get Bobby to come out with his own book on the world champions, including the ones that came after him—you know, those he still doesn't recognize as champions.

MAN VERSUS MACHINE

Q. With all the "man versus machine" matches of the past ten years, I have really enjoyed the comments on both sides. For example, take a few of the comments by Vladimir Kramnik and Frederic Friedel. They said some things to arouse my curiosity. I found them to be rather interesting and also mysterious. Vladimir Kramnik said: "I have to change my way of playing from normal chess. What matters is to develop the most unusual tactics possible. I have to keep the computer from using its calculating skills. And I will do this while provoking moves that it doesn't understand. The machine has to feel uncomfortable, so to speak." I don't know what Kramnik meant exactly by the term "unusual tactics." And I understand that computers are superior to humans at tactical play, so why doesn't Deep Fritz "understand" these unusual tactics? And how do you "provoke moves that it doesn't understand?" Does he mean he will make the machine do things it has no idea of? Why would the machine make moves it does not understand? Strange! Then there is Frederic Friedel: "But I confidently predict that within five years Fritz will be able to beat any human in any type of match. His speed and sophistication are going to continue increasing exponentially." I am astonished that humans will become such useless players so quickly! In five years only! I understand the speed aspect, but I wonder whether the speed of calculation will help it only in the tactics department. As for sophistication, is it not the *humans* who teach the machine that, hence humans will always know more in that department?

—*Kenya*

A. I expect it's likely that Russian World Champion Vladimir Kramnik and German computer/business genius Frederic Friedel were trying to engage interest in the match Kramnik and Deep Fritz played a couple of years ago. We might want to keep in mind that these two intellectual giants had to reduce complex ideas to a level that could be understood by various journalists and their readerships, many of whom may not have been familiar with the most elementary of chess concepts.

Since Kramnik and Friedel are two of the smartest and most gifted people on Earth, I'm not certain I should pretend that I understand exactly what they were trying to convey. But since you've asked me to, I'd say Kramnik intended to play the match with a different mindset, one emphasizing unusual aspects of positional struggle to which computers might have trouble assigning verifiable numerical values. His programmed opponent might attribute weight to irrelevant matters or miss certain intangible subtleties that the experienced human mind would be able to judge better, however intuitively. By invoking the term "tactics" it appears he was not using it as is often done, to mean short-range immediacies to advance a strategy. It seems he was really employing the word in a more strategic sense, to indicate a methodical line of attack or overall approach.

Friedel's remarks also seem perfectly plausible. Programs are becoming so sophisticated that they should be playing better than the world's most adept players within a couple of years. But nowhere does Friedel say or imply that humans will thereby become useless. They are the programmers—at least for now. I'm sure they're resourceful enough to find some way to keep people on top, even if that means merely having a better seat from where to observe the proceedings.

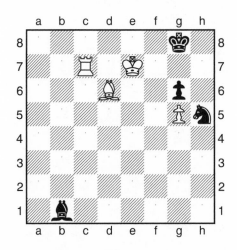

Kasparov-Karpov, New York 1990
Black resigns a 102-move war game.

HIGHER AUTHORITIES

Q. Do you have any clue as to how many grandmasters (both male and female) there are currently in the world? Are there separate norms between the genders? I remember reading that somewhere. Why bother making the distinction? If the Polgar sisters can do it, why shouldn't other females be expected to raise their game?
—*Canada*

A. A grandmaster is a grandmaster, whether it be male, female, or email, unless the title is not "grandmaster" but something else, such as "other type of grandmaster," or some diminishing "other" appellation. Judit and Susan Polgar have achieved the actual grandmaster title, with no qualification, and they aren't alone. Most women now play without expecting any quarter, and considering the nature of the typical male player, that's the way it should be. Currently there are anywhere between 550 and 600 grandmasters in the world. I do not know how many of these are or claim to be men. I think there may be about 100 women who have won the lesser distinction of women's grandmaster, and some of these have garnered the actual grandmaster title and a few of them may even be better than that. I'd suggest the creation of an even higher title, but someone important might take me seriously.

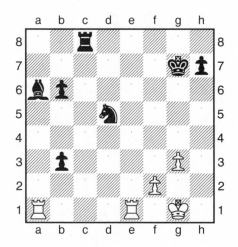

Kramnik-Deep Fritz, Bahrain 2002
White resigns.

GMS SEEK FUN

Q. My question is, as a matter of fact, a curiosity I believe you can tell me. Do GMs still play chess just for fun? Do they take the board and say "How about playing a chess game?" If they do, whom do they play against?
—*Brazil*

A. Only a few of them have been caught saying such curious things to a board. But it's common knowledge that many of them say other things while playing chess for fun with various adversaries, most of whom pos-

200

sess human qualities. Sometimes they play against a woman who goes by the name Caissa while disguising herself as different men and women; sometimes they plunge into a consuming dimensionless void known as ICC that hides the identities of countless genderless entities; and sometimes they face off against the self and the monsters within. Much of it can be fun, especially when the grandmaster wins.

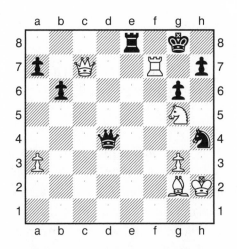

J. Polgar-Kramnik, Kasparov Chess Simul, 2000
White mates after 1. Rf8+!.

FISCHER AND ART

Q. Do you agree with the affirmation that "Bobby Fischer was the first who demonstrated that chess is art?" May I explain that I heard (maybe in bad translation) these very words spoken by the personage played by Ben Kingsley. For me, personally, Fischer was a great follower of many artists, like Morphy, Pillsbury, Marshall, or Fine.
—Brazil

A. Bobby Fischer doesn't think that. Ben Kingsley doesn't think that. You don't think that. I'm willing to bet that even the translator doesn't think that. So why should I think it, regardless of the translation? It should be clear to perceptive beings universally that thousands of people, and yes, even some nonpeople, have contributed to the development of the chess art form prior to the first manifestation of the Fischer godhead. I love being counterintuitive and paradoxical, but not to the extent of being slavishly devoted to a fallen idol who seems to live by his own kind of inviolable logic—a logic the four chess artists you've named might not quite take to heart, individually or as a foursome.

EVERGREEN

Q. I understand the names given to some games ("The Immortal Game," "Game of the Century," etc.), but what does "The Evergreen Game" mean in reference to Anderssen-Dufresne? Thank you!
—*USA*

A. An evergreen tree is one that has foliage that remains green throughout the year. The Anderssen-Dufresne, in turn, will always be new and vibrant to new generations of chess players. It also has many possible variations that "branch out" and form analytic trunks, some of which are extremely difficult to follow. So the word evergreen applies to the game for two reasons: the game will always be fresh, and it leads to all kinds of branching variations.

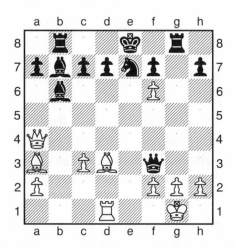

Anderssen-Dufresne, Berlin 1852
"The Evergreen Game." White wins with 1. Qxd7+!!.

THE GREAT KHAN

Q. In your opinion, where does Mir Sultan Khan rank among the most naturally talented chess players of all time? Do you think he was a grandmaster by the standards of his time? Did his contemporaries consider him a grandmaster? I read somewhere that Capablanca once called him a genius. Would you agree?
—*USA*

A. Yes, I'd have to agree. Sultan Khan (1905–66) was extremely gifted, and for a stretch was one of the world's strongest players, certainly a grandmaster by the criteria of those days. He had several outstanding tournament and match results in the early 1930s, and he won the British Championship on three occasions (1929, 1932, and 1933). Besides, if Capablanca thought he was a genius—and he did—that's good enough for me.

STEIN AND CHAROUSEK

Q. I am a big fan of both Charousek and Leonid Stein. Is there any way you could include more games from them in your "Solitaire Chess" column in *Chess Life*? I love Stein because I am learning the King's Indian Attack and I love Charousek because I am learning the opening game to improve my tactics, and no one played tactics better than Charousek. Thanks.
—*USA*

A. Like you, I admire Stein, though I suggest that the reason you offer—that you are learning one of his favorite openings—is a bit off the mark. If we put our heads together I'm sure we could find better reasons for revering him. I also appreciate the tactics of Charousek when he played at his best, though I admit I find it a tad curious to suggest that his was the highest level of tactical play ever achieved. I think Capablanca, Alekhine, Keres, Tal, Spassky, Fischer, and Kasparov would have kicked his aggressive tendencies you know where. But I will do what I can. It's what I do best and it's the least I can do.

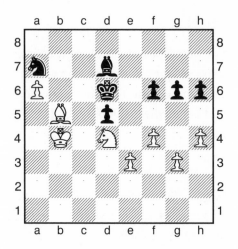

Stein-Tal, Kislovodsk 1966
Black (in Russian) calls it quits.

SANTASIERE'S ART

Q. I am from Rome and I am 38 years old. I am also an admirer of yours, since the time you appeared in the movie *Searching for Bobby Fischer.* What do you think of the rare book of I.M. Santasiere on the Santasiere Attack of the Wing Gambit of the Sicilian? I am not sure of the title. Did you ever meet him?
—*Italy*

A. Santasiere wrote lots of articles and various monographs on openings and different aspects of chess, but I don't recall one in particular on the Wing Gambit of the Sicilian, not that he didn't play it (or write about it). He loved to play b2-b4, whenever he could, which is why another name for the Orangutan or Sokolsky's Opening is Santasiere's Folly (1. b4). He was a creative man.

I met him only on one occasion, at the Marshall Chess Club, when Carrie Marshall introduced him to a table of people I was sitting with. I was just an obnoxious kid, so I don't remember much about it. What I do recall is that Mrs. Marshall was all aglow as she guided him around by the arm. Those were the days.

MELVILLE'S CHESS

Q. I apologize in advance for troubling you with a question that is not strictly related to chess play. However, from interviews I have read, you seem to be quite well read, so I thought I would ask your help with an interesting conundrum. I read *Moby Dick* in a somewhat cursory fashion when I was in high school, and did not get much out of it. I was recently encouraged to reread it, though, and I was shocked at how much better it had gotten over the years! The question: I thought that I had read somewhere that Melville has a few chess scenes in the tome. Since I had read it in such a lackadaisical manner way back when, I wasn't surprised that I didn't remember them from the first read. But I also did not run across them in my second, more diligent reading. Have you heard about chess scenes (or references) in *Moby Dick*? Must I read it a third time, looking only for chess? Do I somehow have the wrong edition of the book, or the wrong book altogether? Is there another whale of a book I have it confused with?
—*France*

A. I knew we'd eventually get around to a question having to do with chess. There's no evidence that Herman Melville played chess. Nor, to my knowledge, did he write about the game with any real insight. The only allusion to chess in *Moby Dick* that I know of occurs when he refers to the harpooner Daggoo as looking "like a chessman," but he doesn't say which chessman. Nor does Melville show any special appreciation for chess in any of his other works—he actually writes with greater admiration for checkers.

Melville does, however, use chess here and there metaphorically. Besides reducing Daggoo to a kind of pawn in *Moby Dick*, references to chess can also be found in Melville's *Omoo*, *Redburn*, *White Jacket*, *Pierre*, and *Billy Budd*, with the latter novella providing: "Life is not a game with the sailor, demanding the long head; no intricate game of chess where few moves are made in straightforwardness, and ends are attained by indirection; an oblique, tedious, barren game hardly worth that poor candle burnt out in playing it." I love Melville's work. He was a true literary artist. But I think there was a lacuna in his artistry when it came to chess.

PASSION CHESS

Q. Recently I persuaded a friend of mine who didn't play very often to play a game with me. The result—she turned into a chess maniac. But I think she will soon be frustrated because she doesn't have the feeling that her game improves (although it does). So my question: Are there any exercises or something that you could recommend to her?
—*Austria*

A. You may want to pick up a copy of *Das Leidenschaftliche Spiel*, by Gustav Schenk (Carl Schunemann Verlag, Berlin 1936). The English version is called *The Passionate Game*, and since the book is all about a kind gentleman who teaches a female companion chess, both you and your friend might benefit from the reflection it provides.

I think it's best that you recommend the exercises. Beyond that, she probably needs some winning and a little encouragement. For the typical chess player the two are practically synonymous. The problem could be that she's only playing you, and losing all the games. If so, find her other opponents to play, preferably some for whom she could hold her own. But if she's been beating you, then something is not quite right in Austria.

FLIPPING THE NEGATIVE

Q. Have you ever looked at the position on the cover of Lasker's *Manual of Chess*? I think this came up before but please refresh me with the solution (or is Lasker lost there?).
—*USA*

A. Lost, or lost in thought? I haven't looked at that position in years (other than the time I may have already answered this question), not that I haven't thought about it. For one, if my memory serves me right (I can't seem to find my actual copy), it's not a full position. Furthermore, in the edition I had, I don't think it was even a legal position. I recall a dark square being on the right. Since Lasker and those who loved and admired him must have known about the light-on-the-right rule, I'm going to assume that a gifted person in the art department flipped the negative. Would you care to join me in that assumption?

SEVENTH SEAL

Q. It seems like a while since someone has asked you an innocuous, non-instructional (but still diverting) chess question, so I thought I'd try to fill the gap. I recently saw *The Seventh Seal*, Ingmar Bergman's great film, famous for Max von Sydow's portrayal of a medieval knight playing a game of chess against Death. It didn't occur to me until the film was well over that it would have been interesting to look closely at their chess positions (I was distracted by the themes about the meaning of life, the existence of God, and the possibility of personal annihilation at death). Have you seen the film lately? Have you ever noticed any specifics of their game? Does it comport with their descriptions of it? In your opinion, is Death a "skillful tactician," as the knight says? Can you tell if the knight was planning on breaking his flank with a combination of bishop and knight? Also, as a matter of curiosity, what would happen if a real chess player tricked his opponent in order to learn his strategy (as Death did)? It's certainly unethical, but is it considered cheating as well? Thanks, chess column is my favorite!
—*Scotland*

A. The movie is great, one of the masterpieces of world cinema, but the chess positions make no sense. Worse yet, except for one scene, they always put the corner light squares on each player's left, and the positions themselves are afflicted with plague. Generally, whether it's film or advertising, it often seems that the board has been set up incorrectly, with a dark square on the right, when actually what they did was turn the negative because someone thought it made for a more interesting shot.

Still, you have to like the dialogue. Who wouldn't want to break the enemy's flank with a knight and bishop combination? I'm not sure, however, that Death cheated the knight by deceiving him. It has long been accepted that hornswoggling your opponent is standard operating procedure at most chess events, whether dressed to kill or not, on light squares or in the Dark Ages.

CHESS ON TV

Q. Recently I've been surfing the cable channels and have stumbled upon a show that has quickly become one of my favorite TV shows. That show is, surprisingly, the World Poker Tour. This is a surprise because before starting to watch this show I really knew little about the game of poker. Now, not only do I know how to play Texas Hold'em, but I also know how to bet, who the players and personalities are, and much about the locations of where the tournaments are held. Also I was surprised at the amount of suspense and excitement that comes from each hand of poker played. Now the chess question, why can't this be done for chess? I've seen the 1995 Kasparov vs. Anand World Championship on ESPN and it just wasn't as interesting as poker. Daniel King's over-exaggerated commentary was just too phony. On the other hand the coverage of the 1972 Fischer vs. Spassky World Championship on PBS with Shelby Lyman was fantastic. It would seem to me that there is some kind of similar relationship between the games of chess and poker. Chess and poker players, aren't they of a similar kind of mentality? Wasn't that noted by American chess master, Ken Smith, also a noted world-class poker player? So, why not chess and TV? I can see nothing that can promote the game of chess more, if done right. Any thoughts on the subject would be appreciated.

—*USA*

A. Chess should be on television. That kind of slick programming could help promote and popularize the game. Many chess fans, nonetheless, don't need the seamless transitions and state-of-the-art pyrotechnics today's typical viewer requires. For them, the ongoing process of trying to guess the next move is usually sufficient to keep their interest. But for the uninitiated, coverage must hold sway over content. So it's natural for those who analyze chess positions on the tube to emulate those who announce sports, adopting and adapting the broadcasting tricks and techniques of baseball, football, basketball, hockey, soccer, and whatever else relies on scoring and winning, such as cheerleading and poker. (I think David Letterman had it right when he said: "There just isn't enough televised chess.")

To be sure, chess can be seen on the telly now and then, and expert commentators such as Daniel King, Yasser Seirawan, and Maurice Ashley have done a splendid job trying to make Kasparov kingside attacks sound like Laker fast-breaks. Though this doesn't necessarily appeal to everyone, it generally has broadened the spectator base to include many non-core chess people who otherwise might confuse chess with checkers, both of them being war games. In fact, such members of the lost generations often make the same mistake even after following the televised analysis. Too bad chess programming has not tempted the corporate world to invest the power money that big-time sporting events have.

Television reporting of the 1972 Fischer-Spassky Match was pretty special, even though there was virtually no financial backing available. But it was the first of its kind, so it was compellingly novel. Americans (including, supposedly, Henry Kissinger) thoroughly enjoyed the spectacle of Bobby Fischer challenging Russian hegemony when it really meant something. Spice in Shelby Lyman's utterly charming and diverting on-air stewardship, and you had a winning formula for all future coverage of chess competition, with or without sponsorship. If only all of those conditions could be fulfilled with every small-screen presentation, then the game could really give poker a run for the play money.

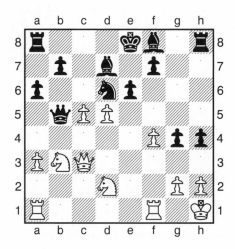

**Spassky-Fischer, Reykjavik 1972, 11th game
White traps Black's queen with 1. a4.**

X-MENTALITY

Q. At the end of *X-Men*, Professor Charles Xavier (Patrick Stewart) plays a game of chess with Magneto (Ian McKellen). I doubt you've seen this movie, but if you have, is it a real chess game? Also, my dad says I should ask you about the chess game that HAL plays in *2001: A Space Odyssey*.
—*USA*

A. In point of fact, I did see Ian McKellen in *X-Men*, though I preferred him in *Richard III*, where he didn't have to draw upon his skill at chess. I'm not sure the position against Patrick Stewart evolved out of a real chess game, but that's never stopped Hollywood before. Perhaps Paramount found the basic setup in an outtake from the old *Star Trek*. The final position seemed Spock-like, although I wasn't as focused on the chess as I was on my watch, which glows in the dark. You can tell your dad, however, that I am familiar with the chess situation in *2001: A Space Odyssey*. Indeed, HAL does give a winning three-move combination, when actually there's a mate in two. Either that's the first sign that HAL has a screw loose or it's his use of descriptive notation. Please give my best to your dad.

PUPPETRY

Q. I am a 33-year-old class A player and the father of a three-year-old-girl (and a three-month-old baby boy as well). Like all dads, I think she is brilliant. Let me spare you and your readers why I think so. In any case, I can't wait to teach her to play chess. In fact, I have already begun to do so. She knows the name of the pieces but I have not been able to go much beyond that (although I am a professor by trade and I have been quite successful teaching her many other things). I don't want to force her into something that she is not ready for yet. However, I was wondering if you knew a fun way for young kids of that age to improve their understanding of the basics of chess. I actually think this age bracket is an unexploited niche in the chess market. If I had the connections, the skills and the money, I would produce a *Sesame Street* kind of show about the chess game. I see bishop monsters going sideways, etc. What do you think about that?

—*USA*

A. You can teach her by play-acting the game, using a large floor mat or rug, partitioned like a chessboard (though you can start with fewer squares). Find stuffed chess pieces, make them, or come up with generic surrogates that can substitute for knights, pawns, and the rest of the crew. Then use your academic imagination to fashion engaging narratives that keep her enthralled and wanting to participate further. Over time she will have been tricked into learning how to play chess, enjoying every moment she spent with her loving father. You can get further use of the materials in three years, once your three-month-old is ready to imagine his own stories.

The *Sesame Street* idea isn't a bad one. In fact, Jim Henson asked me many years ago to come up with a concept to teach chess in the puppet format. And I would have, but I got sidetracked with my work at the Manhattan Chess Club and the developing Chess-in-the-Schools program, known at the time as the Manhattan Chess Club School. Those activities became so demanding that I lost my way for a year or so and couldn't do anything else. I actually forgot about everything else, including *Sesame Street*, and the phone calls and letters they sent me. Wow, was that stupid.

CHESS PREHISTORY

Q. I am something of a chess historian. There are many facts we do not know or may never know about chess history such as how far back the game goes in history (the invention of it and the rules; also, where it comes from; I think China, I disagree with India). Additionally, the rules are interesting. I believe chess may have been played many thousands of years ago, in some version, and survived without a written record. Early man carried the game with him as a form of religious worship. It was a way to become one with their environment and to receive spiritual sustenance. I also love the lore of the great players and the grandmasters. (I do not believe women had anything to do with it, as you said in one of your

211

past columns.) Everything about them fascinates me, as it does most people. You cannot get much on their private or secret lives or what has enabled them to become so developed at chess. Why don't we have chess games per se recorded prior to the Renaissance? I realize the openings were different. But they left none of that for us to read. You have been writing about chess and teaching it and maybe you have information you could provide on this. I would appreciate any insights you have on the above problems.

—*USA*

A. I'm not sure what problems you're referring to. You mean the ones way above, like in the sky? I was hoping we could come back down to the planet's surface. You want to know about grandmasters and chess history? Here's the little I've been able to glean, possibly from the same sources you've been exposed to. (I'll leave out the women.)

For centuries great players and grandmasters have mystified the public with their play and strange garb (though not always in that order). These geniuses have preserved a modicum of privacy by remaining aloof and keeping unlisted phone numbers. But it wasn't always so, at least not in primeval times. Pawns, rooks, knights, phone numbers—those were practically unknown then.

In those days, before checkmate and resignation became popular, the pieces didn't have names and they weren't even pieces. Furthermore, I think there were only three ways to lose a game: being called for touch move, a defective sundial, or the sudden intervention of an annoying kibitzer.

According to what I was told, and as you imply, the initial school of good players came on the scene a long time ago. But certain experts say that they really appeared ten years before that. Nonetheless, grandmasters hadn't been invented yet, and we can say for sure that no chess games were recorded prior to 10,000 years ago (I'm certain of it). That's because the average player didn't wear a shirt and therefore had no place to put pens.

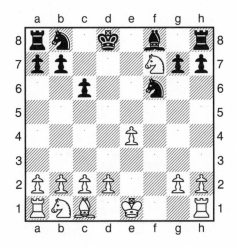

Ruy Lopez-Giovanni Leonardo, Rome 1560
White wins one of the earliest games ever recorded.

CHAPTER 7

Going Through a Phase

The seventh section deals primarily with questions on the phases of chess. The opening, the middlegame, and the endgame received some attention, although I detected a definite prejudice for exploring opening ideas. Readers asked which opening move is best, how many different lines one should have at his or her disposal, and how to create an opening repertoire. Some of the questions could have fit nicely into other sections, such as those on improvement and the new technologies, but in the end they wound up here. Besides, opening questions are the second most-asked, so it made sense to group them together. (Chess relies on a special kind of logic.)

I've also included questions on planning and tactical play, and how to win certain kinds of basic positions. A couple of questions in this chapter fuel a debate that has been ongoing for 100 years: whether to start one's study with the endgame or the opening. Experts come down on both sides of the question, but since I don't like siding with any of them, I went my own way and said something else. That's chess, and that's what this section is about.

LAST SHALL BE FIRST

Q. In your opinion, is there an accepted advantage to playing either Black or White?
—USA

A. That depends what you mean. If you're talking about at the game's start, when it's advantageous to go first, it's better to have White. But if you're talking about at a later stage in a game, when it's mate in one move for Black, it's better to have Black. Which of those two situations were you referring to?

OPEN SAYS ME

Q. Every book I read always says matter-of-factly that queen-pawn openings lead to quiet, positional games, whereas king-pawn openings lead to sharp, tactical games. It is not clear to me why this should be true. Why should one lead to positional play and the other to sharp play?
—USA

A. The distinctions you refer to are not hard-and-fast absolutes. Many queen-pawn openings are more likely to lead to quiet, positional games. But some queen-pawn openings can be busy and overtly aggressive. For example, the Colle can result in an abundance of sudden attacks. Meanwhile, king-pawn openings don't automatically trigger sharp, tactical battles. Just consider a few of the blocked up lines in the French Defense or some of the closed variations of the Ruy Lopez. Nor do these much-vaunted distinctions take into account the possibility of transposition, where a clever, dumb, or even standard shift in move order can change either type of beginning into the other.

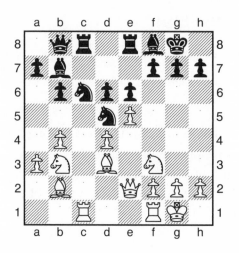

Koltanowski-Reilly, Barcelona 1935
White's Colle led to a furious assault.
After 1. Bxh7+ he won in 13 more moves.

The differences between open and closed games mainly focus on the center and how quickly it clears of pawns. If the center opens fairly early, then it's more likely the game will take a tactical turn. If the center doesn't open up so rapidly, then it's usual for the game to become slower and more positional. But still, this type of generalization lacks the degree of certainty we've come to expect from the Second Law of Thermodynamics.

Generally, the center opens by exchanging some middle pawns so that there are fewer obstructions to piece movement. For the most part this comes about when at least one side (usually White) pushes both central pawns far enough ahead—ordinarily at least to the advancer's 4th rank—to encounter the enemy center directly.

Which beginning move for White (1. d4 or 1. e4) is more likely to lead to such early central activity and therefore an open game? The answer tips toward the king-pawn (1. e4). This is chiefly so because the queen-pawn has a natural protector backing it up (the queen), so there's a greater chance its two-square movement could be delayed without disadvantage. The king-pawn, on the other hand, starts the game in front of the king, which is powerless to support its advance. Delay the king-pawn's two-square opener and the opponent may actually seize control of e4 and prevent this advance altogether.

216

Factor this into the brew. When White starts by pushing the king-pawn, he can usually castle faster than when he opens with the queen-pawn. It takes at least one extra move to castle on the queenside because the queen must be moved. The additional king safety attained by castling sooner makes it less perilous to open the center by double pawn advances. That's another reason open games are more likely to ensue from king-pawn openings.

So if you want to open up the game and increase the likelihood of tactical play, you have a slightly better chance if you begin with e2-e4 and then, at a timely moment, follow up with d2-d4 (or d3-d4). But chess doesn't really lend itself to that kind oversimplification, which is why I either avoid responding to this type of question or resort to flippant answers. I usually prefer the latter.

ATTACK IT

Q. I am an Internet chess player, with a lowly rating of 1178. I am curious about what to do when the opposing queen moves out early. Many chess books advise one not to move the queen early as it is easily attacked. However, I was playing this game when suddenly the Black queen developed on move three. I was at a loss. This player made a mistake, but how to exploit it? Due to my confusion, my enemy easily took the initiative, until he made a blunder and allowed me to force mate. If only he had played better.
—*Malaysia*

A. The books aren't wrong, at least not about this. The queen shouldn't be moved out early unless the situation renders it necessary. Now maybe you played imprecisely, missing ways to capitalize on your opponent's violation of principle. Or perhaps you didn't miss anything and only think you did. But whatever the circumstances, and here there are many possibilities best left unmentioned, something tells me you shouldn't base your interpretation of chess theory solely on the conduct of that one game. I suggest you play a few more before coming to any definite conclusions.

THEORY

Q. Well, firstly I want to say keep up your good work of teaching chess. I am 16 and a Zimbabwean chess player. I participate in many tournaments, but the problem I have is that I do not have knowledge of theory. How should I get theory? Must I do this from a book?
—*Zimbabwe*

A. I'm not sure what you mean by "theory." Perhaps you mean the theory of positional chess, which are the methods and principles by which chess should be played. You might be referring to endgame theory, which consists of all the known winning and drawn positions, as well as their underlying concepts and supportive analysis. You could also be thinking about endgame theories within endgame theory, such as the theory of corresponding squares.

But most of the time, when people talk about theory, they're referring to opening theory. I'm going to assume that's what you mean. There are many books that treat opening theory, such as *MCO* (*Modern Chess Openings*), where reasonable moves and lines are presented, together with the judgments of the analysts.

If you really wanted the latest theoretical ideas, however, it wouldn't be so practical to rely on books, which, in today's world are dated before they come out. It would make more sense to pick up magazines and tournament bulletins containing the latest games and theoretical articles. Scan the Internet. Nothing is faster, and the critical response to recently played games is immediate and worldwide. So if you really want to study theory, start by clicking the various online sites, where you can often follow the best players in the world (don't follow them, just their games) as their games are actually being played.

THE LONG AND THE SHORT

Q. For White I play fine against the Sicilian Defense. My favorite system is Rossolimo's Variation, with 3. Bb5. With White when I play 1. d4 I like it when my opponent goes into a King's Indian but not a Gruenfeld. I'm also having trouble sometimes with the Benoni and I don't like to play against the Benko. That's why I'm going to stick with 1. e4 and try to get either a Rossolimo or maybe a Wing Gambit, which I've had success with. I'm not sure what I should be doing, although I currently owe a word of thanks to Eric Schiller's book, *Unorthodox Chess Openings.* Schiller gives facts, and I like that. My question is I notice that you often give long answers to short questions. Do you ever do it the opposing way, getting right to the point? —*USA*

A. Occasionally.

THE REASONS WHY

Q. I have purchased a few chess books (including some of yours) and I really want to learn the openings. I don't want to memorize a bunch of moves. I would rather learn why certain moves are made, and the principles behind the openings. Is there a book that could help me?
—*USA*

A. Reuben Fine's *The Ideas Behind the Chess Openings* was one of the first books to explain the opening concepts of particular variations. But through the years texts that elucidate chess openings have proliferated and now their combined weight is warping the shelves at fine libraries and book emporia near you.

I suspect, however, that you're not necessarily going to be satisfied by any one title. You can read the best book and still feel frustrated if it doesn't answer your questions suitably. Indeed, the answers you seek might not be found in good books. It could be that you have to get your insights from a few bad books or from no books in particular. Perhaps you'll have to make your most meaningful advances over the course of time by continually facing and overcoming challenging real-game hurdles. That's one of the most reliable ways to gain discernment in chess or anything else: to accumulate enough experience so that you can say with Socratic wisdom that you don't really comprehend very much at all.

But at that point you should know at least two things. The first is that no one book, whether it's the *Bible* or the collected jottings of the greatest chess player who ever lived, can tell you everything you need to know. The second is that failing to find that book won't stop you from enjoying the study and play of the world's most fascinating game.

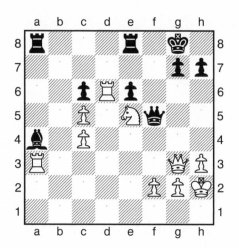

Fine-Botvinnik, Holland 1938
Black resigns.

OPENING CHOICES

Q. I have been playing competitive chess on and off for more than ten years. My rating fluctuates between 1700 and 1800. I have a couple of questions. My first question is, how do I find out what style of play I am best suited for? I play Nf3, d4, and e4 openings. I like tactics and I like attacking, but some of my best results have been with slower openings. —*Canada*

A. You're obviously a fairly strong player, with some real experience behind you, so it's likely you're not entirely in the dark. You should have some sense for when you feel chessically contented. Since you like to attack, but seem to perform better in some of the slower openings (I'm going to take the liberty of presuming that you mean openings other than 1. e4), it sounds as if you proceed more effectively after your position has been built up. I'm going to go out on the limb and counsel that you narrow your choice of openings, opting to play 1. d4. But this is general advice, and you're a specific person, so you might want to have your games critically analyzed by a master or strong player for confirmation or a second opinion.

IT STARTS BEFORE IT STARTS

Q. I've been playing chess seriously for about four years. I've recently noticed that there is a huge difference in my playing strength between regular and irregular openings. If I can play a regular opening (of course mostly when I'm White), I get to have more influence. With White I always play 1. e4 and usually reach a playable middlegame, having a calculated strength of about 1900. But when I'm drawn to some weird lines early on (which now happens quite often because people I play regularly have noticed this too), I usually am in a dire situation by the 10th move and have a much lower playing strength. Is there a way or a system that I can apply to turn unusual openings into more regular familiar lines? Can I force my games to look like I want them to by countering weird openings (1. Nf3 or 1. c4 for example) with certain moves?
—*Israel*

A. If I understand you, your problem may be that you're encountering special difficulties when playing Black. This would be natural, because Black is much harder to play than White. White has the first move and slightly greater control of the game's flow. Either you must opt for defenses that instill distinctive character and a measure of counter-control early on, or you'll need to play enough times to insure getting a fair share of the White pieces.

It could be that by "regular" openings you mean king-pawn openings, or even more restrictively, double king-pawn openings. Perhaps you feel more at home in symmetrical lines, though I must admit I'm only guessing. There are plenty of asymmetrical responses, such as the Sicilian Defense, which aren't considered "irregular" at all, let alone "weird." Moves such as 1. Nf3 and 1. c4 are fairly standard in today's competitions, though inexperienced players often have trouble appreciating them, and therefore tend to go awry. If this is what you're referring to, and I'm not saying it is, you might start to familiarize yourself with these openings a little more in depth. You can do this by hunting down games that show those openings, drawing the material from accessible magazines, books, and software.

Is there an approach to help convert the irregular to the regular? Not to my knowledge, though it probably wouldn't hurt to grasp openings and their possible transitions as well as Garry Kasparov. But even if this isn't who you are, and regardless what your opponent throws at you, it's almost always possible to direct the game to a less repellent line. It may be that you simply need to acquire a larger basket of experience so that you have more varieties of produce to sample.

One other piece of advice: don't play the first few moves mechanically. Too often we don't start thinking until after the first five or six moves are played, and by then it may be too late to spot an opportunity to give the game an unusual twist—or to stop the cutting edge of theory from twisting the other way. It's an argument for working hard from move one on, and even slightly before. That's right. It helps to think before you have to think.

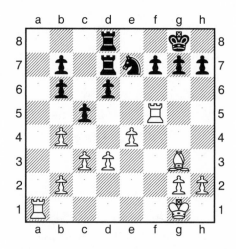

**Kramnik-Leko, Dortmund 2003.
They agreed to a draw.**

DRAW FLAW

Q. When playing people of higher strength than me, which openings give the best chance of a draw?
—*USA*

222

A. You haven't stipulated your strength. For all I know, you might be a world-class grandmaster and you'd like to understand how to maximize your chances of drawing with Kramnik. If so, I really can't help you. It's also possible you're merely a beginner and you'd like to know how to draw with other beginners. There, too, I couldn't help you, mainly because I wouldn't, since I don't believe anyone should be encouraged to seek draws as a playing strategy. Instead of trying to draw, why don't you resort to the more standard approach and play to win? It has worked in zillions of chess games, going a long way back, so there must be something to it.

If I were to answer your question a different way, the truth is that when most of us aim for a draw we wind up playing too passively, and that's often the surest way to lose. So if you want or need a draw, it's best to play actively for a win, but without taking unnecessary risks. However, I'm not going to advise you on which openings to play in order to increase opportunities of achieving drawing nirvana, primarily because following specified setups blindly is antithetical to the way chess should be played and the way I've been taught. But that's just the rational being in me.

PAYBACK

Q. I have a question regarding opening training. As Black, I want to develop a repertoire against 1. d4 and 1. e4. So against 1. d4 I might want to try the Nimzo-Indian and against 1.e4, I might want to try the Sicilian. The problem is that under each general defense, there are large numbers of variations, such as the Dragon or the Najdorf in the Sicilian. Moreover, what I end up playing is going to depend on White's second move. So, I'm not sure exactly how I go about developing a small and focused repertoire. Can you offer advice?
—*USA*

A. There are a lot of variations to learn when developing an opening repertoire, because you must arm against all reasonable choices. It's going to require some work, and there's no getting around it. You can't succeed merely by memorizing a few tricks. Chess doesn't work that way. If it were that simple everyone would be an outstanding player, and the game would be no harder than eating crackers.

Moving ahead (I suppose the time has come), you could take any of several different approaches to develop a serviceable repertoire. Numerous books treat this very problem, offering the reader a set of consistent replies, for both White and Black, to whatever reasonable moves might occur in the opening. You could go to a large bookstore and review the titles, looking for an appropriate one. Quite possibly you'll find a treatise that works for you. You could also go through the online catalogs, many of which provide a sufficient description of hundreds of new books and see what you can find in those.

Another idea is to adopt the opening repertoire of a particular good player. They've already done the assignment for you, so to speak, and they wouldn't have gotten terribly far unless their own systems were decent ones. Just pick up a game collection or two of a player you admire and use that as the backbone for your own set of openings and defenses. You could even assume the responses of your favorite software, not that the logic there is likely to be as strong as it would be in the games of a great competitor. Even so, it's a starting point, and you can always modify the variations as you become more accustomed to them.

You might also consider asking a strong player or teacher to evaluate your game, to see what lines he or she thinks are suitable for you. And finally, perhaps you don't have to worry so much about studying lines at all. Maybe you could do what thousands of players do: just play and go along with what comes into your mind over the course of time, from move to move and session to session, experiencing the joy of learning by losing hundreds of games to good players. They'll show you what to do and not to do (by taking your pawns and mating you), and you'll have the additional satisfaction of knowing that you've given them many moments of incalculable pleasure. What goes around comes around. Eventually you'll get paid back for your time, effort, and magnanimous spirit—if not in the next chess game, perhaps in the next world.

COMMON SENSE

Q. I am currently an unrated player, but I have been playing and beating players up to ELO 1700. I am having problems with the opening. I usually play it with "common sense" moves. What is the best way to study an opening, and which openings do you recommend for open, tactical games?

—*Jamaica*

A. King-pawn openings and double king-pawn defenses are usually tactically abundant. Many (though not all) of the concepts relevant to them are direct and immediate, so students usually see the point more quickly.

As a relatively new player, you probably should answer queen-pawn openings with double queen-pawn responses. But none of this is necessary. You can play any reasonable moves you want, as long as you're really trying to understand what's happening. If your opponents wind up zapping you along the way, eventually you'll find out why and your game will grow naturally.

A good approach to opening study is to collect 50–100 annotated games in your opening of choice. Play over the material, trying to absorb some of the fundamental ideas. Make notes as questions arise. As you accumulate a number of such problems, try to get them cleared up by a stronger player.

Then, even if you don't yet understand as much as you'd like, just start playing the opening in offhand games. Whenever you encounter difficulties, ask your opponent or other strong players about them afterward. Later, you can hit the books and see what they have to say about pertinent positions and those similar to them. That may not be the ideal way to study the opening, but it's a good way, and it should increase your knowledge of particular systems while expanding your overall chess comprehension. If not common sense, at least that's the theory.

AMBITIOUS PREPARATION

Q. I am a sophomore in high school with a provisional rating of 1100. I have been playing for about two years and have slowly progressed in skill. I feel that I am now at a point at which I need to begin to develop an opening repertoire. I have read that it is good to have a pair of White openings and a pair of Black defenses. I have studied queen-pawn openings (Queen's Gambit) and have enjoyed some of the positions at which

I have arrived. What would you recommend that I put in my repertoire? Also, what books do you recommend in this area?
—*USA*

A. I don't know how you've arrived at your proposed program, but I think it is ill advised to memorize specific openings too deeply at your level, so I won't recommend anything in particular. Furthermore, it would be imprudent for a player of your rating to plan on satisfactorily playing radically different opening moves (such as 1. d4 and 1. e4) on an alternating basis. It would necessitate a great deal of apparently contradictory study, requiring you to spend the better part of your free time memorizing—much of it by rote, and most of it terribly needless—even just a few of the reasonable possibilities stemming from these disparate beginnings. Then there are the Black pieces. At the very least, you'd have to equip yourself with viable lines against 1. d4, 1. e4, 1. c4, and 1. Nf3, and even these preparations wouldn't leave you fully covered.

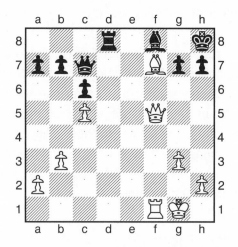

Reti-Bogoljubov New York 1924
White played 1. Be8! and Black resigned.

Why don't you pick up a manual presenting some of the ideas important to the opening phase in general, such as Richard Reti's *Masters of the Chessboard* or Reuben Fine's *The Ideas Behind the Chess Openings*. After going through either or both of those volumes, or works analogous to them, you'll have a much better sense of which variations work for you. Isn't that what you're after?

SIMPLE SOLUTIONS

Q. It has been suggested that for openings one needs something as White and a defense for king-pawn and queen-pawn openings as Black. What are the simplest solutions to this to get a playable middlegame?
—*USA*

A. There are no simple solutions to insure getting a playable middlegame. If there were, I too might be a player. Therefore, I usually shy away from recommending specific openings and defenses without knowing something about the individual, and even here I'm cautious, for students tend to take such suggestions as gospel.

Nonetheless, if I had to advocate something without regard to the person at hand (which I never do in real life), I'd probably advise that White start by moving the king-pawn two squares ahead. I would stress quick development, reasonably early castling, aggressive action, playing with a plan, and all this while actually looking at the opponent's moves. The latter is very important. And when one has the Black pieces, I would urge trying to get the White ones as soon as possible, whether the opponent has opened with the king-pawn or the queen-pawn. Steal the initiative and you can seize the day!

BREAKING THE PIN

Q. I would like to forward to you a question that has been puzzling my mind for a very long time now. In the Ruy Lopez, many variations start off like this: 1. e4 e5 2. Nf3 Nc6 3. Bb5 a6 4. Ba4, and now Black has several options. But after Black's 4th move (4. ... Nf6, 4. ... d6, etc.) and the appropriate White reply to it, very often Black decides to play b7-b5 anyway (on the 5th, 6th, or 7th move or so). The question is: If Black intends to play b7-b5 anyway, why not immediately do so on the 4th move? I'm not pleading in favor of an immediate b5—I can easily live with delaying it myself—it's just that I'm curious about it.

—*Belgium*

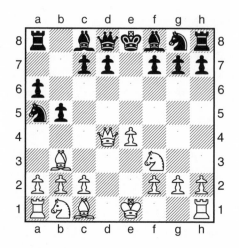

Addison-Fischer, New York 1963
Black gets a "good" game with Ne7.

A. By playing 4. ... b7-b5, instead of waiting to a later point, when circumstances might be slightly more favorable, Black decides to thwart the possibility of capture on c6 once and for all. (Players often describe this as "breaking the pin," even thought the c6-knight is not pinned until the Black d-pawn moves.) But after the bishop is forced back to b3, the position resembles an Italian Game (1. e4 e5 2. Nf3 Nc6 3. Bc4), with two important advantages for White: his bishop is safer at b3 than it is at c4 (where it can be attacked with tempo by either d7-d5 or Nc6-a5); and, by playing b7-b5, Black has accepted certain weaknesses, especially along the d5-a8 diagonal, which he doesn't have in the Italian. To be sure, after 5. Bb3, Black is practically lured into going after the bishop with 5. ... Nc6-a5, which weakens control of e5 and d4. That makes it much easier for White to open with d2-d4, since d4 is not as well guarded anymore. And by playing 5. ... Nf6, Black runs into the dangerous 6. Nf3-g5, when the intrusion of the knight here is more annoying than in the Italian.

So if you want to play an early b7-b5, "breaking the pin," fine. But stay alert and make sure it doesn't break you soon afterward.

THE DRAGON

Q. I am an average 1600 player. I like to use the Sicilian Defense when playing Black. Sometimes I fianchetto my bishop to the black diagonal (g7), and when I do, I face lots of long castling. I am having problems defending against the attack on my castled king. How do I stop the pawn advances without opening direct lines of attack for my opponent?
—*Puerto Rico*

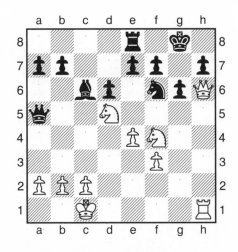

**Karpov-Korchnoi Candidates Final 1974
White plays 1. e5!, and Black resigned
after 1. ... Bxd5 2. exf6 exf6 3. Qxh7+ Kf8 4. Qh8+.**

A. It seems as if you're referring to the Dragon Sicilian and the Yugoslav Attack against it. You can try to meet White's kingside pawn storms somewhat by playing a timely h7-h5, but this doesn't stop the advances. It just attempts to neutralize them. If you're going to play the Dragon, you can't just sit back and try to defend. You're going to have to rely on your own pawn blitzes on the queenside to fuel a counterattack. By mustering sufficient offense there, you might deter your opponent to the extent that

229

White's kingside attack lacks juice and never really gets going. If this suggestion leaves you feeling uneasy, you can try something more akin to your style, either another Sicilian setup or a different first-move response altogether. Remember that in choosing opening lines it's often wiser to select moves that are more comfortable than necessarily correct. If you're not happy at the start, it's unlikely you'll be smiling in the end.

STANDARD FARE

Q. What do you think of the following openings: the Zilbermints Benoni, 1. d4 c5 2. b4! and the Zilbermints Grob, 1. g4 d5 2. e4 dxe4 3. Nc3!. —*USA*

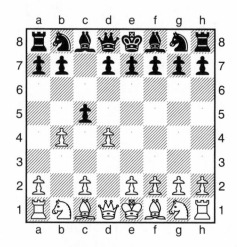

Zilbermints Benoni.

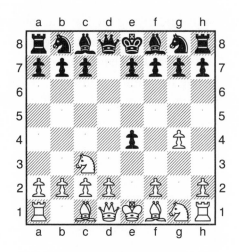

Zilbermints Grob.

A. Interesting, very interesting.

MIDDLEGAME ADVICE

Q. I am a beginner at chess and my experience of the game comes from email chess and games against my chess computer. Although I know all about development and basic tactics like the pin, fork, and skewer, I seem to lose more games than I win. I think I concentrate too much on attacking and not enough on defense. My openings are okay but I get lost in the middlegame. Can you tell me how I can improve my middlegame without a coach? Most middlegame books seem too complex.
—United Kingdom

A. You improve with practice in any art form. So it's a matter of time: time spent playing strong players, solving tactics, analyzing positions, and in this case reading books and essays on middlegame situations. It's clear that you already know some things about pins, forks, skewers, and the like, but it sounds as if you're having trouble spotting them in your own games, or sensing in advance how and when to set them up and ward them off. Let's focus on fundamental tactics and put aside strategic issues, because we need to start somewhere, and in this compass we can only say so much.

You can boost your underlying tactical skill by playing game after game against challenging opposition—learning on the job and over real time. But you should also work with books (or software) examining such tactics in both instructive and random formats. It truly doesn't matter which books you start with—any of hundreds will do. Basic positions are basic positions. I mean, how many ways can you talk about the forced mate in the Paris Opera Game?

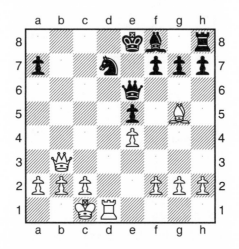

Morphy-Consultants, Paris 1858
White forces mate after 1. Qb8+!!.

Don't let self-absorbed chess people fool you into thinking that how they present a forced two-move mate is superior to the way other, less-skilled people do it, or that their arrangements are more logical, or that they make sure there are fewer misprints. In fact, the test you must eventually pass to enter the realm of tactical understanding requires that you realize for yourself that an error has occurred. That goes for a potentially misleading typo.

Furthermore, the most important logic a problem offers is often what you give to it. That's logic that sticks: what you've figured out for yourself becomes a tool for active future use, with more power than many abstract and lifeless truths (not that it's not nice to know about them, too). This comment, naturally, does not necessarily apply to more subtle positions, that may become clearer under the guidance of a more sophisticated hand.

More pertinent at this building-block stage is that you actually attempt to solve the puzzles yourself, especially without moving the pieces. You should approach such tasks as if they're positions from your own games. A little pretense never hurt any chess student, and it can elevate your practice to a meaningful personal level. Since you're at home over the keyboard, rely on software tactics. If you lose your way, you can usually just click back to the original position without any loss of certainty and with diminished time-wasting toil. It's okay, even desirable, to look at the same problems periodically, and to keep track of how you do. If you solved a problem in five minutes the first time around, aim to find the solution in a minute or two the next time. Your goal is to be able to look at a diagram and know the answer, just like that, almost as if recognition is sufficient for comprehension. You won't need a coach, and that's when the real thinking can begin.

ENDGAME ADVICE

Q. I would like to know your opinion about endings. I have read your endgame course, which I considered excellent, and I really enjoy playing this part of the game. Understanding the endgame has helped me a lot to improve my game, but I am not sure how to continue now. To give you an idea, my ELO rating is 1750, I am 33 years old and my style is more positional than tactical. Is it important to start with pawn endings, then minor pieces, then rooks and then queens? Or maybe I should study rook endings first because they are the most common? Could you also please suggest books to improve the endgame play?
—*Argentina*

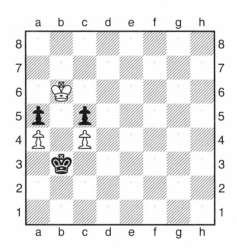

Korchnoi-Petrosian, Candidates 1974
White takes the opposition and wins with 1. Kb5!.

A. Like many things in the conceptual universe, there just isn't one way or place to start when it comes to studying the endgame phase. But however you do it, you'll need to understand something about both endgame theory and practical endgame play.

Almost none of the existing endgame books are so bad—even the really bad ones—that you couldn't get something from perusing their pages. Either they contain basic or theoretical positions worthy of study (true, probably borrowed from other texts, often without credit, and possibly not analyzed well in the first place), or actual endgames played out by good players. Very seldom will you get endgames played out by terrible players, because even thieves want to steal things of at least superficial value. And even if the practical endgames are presented inadequately, you'll have the examples themselves, and these must be of some use regardless how well they're analyzed or presented. To be sure, for some authorities the real pleasure in reading inferior treatments is to deceive themselves (and any thralls who'll listen) into thinking they could have done a better job.

Now the information you provide about yourself is helpful, but I still don't really understand you well enough to offer reliable counsel. It's doubtful you'd want to read a so-called good book just because I recommended it. You might wind up hating it, the apparently indifferent person who advised you, and maybe the game itself. On the other hand, a particularly inept book might appeal to you in some way, so that you devote yourself to it with a passion, thereby deriving much more from it than you might from a sterile presentation of someone who the establishment designates as an expert in the field.

I'm not an expert in any field, but I'll meet you halfway and tender this advice: go to a bookstore or online catalog and take a closer examination at what's available (useful new items are coming out all the time). Carefully look at each offering and compare to the rest. When you encounter a book you like (or possibly even some software), just go with it and have fun. If, once you've gotten a bit into a particular book (or program) and determine it's not working, stop using that course and simply turn to another. If your initial choice is favorable, however, proceed with the same investigative process until you discover another inviting tool. Eventually you should learn something, possibly even about the endgame, and you'll have done it your way, which, according to Frank Sinatra, is why we do anything. And if none of this really helps, just go out and buy any large reference work on the endgame. At least you'll be able to look things up (not that the book is likely to have an index).

OPENING OR ENDGAME?

Q. Capablanca once said, "Chess should be learned starting with the endgame." I have been playing for one and a half years in tournaments and I am getting to the 1500 USCF level. In my personal training I have stayed away from studying openings. Recently, I started taking lessons with a local GM and he suggests that we should put my opening repertoire together first. Coincidentally, I was reading *How to Be a Complete Tournament Player* by Edmar Mednis and he is very adamant about spending most of the training time in the opening. As a chess instructor, what are your comments on the relative importance of opening study and repertoire design for the adult aspiring 1500 player?
—*USA*

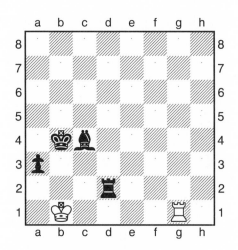

Capablanca-Tarrasch, St. Petersburg 1914
White resigns.

A. Back in the Sixties when I first began grokking the game, many authorities believed that the proper way to study chess was by starting with the endgame. There were a number of reasons for following that course, most importantly several of the greatest chess players of the early 20th century (namely Capablanca and Tarrasch) advocated it. Capablanca's *Chess Fundamentals* and Tarrasch's *The Game of Chess* were books that everyone treated as the last word. And indeed, the views espoused and exemplified in those vaults of wisdom are convincing.

Their reasons for starting with the endgame, whether stated or implied, were essentially threefold. Endgames can assert the power of the pieces in their purest form; endgame concepts and positions are often simpler to grasp; and endgame situations tend to resolve into finality, thus keeping us focused on the goal. Intellectually, the gods of chess may have been right on. But neither Capablanca nor Tarrasch had the benefit of actually working with hundreds and even thousands of students directly, to test out their views in practice, not just in scholarly abstraction. Freed from having to deal with the reality of people, they could afford the luxury of pursuing conceptual ideality on paper.

Because they hadn't done very much heavy-duty teaching, they weren't cognizant of practical problems that can thwart the learning

236

process. Regardless how well present-day teachers explain the logic of starting with the endgame first, they are constantly hit with comebacks such as: "But I never get to the endgame." I doubt that either Capablanca or Tarrasch had to concern themselves with such protestations.

Naturally, teachers have answers. Learning about the endgame also helps students find out how to get to one. Still many students won't learn the endgame satisfactorily. Their own fears and prejudices are apt to put them in conflict with their own best interests. The result is that their passion for study may very well be sapped from the start.

That's one reason many teachers don't automatically emphasize any particular phase at all. Of course they might introduce opening principles and some useful variations. But they'll also feature the types of tactics that are likely to arise from those openings. And they may also examine with their students typical pawn structures relating to the openings under question—not just as they bear on middlegame strategy, but also on how they might conduce certain kinds of endgames.

Instructors who take this more holistic approach, trying to study all phases and none in particular, touch upon motifs as they become appropriate. Rather than showing how to win with an extra pawn in some manufactured framework, they'll wait until the opportunity materializes in one of the student's own games, where the student is a pawn up. Then they'll introduce the theory as they play off that specific position. When teachers wish to discuss planning, they'll springboard from places where the student had real-game trouble. Pragmatic practitioners do not necessarily teach openings they like themselves, unless it's truly apposite to the student's needs. Instead they develop a repertoire they think applies to that student, naturally adjusting it over time as new bits of information come in and the program must be modified.

In a way, this method of instruction fits nicely into the Mednis overview on the matter. He placed greater emphasis on opening study, despite the fact that he was a leading expert in endgame presentation. In some of his finest books, Mednis took the position that if you start your study with certain openings you could connect to many other pertinent ideas in the other two phases. Using the opening as a launching pad, you could segue into tactics, pawn structures, planning, and casebook endgames that are likely to result from those very openings. This is surely a more organic way of handling things, studying without boundaries and in context.

It's doubtful that there's one and only one way to study chess. And regardless of what Tarrasch had to say about starting with the endgame ("the simplest part of the game"), wasn't it also Tarrasch who offered the bon mot that before the endgame the gods have placed the middlegame? Maybe he was on to something—both times. As long as the grandmaster you've contracted cares what happens to you, I think you should trust his advice—for now.

COVERS AND BOOK JACKETS

Q. Every chess player and teacher agrees that learning (i.e., understanding) endgame rules is the best way to improve. However when one looks at chess Web sites one can see quite a lot on openings but little on endings. How would you explain that? Could you give some good links to sites with practical chess endings, exercises, and teaching? I would most of all appreciate a site where the basic rules (like opposition, corresponding squares, how to draw with disadvantage, etc.) are highlighted and explained.
—*France*

A. I'm afraid I don't really believe that the best way to improve is to learn endgame rules. There are many ways to study chess. Although these include starting by studying the endgame, the methods don't stop there. You can also begin with the opening, or basic principles, or tactical exercises, or any number of other approaches suitable to individual needs and tastes. Clearly, what works for one person may fail for another.

I don't mean that in a trivial sense or just to be contentious. We really don't know the best way to improve, and many of us who think we know something think quite differently. Many experienced chess teachers believe the best way to perk up one's play is to have it analyzed on a regular basis. They feel that's how you can come to understand your problems, and once you've understood them, you can start seeking remedies. Personally, I love reading book jackets and back covers. I've learned so much that way; I could never repay the responsible parties.

PRACTICE SOURCES

Q. In one of your recent Q&As you suggested that a good exercise in endgame technique and learning to win "won" games is to take a resigned position from a grandmaster game and play the winning position against a much better player or computer. I wonder if you could suggest some resigned games that would be particularly good for this sort of exercise. *—Canada*

A. Rather than compiling a list of games, I'm going to suggest that you start by tracking down game collections of players known for their endgame technique. Just about any top grandmaster will do, though you might benefit especially from the games of Fischer, Capablanca, Lasker, Rubinstein, Petrosian, Karpov, and Korchnoi. Those guys will give you great product while offering valuable insights into other areas of chess to boot.

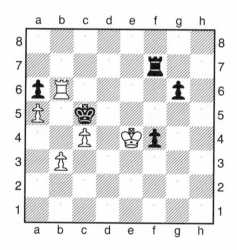

Smyslov-Botvinnik, Moscow 1958
White plays 1. Kd3! and Black resigns.

BYPASS STRATEGY

Q. I have a chess rating of 1675 (USCF) and I have been playing chess tournaments for the last five years. I find myself getting nervous in intense middlegame situations. Once a queenless endgame is reached I feel considerably more relaxed. This is where most of my success comes from, winning endgames. Can you recommend a set of openings that could by-pass the middlegame and lead one to a playable endgame? Also, could you recommend some endgame books to study?

—*USA*

A. Playing good chess is partly about feeling comfortable. If skipping the opening to reach an ending makes you feel at ease, then this strategy is right for you, regardless of the method's general merit. And indeed, it's often quite possible to play the opening in such a way as to reach a favorable ending by skipping the middlegame.

The Ruy Lopez Exchange Variation is such an attempt. From Emanuel Lasker to Bobby Fischer we've seen players cede the bishop pair to obtain a favorable pawn imbalance on the kingside. Whenever you weigh exchanging to reach an endgame, you should factor in the resulting pawn structures and how particular pieces will thrive or falter after the trades. If you have a choice, you certainly don't want to trade down to an inferior endgame, with lifeless pawns and scopeless pieces.

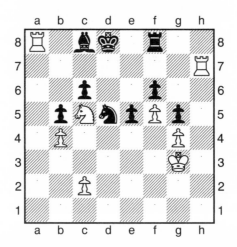

Lasker-Capablanca, St. Petersburg 1914
White's strategy worked and Black resigned.

A number of books present openings according to the types of endgames they are likely to lead to. There are also various computer tools available to help you track down similar material. Using software, search for games stemming from favored opening variations. Make certain they go on for a definite number of moves (let's say 40), so that it's likely they've reached the endgame phase. Request games with a decisive outcome, where your side scores the point. Later you can do a similar search to see how the other side wins the same kinds of endings, if only to learn what to avoid. Then you can round off your efforts by looking at draws, for those can be just as important.

So if you feel more contented with the queens off the board, go ahead and trade them. Yet make sure you realize that an ill-considered exchange could lead to a losing position, whereas keeping queens on the board, as displeasing as it may be to your aesthetic, might at least offer some chances. But the choice is yours (actually, it's not, but that's another question).

OLD OR NEW

Q. I've been reading some interesting books on chess. In the beginning of one of them, the author outlines chess fundamentals put forward by the old masters. In the second part he is able to thwart these ideas. My question to you is: Should a player still take the chess fundamentals put forward by the old masters seriously or should we try to emulate the ideas brought forward by the new masters?
—USA

A. The fundamentals are the fundamentals. Normally, it's still better to have more scope for your pieces, to avoid weaknesses, and to control open lines instead of abandoning them to the other player. A knight is still worth about three pawns, or as my teacher used to say as he pilfered one of my knights or bishops, "a piece is a piece in any country in the world."

But while those ideas remain essentially true, there are always new and different ways to interpret them. Successful players must be aware of their corresponding applications. Moreover, all those general ideas have numerous specific exceptions, and inventive players are constantly looking for exceptions, sometimes saving them to be unleashed for surprise effect.

In the opening, for example, "new ideas" come along all the time. Sometimes they're not really so new. In fact, they may be quite old, and somewhere along the line simply fell out of style. It's not unusual for some of these re-emerging ideas to succeed at first and then be refuted or neutralized as subsequent tournament praxis employs them. During the 1930s, 1940s, and 1950s, it was de rigueur to assume hideous weaknesses to garner dynamic attacking prospects. But those were not really new ideas (today's players usually try to avoid most weaknesses altogether).

The older masters simply had fewer examples from which to draw. The game needed a longer (and written) history so that thinking about fundamentals could evolve. Many innovative ideas were actually explored in the late 1800s and early 1900s, but went unappreciated until more contemporary eyes were able to judge them in hindsight and through new lenses.

The endgame is the least likely to see changes. Some original endgame analyses are added to the lexicon every year, and occasionally a clever resource is found in a tricky endgame. But when you're up a pawn, the best way to win is essentially the same as it used to be. Philidor's draw in rook-and-pawn endgames is still guaranteed. The outside passed pawn is still an advantage. The stronger king's position was important then, and it's still important now.

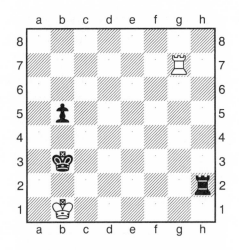

Mason-Zukertort, Paris 1878
White cuts off the Black king by 1. Rg3+,
and the players agreed to a draw.

A final thought. Even though the new treatments may seem more relevant to you, because you see them more often in your own tournament practice, it still helps to understand how they came about. In fact, knowing the history of an idea is a very good way to understand the idea itself. So don't assume early ideas are passé. The great players of the past helped us get to the present. It's as Isaac Newton said. Now we're the ones trying to stand on the shoulders of giants.

TWO ARE BETTER THAN ONE

Q. I am a relatively new (adult) recreational player. In my studies, I have come across a statement that in an endgame of only two knights and king versus a bare king, there is no forced checkmate. Is this true? If so, does that mean there are hypothetical games where one side has the large advantage of two knights in the endgame, and still the game is a forced draw? Obviously, careful play is needed on the part of Black to avoid checkmate, but a draw could be had simply by a 50- or 100-move rule. Has such a draw ever been reached in any recorded game?
—*USA*

A. It's possible to set up a checkmate with just two knights and a king versus a lone king, but the win can't be forced. Either you would need your opponent's cooperation or the situation would have to arise from entailed tactics, with other forces playing a role. It's possible with a king and two knights to drive a lone king toward a corner, but one move before delivering checkmate, stalemate would raise its hideous head. For that reason there are all kinds of remarkable studies where the defender is allowed to keep a single blockaded pawn so that stalemate can be dodged at key moments.

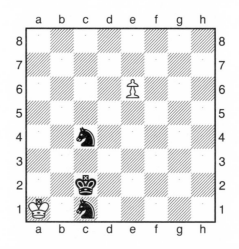

Motwani-Gurevich. Hastings 1991
Black forces mate by 1. ... Nd2,
when White's pawn ensures no stalemate.

Of course, there are additional ways to draw when behind by two knights. For example, such a game could be drawn by perpetual check or perpetual threat, neither of which are official rules. Those are actually sub-classes of drawing by threefold repetition of position. If behind by two knights, sometimes the defender might be able to survive by setting up a fortress. That's a kind of impenetrable barrier. A deficit of two knights could also be circumvented by the 50-move rule (there's no 100-move rule since they've changed it back again), or even by one side foolishly accepting a draw in a winning position. And in speed chess an advantage of two knights or greater against a lone king would become a draw if the superior side forfeits on time. But for the most part, if you have the advantage of two extra knights, with other material still on the board, you can almost always force an easy win. Has such a draw ever been reached in a recorded game? Are you kidding? Come by any of my classes sometime and see for yourself.

BISHOPS AND KNIGHTS

Q. I am a true student of the game. I believe in working, so I do not want to ask for help, but I want to know: bishop versus knight, which is the better piece?
—*Ukraine*

A. Bishops are better than knights in a majority of positions, but there are many cases where knights come out on top. And even when a piece is not suited for the given circumstances, it may have a future.

If possible, players should try to understand the nature of the position looming ahead and realize which type of minor piece will function better. Then they should play to obtain the right minor piece for the given position while trying to stick their opponent with the wrong minor piece. And if they wind up with the wrong minor piece they should then play to exchange it off for a good one. Players can also try to strengthen an impaired minor piece or steer the position into a situation where the deficiencies are neutralized or the poor minor piece eventually acquires resurgent strength.

I won't go into an analysis of all the factors that favor each minor piece. But you should probably keep in mind that knights usually can get the edge in only three ways. They can be better if (1) they can exploit their ability to guard squares of both colors; (2) they can occupy unassailable points in the enemy's terrain; or (3) they can capitalize on closed positions where opposing bishops are severely hampered. If you'd like to understand more about these distinctions, you can find plenty of explained examples in any number of books, or you can come up with terrific examples online. There the real fun is in doing the research on your own, without advice coming from anyone else. As a true student of the game, I know you'd rather have it that way.

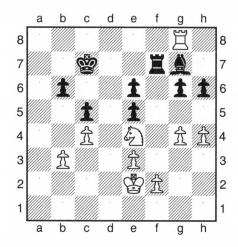

Alekhine-Euwe, London 1922
The knight gets the upper hand over the bishop.
White maneuvered for a win in 12 more moves.

ENDGAME HOLD 'EM

Q. Which is your favorite endgame? Which pays off to study?
—*Spain*

A. What is this, poker? All right, I'll hedge my bet and go with Cohn-Rubinstein, St. Petersburg 1909. But don't ask me why.

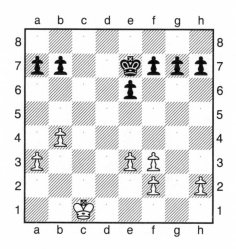

Cohn-Rubinstein, St. Petersburg 1909
Black won in 13 more moves.

CHAPTER 8

Mishegaas: Rules, Etiquette, Notation, and More

Finally, we reach our goal. It's not Mount Olympus, but wherever it is, you'll find questions about rules, etiquette, notation, and whatnot. I didn't know where to put some questions, and some of it I didn't want to put anywhere. Still, some of the more amusingly troubling ones ended up here, and not necessarily against my better judgment.

A number of questions concerned pawn promotion and that funny French rule which is so hard to spell. Obviously there were questions about chess symbolism—not what the game stands for, but how its moves are recorded and its ideas are encapsulated. Touch move is touched upon, and there was even a compulsive question or two about compulsory moves, which I felt compelled to answer and include in the present volume.

There are questions about castling, winning streaks and percentages, long games, beauty, and the strange terminology of chess, such as the question about the pig. I can still smell my answer from here. But there are also questions about winning, teaching, and taking a vacation. According to the last inquiry in the book, I don't know how. Maybe that's why I had such trouble answering the question.

HOW TO PLAY

Q. I received a chess game for Christmas this year and I haven't got a clue how to play the game. What can you suggest to get me started?
— *Canada*

A. You can find the rules all over the Internet. Just type in "rules of chess." You can also find basics, principles, tactics, strategies, and all kinds of advice on how to get off to a good start. You can even get practice opponents there, whether it's through Yahoo, ICC, Chessgames.com, or any of the other online playing sites. If you want to follow up with actual books, go to the library and take out four volumes that seem appealing, as long as they clearly indicate they're for beginners. Read them at the same time, comparing, step-by-step, how the same points are covered in each of them. By the end of that exercise you should know how to play chess. And if you don't, at least you may have laid the groundwork for being able to give your first simultaneous exhibition.

THE OTHER SIDE

Q. I'm not a big player of chess. I was playing my brother and one of my pawns reached the other side. When I was young, I remember someone saying that if the pawn reaches the other side, you can take back a captured piece. If this is true, where do you place the recaptured piece?
—*USA*

A. If a pawn reaches the other side, whether by advance or capture, it must be promoted. That means it must be changed into a piece—any piece, except the king. It can't continue to be a pawn. Most of the time players make a new queen, even if the original queen is still on the board. In fact, if somehow all eight pawns sneak through, eight new queens could be made, though one extra queen is almost always sufficient to force checkmate.

The promoting player doesn't have to change the pawn into a queen. He or she can take any of the other pieces, converting the pawn into a rook, bishop, or knight. Changing a pawn into anything other than a queen is called underpromotion, because none of these pieces (rook, bishop, or knight) is as valuable as the queen.

Occasionally, underpromoting to a knight is purposeful, either because of the knight's ability to give a forking check, in a way no line-piece (queen, rook, or bishop) can do, or for some other tactical reason. Since most of the time one makes an extra queen for its sheer power, promoting is typically referred to as queening.

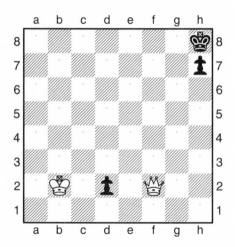

Black underpromotes to a knight and wins.

You do not have to draw your new piece from the stockpile of previously captured pieces, and it doesn't matter which ones have already been taken off the board. Their type and number are irrelevant. Put the new piece on the square that the promoting pawn has just moved. You simply replace the pawn with the new piece on the same square.

What to do if a queen is not readily available on the side of the board? Or, to pose a related question, how can the promoted pawn be distinguished from an ordinary pawn?

Option one: take a captured rook and turn it upside down, if the top is flat enough. Option two: tie a rubber band around the promoted pawn. If this can't be done, use scotch tape. And if this doesn't work, you can turn the pawn sideways, or you'll simply have to remember which pawn is no longer a pawn. It's a challenge, like most moves in the swirling chess ocean.

COMPULSORY CAPTURES

Q. My brother and I have been playing chess for quite some time. We always seem to fall upon a disagreement about if a pawn can "pass up" taking another pawn when it is diagonal to it. In other words, if you have the opportunity to take another pawn, but instead go straight one square without taking it, is this legal? Even if both pawns have already made their initial move?
—*USA*

A. Ostensibly, your question appears to be about en passant, but what you really seem to be asking is: Are certain captures in chess compulsory? There are only two situations in which the rules of the game necessitate a capture to be made. You must take a particular unit if it is the only legal move possible; and you must capture in compliance with the touch-move rule (if you've touched the enemy unit and can legally take it, or if you've touched one of your own units and its only legal move is to capture a specific enemy unit). No other circumstances in chess compel capture, so you and your brother can go right on passing each other like pawns in the night.

TOUCH-MOVE

Q. What is the rule regarding the following: A player picks up his piece, moves it to the square he proposes, removes his opponent's piece from that square, then, without releasing either of the pieces, changes his mind and moves his piece to another square?
—*England*

A. Unless you're playing where the touch-move rule doesn't apply, the touch-move rule applies. The player must take the enemy piece he's touched with his own piece that he's touched. But again, that's only applicable when players abide by the rules, not when they don't.

YOGI'S RULE

Q. A friend and I played a game over lunch, and this time I won. I often record the moves and then enter them into ChessBase Light to see where I could've done better. The problem is that the computer showed I had inadvertently played an illegal move (castling after moving the king many moves before), but neither of us realized it at the time. I know the rule, but had forgotten the king had moved to d8. I checked the FIDE Web site, specifically rule 7.4, but all the rules seem to begin with "If during a game it is found that . . . ." I was glad when he tipped his king, but don't want to have won this way. What happens if "it is found" after the game is over?
—USA

A. Rule 101 of the Common Sense Handbook tells us that if the game is over it's over. Whether the mistake was discovered during the contest or one of you purposefully tricked the other, or some third unforeseen event transpired (there must be at least one that would work here), it doesn't matter. So keep your point, and be thankful ChessBase Light lacks a sense of humor and a chance to eat lunch with your friend.

PROMOTING

Q. I work in a school and run a chess club. As a club player I figure I should be able to answer any chess question that may arise. However, one that got me stumped regards touch-move, vis-à-vis promotion. The question is: With the pawn on the 7th rank and a queen is placed on the queening square, when does the point of no return precisely happen? Can the queen be let go then subsequently be replaced by a knight before removing the pawn? Can you place the piece on the 8th rank, touch the pawn, change your mind about the promoted piece and finally remove the pawn?
—Scotland

A. If you touch the pawn, you must move it to the promotion square. If you touch an enemy piece on the 8th rank, you must take it with the pawn. Touching a new piece on the side of the board, even lifting it, does not constitute the completion of the move in itself, and has no required consequences. As Glenn Petersen informs us, according to the 5th edition of the USCF rulebook (Page 22, Rule 10-h), there is no penalty for touching pieces on the side and the move is not completed until the new piece is released on the promotion square. So, if I understand you rightly, and I understand very little these days, you still have options until you let go of the new piece on the last rank's square. I'm not absolutely certain that I know what I just said, and I feel rather sorry about it, for all concerned.

SIMPLE SYMBOLS

Q. I have loads of chess books (like a good chess fan should) and one thing which really bothers me is the annotation "?!" (dubious). Why isn't "?!" equal to "?"? It seems to me that "?!" always works out badly for the person who played the move, so is "?!" actually bad and therefore equal to "?"? What do you think and what is your interpretation of "?!"?
—*USA*

A. You can be winning, but that doesn't mean you're going to win. You can blunder and not lose the game. The symbol "?!" means the move is probably bad but can't be analyzed for sure. The opposite symbol is "!?". It means the move is probably good but can't be analyzed for sure. Neither symbol refers to a definite mistake, as the symbol "?" does.

But let's not get carried away here. These are just symbols. They never mean quite the same thing, even when employed by the same analyst under similar circumstances, because they are not precise synonyms for the ideas they represent—the moves of a chess game. It's like translating and interpreting, and all translations and interpretations tend to lose something in the process. I have to laugh at all the times I've seen a writer give a particular move two exclamation points in one publication and only one exclamation point in another. Still, it's good to have standards, especially when we know what they are.

EQUALITY

Q. When we prepare for a particular opening for Black with the help of *Encyclopedia of Chess Openings* (*ECO*), after adopting a line we come across a symbol "=" (equality). Though we know that it would be sufficient for a player with Black if he gets equality at the earliest, what would be preferable for the White player? Would he prefer "unclear" over an "equal" line (leave alone "slight plus for white")? Also, what is the exact meaning of "equality"? Whether both the players can easily identify the equality position on the board during the play? Kindly clarify.
—India

A. Don't place too much emphasis on these evaluations. Emanuel Lasker said that one out of every three of them is wrong. (Actually, he said he'd be willing to argue the other side.) Work on understanding the reasoning that produced these symbols, rather than merely accepting them.

Of course, White wants to at least maintain his opening initiative, emerging with the better middlegame prospects (some definite advantage, such as greater space, continued initiative, superior dynamics, or some combination of elements conferring a playable edge). But when we say the position is equal, that doesn't mean the game should end in a draw. It could mean that both players have about equal chances to win, which indeed may result in a draw, or that White's strengths are offset by Black's, or both, or even something else.

In all cases, it really helps to spell out what is meant by the term "equal." And when a move or position is said to be unclear, that generally suggests that it's impossible to say for sure who will get the upper hand, mainly because analysis isn't conclusive. That's why symbols can't compare with language, where so much more can be explained and clarified. Symbols tend to delineate either too little or too much. We usually rely on words to paint in the color.

I'm not saying that you should ignore these assessments. But try to comprehend their source and don't be afraid to question them. When you can do that—when you're not dependent on other people's detritus—that's when you know you've really arrived. Good luck. You sound like a sincere chess player and I'm sure you're ready to rely on your own thinking.

CASTLING NOTED

Q. An individual at a club I attend has asked a number of people the same question but as of yet no one has been able to answer it. When we write chess notation we use 0-0 or 0-0-0 to record castling kingside or queenside. Where or when and why was it decided to use these notations to indicate castling?
—*USA*

A. These changes took place sometime late in the 19th century. Before then the words were written out. If there were only one way to castle, the indication might be "castling." If both types of castling were possible, one might see either "castles kingside" or "castles queenside," whichever applied. Obviously, as chess literature proliferated, writers and readers required more economical ways to communicate moves and information. The notations 0-0 and 0-0-0 refer to the numbers of squares the rook passes over in castling.

COMPOSED PROBLEMS

Q. I wondered what you thought about composed problems. Some composed problems may never happen in a real game, so do you feel they are of any real value? Do you use any composed problems in your teaching? One of our club members made up this composed problem: What is the earliest possible move in a game when the White player can castle to either side? The answer was: White on his 6th move can castle either way by the following moves. 1. e4 Nf6 2. Bc4 Nxe4 3. Nf3 Nxd2 4. Qe2 Nxb1 5. Bd2 Na3. There are more solutions that involve White making different moves but Black is required to make the same moves. Of course this will never happen in a game.
—*USA*

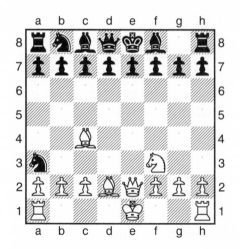

White can castle on either side.

A. Certainly I would use them if they worked in a particular lesson. Most of us turn to chess not just for engaging competition, but also to experience the beautiful and the sublime. These qualities are given defining shapes and forms in the great chess compositions. Occasionally they give us a good chuckle, too, as does the composition offered by your inventive club member. Thanks for sharing it with us.

BEAUTY

Q. I am a 14-year-old with a 1380 rating. I am trying to improve by reading Bronstein's Zurich games and doing problems from Laszlo Polgar's book *Chess*. My question is about the latter. About a third of the way through the book, the problems become all study-mates (e.g., White has a queen, two pawns, a knight, and a rook versus a king and maybe a few Black pawns. Find mate in two). I am wondering if it is worth my time doing these problems that probably won't come up in a game, and are obviously won for White anyway? Or should I skip the study-mates and go on to the more life-like problems later in the book?
—*USA*

A. If you're seeking to speed up improvement, it's better to work with tactical positions that are more likely to pop up in your own play. Nevertheless, don't automatically equate how often a situation occurs with its practical worth. It's true that you won't often get a chance to mate with a bishop and knight. But knowing how these two minor pieces coordinate can be of immense value, and you might not appreciate this until you've actually invested time and studied the bishop-and-knight basic mate itself.

The same is true of chess compositions. It might seem that the actual positions never arise in everyday play, and working on them may require enormous effort. But don't rule out trying to solve composed positions altogether, especially endgame studies. They often touch upon essential themes and radiate great power. Trying to analyze these aesthetic conceptions can stimulate creativity. Indeed, the best ones show the art of the game in its purest form.

You're obviously a very perceptive young man, capable of making intelligent decisions on your own future. It seems to me you can trust your own judgment and skip over the study-mate problems in Polgar's book if you like. That is, with an eye to advancing your skill, it's okay to move ahead to the book's other practical sections, such as its wonderfully organized collection of 600 games. But I wouldn't turn off to composed problems completely. They offer truth and beauty, and seeking those two ideals needs no special justification.

GIVING ODDS

Q. I am a casual chess player, far away from any club in rural Alberta, but I often introduce others to chess. However, they usually get weary of being beaten in the learning process, so I spot them a queen or whatever to make it a challenging game for all. I heard a reference to a detailed chess handicap system (similar to the formal Japanese Go system which I also play), but never found any more information. Does such a handicap exist, and if so, how does it work? If a "formal system" exists, then my opponents won't feel I am just taking pity on them, but using a recognized system. Even if such a system does not involve eliminating pieces, it could be, say, three free pawn moves or whatever. Any instruction would be a help. Also, just a general question from a former member of both chess and Go clubs: Is the popularity of Go catching up to chess?
—*Canada*

A. To my knowledge, no such formal system for handicap chess play exists. Besides, chess players usually look upon giving odds unfavorably. They believe that it distorts the nature of the game. But I see nothing wrong with what you're doing. If this helps you bring people into the fold, I'm in favor of it.

Most chess players who specialize in such contests give time odds more often than material ones. Chess may not exactly have a nine-stone handicap, but it enables the odds-giver to offer a knight, a rook, or even a queen. The standard way of playing such games in the old days was to offer pawn and move (usually the f-pawn). One player I know offers pawn and two moves, though not necessarily to all comers, for such circumstances practically lead to a forced loss.

Is the popularity of Go catching up to that of chess? Maybe, but as chess players we don't have to believe it (thank you, Edward Lasker).

LONGEST GAME

Q. I was told that the longest chess game ever went 241 moves. It must be possible to go much longer than that in over-the-board play. Do you know how long the longest theoretical chess game is? What are the calculations? If you don't know, do you know where I could find this information, or how I could figure it out?
—Germany

A. The game Nikolic (I.) versus Arsovic, Belgrade 1989, went 269 moves and, to my knowledge, is the longest actual chess game in terms of moves ever played. I don't really know what the longest possible game is. Years ago, the mathematician Donald MacMurray did a calculation in *Chess Review*, which I think has since been corrected. I can't seem to find his actual piece, but his analysis took into account the 50-move rule). Since the kings must stay on the board, the greatest number of possible captures is 30.

Each pawn can move six times at most, which means there could never be more than 96 pawn moves. Adding captures and pawn moves together he got 126. He then multiplied 126 by 49.5 (to avoid a 50-move draw) to get 6,237. But this is not quite right, for some of the captures would undoubtedly result in pawns being eliminated from the board, so the actual figure must be somewhat less than 6,237 moves. I wouldn't be surprised if some of our readers knew the correct answer. If any send it in, along with the explanation, I'd be happy to publish it in the next column.

Kevin Bonham (Australia) writes:

In your column you ask the length of the longest possible game assuming that the 50-move draw rule is used. I have often seen a figure of 5,949 moves quoted. That was before king versus king was an automatic immediate draw, but the calculation was also incorrect anyway and I believe (though I'm not absolutely certain) that the longest game is presently drawn with Black's 5,898th move. Note that the figure changes with slight changes in the *Laws of Chess.*

The calculation given by MacMurray is wrong for two reasons. Firstly, while there can be 96 pawn moves and 30 captures, unless some of those captures are by (not of!) pawns, then the pawns never get past each other and make all their moves. It is necessary to have eight captures by pawns so all the pawns can pass each other and promote, so the figure to be multiplied is 118 not 126, as eight of the pawn moves are also captures.

Secondly, while McMurray multiplies by 49.5, this is wrong. The game is drawn only after 50 moves by both players without a pawn move or capture, so long as the side making the pawn move or capture is the same one to make the last pawn move or capture; then that adds 50 moves to the total, not 49.5. So the base figure is 118 by 50, or 5,900.

It's a bit trickier than that because there must be several changes in whose turn it is to make the pawn move or capture through the game. Assuming Black makes the first capture, we need a switch to White making the captures so that White can get pieces out and give them up on squares which double White's pawns on files to leave gaps for Black's pawns to pass through. Then we need another change back to Black making these captures. At this stage both sides have unpromoted pawns so we need another switch for White to promote those pawns and take Black's pieces, and a final switch for Black to take White's surviving pieces. Each switch costs half a move, so on Black's 5,898th move, a king capture of White's remaining piece, the game is drawn as only two kings are left and FIDE Law 1.3 applies immediately. (Does the USCF have this law too?)

To illustrate how to do a 5,898-move game, here's an example. Both sides just move other pieces around in the meantime without triple-repeating; Black takes White's knights by gxh6 and bxa6 (100 moves); Black's knights take White's queen and rooks (150 moves); White plays d3 and e3 (99.5 moves); White takes four Black pieces with pawns: hxg3, exf4, dxc4, axb3 (200 moves); White takes Black's other three pieces with bishops (150 moves); Black takes White's bishops: fxe6, cxd6 (99.5 moves); White's pawns are on the b, c, f, and g files, Black's are on the a, d, e, and h files; Black makes 44 pawn moves including eight promotions (2200 moves); White makes 42 pawn moves including eight promotions (2099.5 moves); White takes Black's eight promoted pieces (400 moves); Black takes White's eight promoted pieces (399.5 moves); king versus king, game drawn immediately by FIDE law 1.3.

This makes a total of 5,898 moves. If anyone thinks they can make one go for longer, I would like to see them construct an outline game like the above to prove it rather than just supplying an abstract 'calculation.'

SKITTLES

Q. I have played in some chess tournaments in the past year. I am curious about something. Why is it called a "skittles room?" I know it seems silly, but my engineer brain wants to know why.
—*USA*

A. The word skittles originally had nothing to do with chess. It refers to the British game of ninepins, which is a kind of bowling. The term often appears in the expression skittles and beer, suggesting that the play can be more social than competitive. To play skittles could mean that you'd be willing to use the game as a vehicle to have an entertaining evening or afternoon with your friends.

And that's the way we use this word in chess, where skittles signify casual play, usually without a clock, often noisy and full of kibitzing. The skittles room is the location at a club or tournament where you can go to play or analyze your games without having to worry about disturbing the progress of more serious games played in nearby spaces or other areas. Despite what some impish tournament directors have implied, it's not the place where they send undesirables or people they simply don't like. Rather, it's where they offer a certain kind of candy.

THE PIG

Q. I recently picked up a Graham Burgess book, *Chess, Tactics and Strategy*. In the book Burgess says, "Of all the masters I have known, only one has used the term pigs for rooks—Seirawan." Waitzkin, in *Attacking Chess*, says you used the term in your lessons with him. Where did you learn the term "pigs?"
—*USA*

A. The term was very popular in American chess circles back when I was a kid, especially in Washington Square Park and at the Manhattan and Marshall Chess Clubs. But it didn't signify any old rook. It referred particularly to a rook on the 7th rank. Now that was a true pig.

When I was a teenager, I asked Al Horowitz why such a rook was called a pig. Horowitz—who was a real tough customer—proceeded to use his rook to chomp a bunch of his opponent's pawns in a money game. "It just eats, and eats, and eats," he noted dourly. Once Al Horowitz explained anything, it stuck.

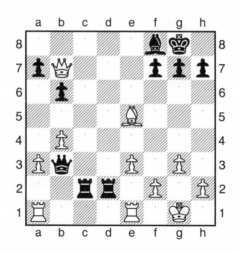

Nimzowitsch-Capablanca, New York 1927
Black's doubled pigs eat up. After 1. ... Rxf2,
White resigned in 12 more moves.

MEANING OF CONTROL

Q. What is the appropriate way to address oneself to a chess Master/IM/GM in the context of chess? Should I have written instead "Hello Master Pandolfini?"

More to the point, every bit of chess strategy I have read so far often refers to the concept of "control" over this or that square, this or that file or rank, or some other set of squares. Fine. But what is control, really? At some shallow level, I have no problem with this concept. If my rook sits on an open file, it "controls" that file. But what if another piece, perhaps several other pieces, also control the set of squares in question. Say, there is an enemy rook sitting on the other end of that file. Who controls the file now? One could say that whoever can control the square(s) when all pieces are exchanged controls it. But, first, the game is constantly in flux, so that I may control that file three moves down the line, but maybe not four moves down. Also, at what cost? If, after exchanges, I am in control of a file, but also down a queen, what kind of control is that? To put it another way, for all practical purposes, is there an unequivocal way of defining control? Foremost, I would like to read how you think a low

1900-rated correspondence chess player can usefully fit the concept of control into his play?

—USA

A. Frankly, I don't even know how to control my response to your question, let alone define the meaning of control in chess. But I shall strive to endeavor an attempt at trying.

When you control a square or line in chess it means not only that you guard it but that you can use it to your advantage. Furthermore, by having control you at least temporarily prevent your opponent from meaningful use or access. And even if your opponent can neutralize your control by comparably opposing you, you'd still have control if you could exploit the situation thereafter. But, to be sure, control can come to an end just like that, which apparently is the way I'm choosing to close this answer. Love your question.

EN PASSANT MISPELLED

Q. What is "umpaso" or something similar sounding?

—USA

A. Now that's more like it. I'd tell you it's the en passant rule, but I wouldn't want to treat it so blithely umpaso. If you're referring to that rule, which indicates a type of pawn capture by another pawn, you can find it explained perfectly in any number of places on the Internet. Just type in "the en passant rule," or something like it, and that should enable you to clear things up fairly quickly. If you're not referring to that rule, I don't think my answer is going to help you.

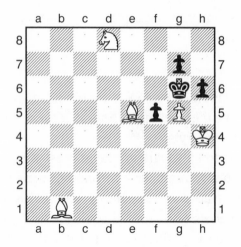

**White mates in one move by an umpaso capture,
1. gxf6 e.p. mate.**

THE QUEEN RULES

Q. There are some ways to put eight pawns on the chess board so that they don't attack each other, considering them as queens. It's kind of hard to explain. I hope you know what I mean. An example: a2, b5, c7, d4, e1, f8, g6, h3. Do you know how many possibilities there are to do this?

—Switzerland

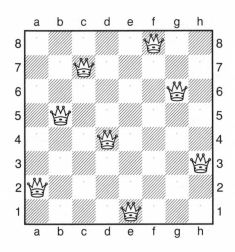

**Eight White queens on a2, b5, c7, d4, e1, f8, g6, h3
None of the queens can take each other.**

A. You're referring to the eight-queens problem. At one time or another everyone tries his or her hand at this puzzle. Dr. Nauck (if he really was a doctor) worked out the solution in 1850. If memory serves me right, there are twelve unique answers. With reflections and reversals I believe the number increases to 92.

A related problem concerns the fewest number of queens needed to guard every square on the chessboard. The answer is five, and there are numerous variations. Many people have explored this question too, from Sam Loyd to Henry Dudeney, to the famous mathematician Karl Friedrich Gauss, to thousands of school kids across the globe. I've actually met some of the latter.

CHESS MATH

Q. Many years ago, when I was a kid, I came upon a cute chess problem (mate in seven moves). The game was played around Christmas time with appropriate wagers between Santa Claus and the devil. At the end of the problem, and with the devil winning, a perfect cross was formed by the piece arrangement and you know how the devil feels about crosses— I've lost that problem, any idea where to find it?
—*USA*

265

A. I'm not sure what your problem is, though I have an idea. It sounds as if it has to do with a cross-pin. Perhaps the final position is similar to the diagram. Of course, as always, it would depend on where the other units are, but here Black's d4-bishop is pinned two ways and that is troubling. I hope this rings a bell. If it doesn't, perhaps some of our readers will be familiar with it and inform us accordingly. If so, I'll let you know. If not, maybe you should go to Santa. And if that fails, you can always go to the devil.

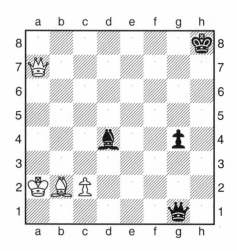

The Devil's Cross
Black to play loses.

COUNTERING BOREDOM

Q. I'm interested in reading chess books and I always remember the things I read. But nowadays, when I read chess books, I feel like I still don't know a lot of things and I'll become bored. I never encountered this type of problem before but now it affects my play in chess and I tend to make mistakes in games. A friend suggested that I should stop reading chess books for a month or two and do other things such as sports, and play more blitz or lightning with friends. Is it a good way to solve this problem? If not, please suggest some other ways for me to solve the problem. Thanks.

—Malaysia

A. I don't think you should do anything that bores you. If you're asking whether playing blitz may be a good way to rekindle your apparent waning interest in playing chess at all, the answer is simple. Maybe. Speed has worked for many others who found serious chess too draining or suddenly no longer exciting.

But it's unlikely that a diet of fast chess will re-ignite your past enthusiasm for reading about the game in general. If you enjoy playing speed chess, it's simply going to encourage you to play more speed chess. Few of us would rather spend time reading about what we could actually experience. Nor is it likely that the thought of the actual thing will rival the thing-in-itself, pathology aside, even for those adept at the art of embellishing rooks in the sky. No doubt a good playing encounter may stimulate interest in all aspects of chess and its study. But if one is particularly concerned with reading about the game (and why not?), surely a better way to fuel such zeal is to find inspiring chess literature and feed off that. One good book might very well lead to another.

Try looking (bookstores, libraries, online catalogs, friends-in-the-know, and so on) with at least the same kind of effort and fervor you've made in preparing this question. You never know what you might come up with, and it may not contain many words at all. A number of the very best works consist mainly of diagrams, often chessic pictures of poetry, and some of those are worth 1000 words or more.

SMALL CHESS CLUBS

Q. Do you think the Internet has been a blessing or a curse to local chess clubs? It has been, I believe, a blessing to chess overall, as witnessed by the number of people in Yahoo's chess room at any one time, and the ability to always have an opponent just a couple of clicks away. As nice as that is, I guess, I wonder if many chess clubs around the nation have not "folded" as a result? I went to the listed location of the Omaha Chess Club this past week and discovered that they were no longer meeting there. I then had a trip planned to Alexandria, VA, and when I did a search for the chess club there, I found an email address which ended up no longer being valid. Although this doesn't mean that they no longer exist, I wonder if you have noticed small chess clubs around the nation

folding as would-be members find it easier to get a game on any number of various Web pages?
—*USA*

A. Not only have small chess clubs suffered recently, the large and famous ones have also been hit hard. It broke my heart when the Manhattan Chess Club was forced to close its doors. Surely, the Internet had something to do with this, but other factors have been playing a role for quite a while. The lure of weekend tournaments offering large prize funds and the opportunity to play against top players definitely contributed, as did the increase in rent and the consequent rise in dues.

Our lifestyles have also changed. Some of us prefer to master satellite TV, interactive media, and other modern-day wonders, many of which can take us across the globe in a nanosecond. A certain percentage of us don't inevitably want to feel trapped inside the confines of a chess club, particularly for what seems to be an infinite number of nanoseconds, where you can't even hang out in your underwear. For these reasons, and particularly the latter, I believe the Internet has mainly been a boon to civilization, even with its attendant collateral damage. But, indeed, I commiserate with all those who miss sitting at the very tables where Fischer and Capablanca once sat.

PRIMITIVE STRATEGY

Q. I am a chess student. I know the opening, and I know many middlegames. But I wonder what is the strategy I should use the most in most chess positions? I have heard it described that there is one primitive strategy I should know very well. Do you know what the strategy is?
—*Libya*

A. If chess shows us anything it's that an appropriate strategy should be determined by the specific circumstances before you. If you're wondering whether certain strategies seem to happen more often than others, I'd answer most definitely "yes."

The two most typical strategies in chess are to simplify or to complicate. All the elements can weigh in here, but let's just focus on material.

You should simplify when you are ahead in material, for example, because you'll want to emphasize your material advantage while keeping control of the situation. In contrast, you should complicate when behind in material because you'll need to preserve the material you have in order to get back in the game. Also, by keeping it complex, there's a greater possibility your opponent could go astray and throw away his or her advantage.

Generally, you simplify by trading pieces and avoiding unclear variations. You complicate by avoiding trades and creating variations that are difficult to analyze. Most of chess is about control. The superior side tries to maintain control and the inferior side tries get control, and so it's natural for the strategies that drive these particular movements to predominate. I don't think I would describe either approach as being primitive, though it might be presumptuous to speak with the same confidence for some of the players who regularly employ these strategies.

TIME TROUBLE

Q. How do you coach your students who have chronic time trouble? I grew up in the late 50s and early 60s playing the classic time limits 40/2. I even remember adjournments in weekend Swiss-system events! I never had time trouble and certainly never lost a tournament game by time forfeit. Slowly but surely, I made progress and my last published USCF rating was 1783. I hadn't played a serious game since 1982 when I formed a team where I worked and starting playing in the Bankers Athletic League, an adult after-work league in New York City, in Autumn 2002. The league plays G/75. I can't seem to adjust. My rating has plummeted from 1783 to 1627 and is falling further because I have lost game after game on time, either outright time forfeits or blunders in the mad scramble at the end. What's most galling is I was winning, either materially or positionally, on the board in all those games! Please point me in the right direction to defeat the time demon and get back on the winning track. I can't be the only guy who's ever suffered from time trouble.
—*USA*

A. There is no known antidote for your problem, but there are methods you can apply in hopes of a remedy. You must start by playing many games in which meeting the time control is the chief condition. That doesn't mean you should neglect the quality of your play, but initially time fulfillment should be paramount. Once you get a handle on the situation, and start increasing your confidence in your ability to satisfy time requirements, you should naturally begin to play better as well. That's the theory as espoused by authorities such as Russian icons Botvinnik, Bronstein, and Kotov, and the methodology adopted by many chess teachers. They expect to ameliorate the obstacle of the clock by encouraging their students to be conscious of it.

Essentially, we get into time trouble because we can't analyze quickly enough and/or with resolution. So improving your analytic skills to the point of efficiency is surely one way to counter the problem, and controlling the amount of analysis we perform is another. Most of us analyze too much. We calculate with great waste and beyond the point of utility.

Obviously, speed chess can be helpful here. In order to avoid forfeiting we have to play more instinctually. In rapid play we are forced to rely more on our intuition and what looks good. Surprisingly, when we analyze less and become more sensitive to structure and pattern, we also become more adept at positional concerns. We think it sharpens our tactical skills, and it may. But the nature of the play also redounds back on our strategic acumen. Eventually we come to sense what's logically sound, almost by appearance. It's uncanny how those immediate judgments are frequently on the money. Think how often good players say things like "that doesn't look right"—and they're right on the money—without any analysis at all.

You're obviously a very thoughtful person and a fine writer, which probably won't help you here. I believe with diligent application you can make headway and solve your problem, but you might need some assistance. Fortunately, there's the Internet. It enables you to play untold practice games, under controlled conditions, at times of convenience and purpose. I suggest you exercise your obvious intelligence and put the medium to good use starting now.

THE GERMAN QUESTION

Q. I have a question regarding openings that has bothered me ever since I started playing chess some 15 years ago. The question is about specializing in the opening. Do you consider it necessary for amateurs (let's say 1600-2300 ELO) to specialize in the openings to improve one's rating? I am 29, ELO 2200, have specialized for a certain period, it worked quite well, but after some time I became bored by the same old positions over and over again. So I thought my chess needed a change.

Then I started playing new openings that fascinated me and my results were also quite okay, admittedly not as well as before. I soon realized that I had some difficulties playing the middlegame and thus spent more time on the clock as I did not know all the typical plans for all the openings I played. And I can say I played almost every opening there is since there is so much that is interesting to discover in chess! Whenever I see an interesting idea or suggestion—from Chesscafe or chess publishing, for example—I would like to try it out immediately! This is a (bad?) habit I seem to share with Carsten Hansen and surely many others, obviously.

I am well aware of the advantages and disadvantages of specialization (deeper understanding of the resulting middlegames and endgames, knowing the typical plans, etc. on the one hand, one-sided and much less creative play, limiting one's own chess horizon on the other hand), but what is your suggestion to stay fresh? I read Giddins' book about building an opening repertoire where he indeed discusses this subject, but I fear that anybody has to find out about it for him or herself! Even strong GMs seem to have very different opinions on this, but I am speaking about amateurs.

Is it okay (and wise?) in your eyes to change to another opening if you know your opponent really well? You can then cut down his preparation and surprise him, but you may even find yourself in a middlegame that is not 100 percent to your taste. And what about playing in tournaments? Do you suggest one should prepare only one opening which you will play throughout the whole tournament (e.g. 1. d4 for White, Sicilian Najdorf and King's Indian for Black) or just play whatever comes to your mind, to just play? My experience tells me that if you want to have fun and fresh positions on the board, you should play just any opening that you like, but only in non rated or blitz/rapid games. If you really want to improve your rating, one should specialize. But if this is really true, I do not know! When you get bored, you may change to a different variation, e.g., from the Najdorf to the Scheveningen as suggested by Giddins and not change the opening completely.

—*Germany*

A. Your questions are reasonable ones. They remind me of the happy days I spent reading Immanuel Kant. But if I were to do them justice it would mean giving them much more space than this column is prepared to give. Furthermore, it might require the intellect of Kant, which needless to say I don't have.

You're not a beginner or an ordinary amateur, but let's start there, since in one interpretation of what you've written you ask me to respond from that perspective. It makes sense to learn the principles and fundamentals before concentrating on particular openings. When one begins studying chess, it's natural to work with open game ideas. They stress things one should know (you know, some finite number of the thing-in-itself), and they're often easier to grasp. As a counter, closed games tend to be a little bit more complex, and they assume that you already know the principles of the open game—when those principles work and when they don't.

Once a beginner has assimilated a firm foundation in basics and open game play, it's perfectly acceptable to specialize, branching out into radically different systems and lines. In fact, it makes the game more attractive and allows for personal style.

As far as improving, we can't do better than playing strong opposition, fairly often, and then submitting those games to thorough analysis. That analysis, which is really like a diagnosis, will direct our next steps, whether it comes from us or other chess doctors. It may suggest openings completely alien to those typically studied by amateurs. It might recommend that we invest ourselves in endgame and strategic work, which most casual players find repellent. But if a strong analyst or teacher told us to give up chess, would we do it? I surmise we wouldn't. So we don't have to take their reasonable advice either. We can do anything we like, as long as we continue to love what we're doing.

272

But you're not a typical amateur. You're already a fairly proficient combatant. You, much more than ordinary players, must submit your games to comprehensive analysis. General baloney from me or anyone like me just won't cut it. If you're serious, and it sounds as if there's a chance you might be, it's time to get down to business. You're not entitled to play merely for the love of the game. You're already too good. And yes, I'm kidding—somewhat. Thanks for bringing me back to my *Cliff Notes* on Kant.

WINNING WON GAMES

Q. I'm having trouble with a particular aspect of my game: I find it difficult to win a won position. I (almost always) come out of the opening with a good position, and I can generally see tactics when they are lurking in the position, but I often start to "drift" and play planlessly. I've identified this inability to finish off my opponent as a weakness, but I don't know how to resolve it. Just last night I found myself four pawns up after a King's Gambit and lost by allowing the Black king to penetrate! Do you have any hints as to how I can eradicate this weakness?
—*United Kingdom*

A. You could try a number of things. You could, for instance, get more practice at playing out winning positions. You can do this on your own, with the aid of a study partner, or by working with a teacher or strong player. If you're doing it on your own, you'll need a source of winning positions to study. A good way to gather them is by turning to the final positions of contests in game collections. Even though almost all of these examples are decisively lost, many of them require some technique to bring home the point. Analyze these positions by yourself, play them out against other human beings, or set them up on computer chess programs and play them out whenever the opportunities arise. The latter approach may be most efficacious, for you can use the computer at your convenience, while avoiding the letdown and inconsistent quality of defense that typically accompanies the onset of the opponent's fatigue. The computer remains indefatigable and resists uniformly throughout the entire session.

You might also invest some effort in endgame study. Such a task also could be pursued with the aid of computers. Just set up positions from a standard textbook, use a clock to simulate tournament conditions, and try to find the right ideas. These labors should have value even when you initially fail to win so long as you subsequently analyze your responses to each attempted exercise. If it doesn't work the first time, analyze it and try again, until you feel you've attained sufficient command to play such positions confidently in real games. Other than the above two remedies you could indeed seek professional chess advice, though this might be costly and certainly isn't necessary.

The other cure is time itself. If you play on a regular basis, stay vigilant to your particular problems. Continually analyze and investigate the positions that give you the most trouble, and you are likely to improve your facility at winning won games. There are no guarantees here, but giving the problem our total focus is the best any of us can hope to do. Logically, this categorical applies to you too.

WORK TIME

Q. I have just started to study chess recently. After some reading and playing, I know and can recognize some basic tactics and strategy. However, I often like to know *why* a move is the best, while the others are not. For example, using ChessMaster 8000, there is an auto-analysis function, and move advice/hint functions. However, I do not really understand the reasons for the move it suggests (e.g., it often tells me the line of moves it sees ahead, and "from this line of moves, you win a pawn"). This does not really help me understand the reasons behind a move. I am trying to find "something" that will tell me why each move in a game is the best in simplest terms. Is there a suggestion or recommendation you can give? Thanks!
—*Canada*

A. Nowadays there are plenty of books that explain the reasons behind many of the moves of the chess games they offer. I suggest that you go to a bookstore that has a large chess collection and spend some time going through the material until you find a text that works for you. Keep in mind that you may not be able to unearth many books that fully clarify all the moves of all their games. And even if you discovered a few such books, you'd eventually run out of them and actually have to figure out some things on your own.

We can't expect everything to be spoon-fed to us. We may have to fend for ourselves, to rely on our own abilities, for no book—nor any consultant or computer—can supply us with all the explanations and answers we might need to succeed during over-the-board play. The best way to become more capable of finding good moves on our own in real games is to find good moves on our own in practice. Surely, we all need a helping hand from time to time, especially to get over certain learning roadblocks and hindrances. But you shouldn't want to be told everything, not if you imagine yourself a real chess player or a thinking being. If we're to grow and improve the right way, some things must be left to the natural process of learning over time.

There are no quick chess remedies that are worth anything. You simply must put greater effort into considering chess positions: asking probing questions, analyzing reasonable possibilities, and considering alternatives to see which seem to be more effective. Sometimes you may have to play positions all the way through before achieving understanding. Then you may have to work further, moving backward from final positions to starting points. This is work, but it often does work, and nothing else works much better.

STRENGTH INDICATORS

Q. I have been reading your column for about two months now and I have noticed the majority of the articles tend to be centered on ratings. I wonder if it is the best thing to monitor your progress with just rating. Are there any other factors that you would say make the same or more difference in your feeling of getting better?
—USA

A. If I had a rating point for every time a chess player asked me about his or her rating, I'd be the highest-rated player of all time, with no one even remotely close. Actual playing strength—not numbers—makes the difference. If you were really getting stronger as a player, you'd probably feel stronger, and this feeling would almost certainly be based on tangible considerations (assuming you weren't prone to delusions). Either you'd be winning a greater number of your games, or you'd be putting people away faster, or you'd have started to beat players you've had trouble with, or you'd be finding resources to save games you ordinarily wouldn't, or you'd be seeing more deeply into positions, or something palpable you could tell others about. It could be practically anything. Whatever it might be, you'd almost surely sense it, as would others. It might not be reflected in ratings either, not that maintaining a rating increase would be irrelevant. That would surely mean something, too.

EXPECTATIONS

Q. I am 25 years old and I have only been playing tournament or rated chess for less than a year. My rating is low right now. My goal is to one day become a national master. Do you feel this goal is attainable for someone getting started this late?
—*USA*

A. An acquaintance of mine didn't learn the moves and rules until he was 18. Within a few years he had become a strong master (just ask him, he'll tell you). Of course your goal is attainable. Human beings can do almost anything but fly by flapping their arms, and someday they'll probably do that, too. But you surely have an obstacle-ridden path ahead of you. It's also not clear what you mean when you say your rating is "low right now." Some people would find a rating of 2400 to be quite low, so I'm not exactly sure where you are or how to assess your chances. It does tell me something, though. It tells me you have considerable doubt, and it's terribly hard to succeed when one is plagued by lack of confidence.

In order to attain your objective—chess mastery, whatever that really means—you must start with the conviction that you can do it. I'm also not convinced that your emphasis is on the right target. Rather than thinking of achieving a certain skill level, one very far down the road to say the least, why not set yourself more sensible goals, realizable ones that are well within your grasp? Bolstered by those measured but steady gains you'll have a decent chance to get somewhere. Even better, ignore ultimate aims altogether and just get into the happening itself. Play because you love it and the experience is its own reward.

TAKING A BREAK

Q. I'm a rather poor player (currently about 1450) who's trying to get better. Lately, however, it seems like the harder I try, the worse I get; the more I think on a move, the more I over-think, and make a mistake. Sometimes, in a game, I'm unable to think at all, other than the first move. My rating has gone down at least 150 points in the last six days, all due to the most simple and ugly blunders in my life. I don't (nor really can I afford) to take lessons from a tutor, so I've been picking up as many books as I can, but I find myself completely baffled by some of the moves. Most of the time (especially in endgame books), I feel like I have the subject down pat, then when the times comes, I lose. Am I doing something wrong? Thanks for your time.
—*USA*

A. You may be doing something wrong, but I can't tell from your question. If anything, you seem to be a little hard on yourself. Numerically, 1450 is not a poor rating. It's an average rating, not a mark of dread. The way you describe it, however, suggests that you're expecting too much. Perhaps you've been pressing more than you should, which makes it additionally difficult to succeed.

It also appears as if you've been playing excessively, especially if you've dropped 150 points in the last six days. You even understand why you've lost. You say you've been blundering. This implies that your mind is not on what you're doing, and maybe you've been distracted while playing. If so, no wonder you've been missing things.

I also understand that you haven't taken any lessons. You've been picking up a variety of chess books to compensate for that lack of constructive criticism. But some of those may be in conflict with each other, which might confuse you further. Nobody can play at his or her best under those conditions, with such uncertainty. Doubt yourself and there's no doubt you're in trouble.

Why don't you get back to basics? I'm not talking about the fundamentals of chess so much as the rationale for playing at all. I presume you turned to chess originally for the fun of partaking in an intellectually stimulating pastime, because you were attracted to the game's positive spirit of competition and its creative aspects. Instead of being concerned so much with getting better, try to get in harmony with the sheer pleasure of play. Quit worrying so much about rating and all that stuff. It's only a number, and even the greatest number pales before human happiness. (That's what they tell us, and for your purpose it's wise to believe them.)

Here's my advice. Take a break, at least for a few weeks. Try to do some other things you really enjoy. See a couple of movies, read a book for fun, sleep an extra hour or two a day, enjoy the sun and walking through a beautiful garden—whatever. After that rebirth perhaps you'll be eager to get back to chess on a new course, and don't be surprised if the new path resembles the old one without the weeds.

NAME-CALLING

Q. I am a chess teacher working in the public school system of a large metropolitan area. I am constantly going into classroom situations in which I am not familiar with the students or their abilities. A big problem for me is how to get control of these classes so that the kids will listen and I can accomplish something. I often find myself talking in a vacuum. Do you have any advice?
—USA

A. Chess classes given in public school systems usually are overseen by two people: a chess instructor and a licensed school teacher (there tends to be two adults even when the chess instructor is also licensed). If that's your situation, I suggest that you try working with the other teacher, to handle the class effectively and to learn about the students quickly. There's nothing wrong with utilizing your assets, and an experienced classroom teacher can be a great asset.

But whether or not you work with another teacher, and regardless of whether you are licensed, there is one vital technique to gaining control of a class. Learn and use the names of the students as soon as possible. That's the seasoned teacher's secret. By repeatedly using the names of the students, right from the start, the teacher actually masters who each student is straight away. Each student feels as if the teacher is speaking directly to him or her, which helps creates the interactivity of a private lesson. The constant use and repetition of everyone's name also forces a class to stay alert, since no student wants to be caught napping.

It's natural to shy away from saying the names too hastily, to avoid making embarrassing mistakes. But it's better to bungle in the first session or two, rather than weeks into the course, when such errors might be much more injurious to a youngster's fragile ego.

If you are unsure if your memory is functioning correctly, soften the negative impact of such miscues ahead of time. Make a game of it from the beginning. For example, in the very first session, you might try calling on students while looking away from them, say, with your back to the class, or even while staring at another student, as if focused on the wrong one. Then, with a friendly smile, turn and look at the right student. Don't be surprised if they are surprised. It's your insurance against future slips. Thereafter the class will never really be sure whether you've made a mistake or merely injected another one of your playful tricks. They'll have to give you the benefit of the doubt, and that should act as a safeguard, strengthening your ability to direct the class.

To students, practically nothing seems worse than a teacher who doesn't know who they are, and probably nothing lifts them higher than a teacher who shows real interest. I'm not saying all that name-calling will make you into Jean Brodie, but it should increase your control while making everyone feel more comfortable. After that, you can get them to listen to practically anything. You might even be able to teach them how to play chess.

LOST WEEKENDS

Q. How do I prepare myself for the five-round weekend Swiss tournaments? I tend to fare well at the local club, with one game a night, but lately my weekend tournaments have been a poor showing. Part of my

results could be due to the fact I have two young children and a demanding job. I would appreciate any kind of advice you could give me.
—*Canada*

A. Perhaps you shouldn't play in weekend tournaments at all, not if you've been much more successful in events that require playing only one game an evening. Maybe five games are just too enervating, which is understandable considering your tough job and consuming family demands. It's really hard to excel when you can't give an enterprise a full and total commitment. So at least for now, why not confine yourself to playing no more than one serious game a day? By ridding yourself of the Saturday-to-Sunday marathon, you'll suddenly have a surplus of time, which could be used gainfully for self-renewal and worthwhile hours enjoyed with your spouse and kids. That won't improve your chess per se, but it might do a lot more for your well-being than a five-game lost weekend ever could.

PIECE CORPS

Q. I am a Peace Corps volunteer living in Burkina Faso. Teaching chess to people around here has been interesting, but finding competition above the beginner level has been difficult. I was looking into correspondence chess over the Internet, but I was having trouble finding sites that would accommodate someone who only irregularly has access. I am looking for something informal just to match me up with some partners who would not mind an occasional wait. Do you have any suggestions?
—*Burkina Faso*

A. It's not every day I have to look up to see if the country of origin really exists. You are to be applauded for the service you are extending to the world of chess and to humanity. Why don't you try a few of these sites: InstantChess.com, Itsyourturn.com, Redhotpawn.com, Chessworld.net, Yahoo! Games, Gameknot.com, Chessgames.com, and Chessclub.com. The latter are two I recommend often. For most of these you can play on very informally, whenever you have access and it suits you. Thanks for spreading the beauty of chess to a distant Shangri-la.

TOURNAMATCHES

Q. I've seen you write on more than one occasion that you recommend going to a chess match to watch. Many people play in chess matches. I can understand that, but I don't understand why they would go to a match they are not going to play in. Can you explain what you get from doing that or why you would want to do that or how a player like me (average) can do it or get anything out of it, or even what I would do?
—*USA*

A. Let's first clear up the use of the terms "match" and "tournament." The public often uses them interchangeably, but they're not the same thing. A match is a confrontation between two players or two teams. Usually, at least two games are played against the same opponent, one game with the White pieces and one with the Black. In a tournament, an individual plays different opponents from round to round, rather than the same one over and over, as in a match.

Some tournaments are truly massive, sometimes with thousands of participants, all trying to keep as quiet as possible. The games can be slow and difficult to follow, but observing the action at these major events doesn't have to be like watching yachts race or grass grow. You can use the time wisely, entertaining yourself while learning about the game.

A good start would be to stake out the top ten boards. If circumstances allow, try going from board to board (usually you can do that unimpeded). Go through the same routine at each one. Begin by asking yourself: Who's ahead in material? You can do that by counting and comparing pieces and pawns, which is an excellent practice for your own games. In fact, even grandmasters do that.

Then you might ask: What was the opening? Or, similarly, how is it likely the game began? Of course, to answer that question, it helps to know something about openings. But even if you do, you're still playing detective. Regardless of your experience, the key to understanding here is determining the type of pawn structure. Most openings achieve their characteristics through pawn configurations. If pawns are placed logically, they tell you where the pieces should be. So adopt the habit of asking questions about pawn structure whenever you try to analyze a chess position. The more opening setups and corresponding pawn structures you can identify, the better.

Another compelling question is, "Who controls the center?" All other things being equal, the side with greater central control almost always has the advantage. Try to gauge how the other side can fight back in the center, and if it can be done at all. You might also classify or describe the center. For example, is it obstructed by each side's pawns, or something in between? Once you understand what you're looking at, you can make certain inferences. If the center is blocked, play must proceed slowly, with much maneuvering. If it's clear, a sudden mating attack could come from anywhere, just like that.

Other questions to consider: "Are any pieces placed well or badly?" "What are the strong and weak points for each side?" "Can the weak squares be exploited or defended?" "Can they be occupied or controlled?" Or you can ask questions satisfying your own needs and tastes, whatever they are. You can conclude your analyses by asking two final questions: "Who stands better?" And, based on the pros and cons of the position, "What is a good plan for each side?"

Meticulous investigation is not easy, but it's fun. If you do it fairly regularly you may very well master the process of analyzing a chess position. If you don't, there's always checkers.

VACATIONS

Q. I am rated about 1700. I study chess with a prominent chess teacher in California. Though I admire him immensely, I find him to be a bit of a workaholic. He works from early morning to late at night, whether it's teaching, studying, or playing. I can almost never get him on the phone. He never refuses a chess lesson or a class or an appearance, if he can be reached, and I can't get him to take a day off. It's like he's afraid to say no for fear of going out of business I think. People tell me you are also somewhat like this. Is this true? Is chess teaching that insecure? Do you ever take a vacation or relax for a day?
—USA

A. Maybe chess teaching does leave us feeling insecure. Most of us have trouble making a living at this activity, and it's not always based on factors under our control. Some of America's very best chess teachers have had to abandon the profession in order to eat and pay the rent. So I empathize with your chess teacher. But I don't consider myself a workaholic. I try to take days off here and there, and I love sitting in parks, walking through museums, and reading big books. Yet it's hard to escape the chess scene completely.

I can remember a vacation day I took a long time ago when I managed the Manhattan Chess Club. I needed to get away, so I decided to head out to East Hampton for an afternoon of sun and no chess players. I think it took about three hours to reach Main Beach, far away from chess civilization. I sat on a beach chair and began to relax with a copy of *Moby Dick*, a book I had always wanted to read. About ten minutes after "Call me Ishmael," I suddenly heard my named blurted out most familiarly.

"Hey, Pandolfini, is that you? Hot dog, it is! Take a look at this."

And there he was, the biggest pest the Manhattan Chess Club ever had, desperate to show me a recent game he had played in the Manhattan Friday Night Rapids on a pocket set. I never did find out why he was there, nor did I progress much with Melville's masterpiece. I concluded two things that afternoon: taking a vacation day wasn't all it was cracked up to be, and the game shown to me on the pocket set was absolutely terrible. I wouldn't be surprised if your teacher has had comparable experiences with similar books and chess fanatics. Take that into account the next time you make out his check.

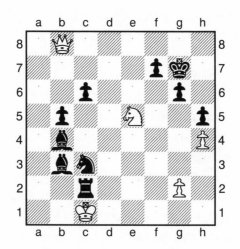

D. Byrne-Fischer, New York 1956
Black elects to play 1. ... Rc2 mate—the
"Game of the Century" the final check in the book.

INDEX

?, 253
!?, 253
?!, 253
=, 254
0–0, 255
0-0-0, 255
50–move rule, 243–244
2001: A Space Odyssey (Kubrick), 210

A

ABC's of Chess, The (Pandolfini), 24
active play, 9–10
advantages, two knights, 243–245
Alberston, Bruce, 77
Alekine, 192–193
analysis
  by computers compared to humans, 166–168, 170
  hindsight and, 177
analytic process, 122
analyzing from opponent's view, 126–127, 185
analyzing games
  of coach, 53
  to find errors, 121–122
  with software, 51, 55
analyzing opponent's move, 116, 125
analyzing positions, 281–282
analyzing without moving pieces, 70–71, 108–110, 114–115, 131
Anderssen-Dufresne, 202
annotated games
  diagrams of, 28–29
  how good players think and, 112
  key moments in, 28–29
  planning and, 112

skipping notes in, 136–137
  as teaching tool, 177
  understanding, 134–136
annotating games, 23
art, chess as, 201–202
Attacking Chess (Waitzkin), 261

B

bad habits, 16–17
beauty and chess, 186
Bergman, Ingmar, 207
bishops, 245–246
Black or White, 215
blindfold chess, 111, 128–130, 131
blitz, 151–153, 172. *see also* speed chess
board compared to computer, 132
boarding school study, 20–21
Bogoljubov, 192
Bonham, Kevin, 259–260
books
  about analysis, 122
  on chess history, 176
  on chess intuition, 151
  for children, 77
  compared to CDs, 155–156
  on fundamentals, 11
  improvement and, 133, 190–191, 219
  most influential, 189
  on openings, 21, 218, 219, 226–227, 254
  for parents and teachers, 78–79
boredom, 266–267
Botvinnik, 192–193
breaking the pin, 227–228
breaks, 277–278
bughouse, 83, 162–165

bullet chess, 162. *see also* speed chess

Burgess, Graham, 261

C

calculations, 109, 114–115

candidate moves, 117, 120–121

Capablanca, 11, 76, 115, 135, 183, 192–193, 236–237

castling, long, 229

castling symbols, 255

CDs compared to books, 155–156

Charousek, 203

cheating, 207

Chess (Polgar), 256–257

Chess, Tactics and Strategy (Burgess), 261

Chess and Children (Kane), 78–79

chess as art, 201–202

chess clubs, 267–268

chess compositions, 255–257

Chess Fundamentals (Capablanca), 11, 236

chess history, 176, 178, 211–212

chess journalism, 68–70

chess pieces, original, 176

chess players, attributes of, 184–187

Chess Praxis (Nimzowitsch), 10

chess software, 51, 55, 166–168, 192

chess symbols, 135

chess variants, 83, 162–165, 170

ChessBase, 51

ChessMaster, 55, 166–168

classroom teaching, 278–279

clock management, 2–3

closed games compared to open games, 215–217

club play, 34–35

coaches. *see also* teachers

  instruction for, 67–68

  and ratings, 41–42

  two at once, 42–43

Cohn-Rubinstein, 246

Collins program, 21–22

commitment to play, 279–280

composed problems, 255–257

computer analysis, 166–168, 170

computer compared to board, 132

computers

  playing against, 165–166

  used in instruction, 146–147

concentration, 3, 104–105

confidence, 5

control in chess, 262–263

control in classroom, 278–279

correspondence chess, 144–146

counterattack, 18–19, 124–125

curriculum for chess study, 60–61, 168–170

D

Das Leidenschaftliche Spiel (Schenk), 206

Davidson, Henry, 176

Deep Fritz, 197–199

defensive play, 123

Devil's Cross, 265–266

diagnosis

  by computers compared to humans, 166–168

  by stronger player, 29–30, 99

Die Blockade (Nimzowitsch), 35–36

Dragon Sicilian, 229–230

draws, playing for, 173, 222–223

Dudeney, Henry, 265

Dvoretsky, Mark, 55, 57

E

ECO (Encyclopedia of Chess Openings), 254

eight-queens problem, 264–265

emotions. *see* psychological aspects of chess

en passant, 251

endgame study, 233–239, 274

English Opening, 96–97

equality, 254

evaluation by analyst, 31–32

Evergreen Game, The, 202

explaining before moving, 86–87

F
fear, 137–138
Feldman, David, 183
feuds, 193
film consulting, 73–74
Fine, Reuben, 219, 227
Fischer, Bobby, 192, 196–197, 201–202
Fischer-Spassky Match, 209
focus, 151
Friedel, Frederic, 197–199
Fritz, 51, 55
From Morphy to Botvinnik (Konig), 21
frustration, 206
fun, 8–9
fundamentals, 10–12, 241–242
future of chess, 148–150

G
game collections, 20–22, 24–25, 102–103, 112
Game of Chess, The (Tarrasch), 11, 236
games, analyzing. *see* analyzing games
games, annotated. *see* annotated games
games, notating, 71–72
games, on Internet, 83, 154–155, 161–162, 280
Gardner, Howard, 183
Gauss, Karl Friedrich, 265
general rules, 124–125
getting started
  playing, 249
  teaching, 58
goals, 22–23, 276–277
grandmasters, 199–201, 211–212
gymnastic chess, 6–7

H
history. *see* chess history
homework, 92–93
Horowitz, Al, 261

How to Be a Complete Tournament Player (Mednis), 235

I
Ideas Behind the Chess Openings, The (Fine), 219, 227
improvement
  books and, 133, 190–191, 219
  diagnosis, 16–17
  endgame, 233–236, 274
  by playing, 30–31, 33–35, 55, 71
  rates of, 13–14, 179
  speeding up, 256–257
  of tactical skill, 4, 122–123, 231–233
  through study, 238
incentives, 90–92
International Master, as goal, 36–37
Internet as a study tool, 218
Internet games, 83, 154–155, 161–162
Internet lessons, compared to face-to-face, 53–54
Internet resources, 172
intuition, 115, 150–151, 185

J
journalism, 68–70

K
Kane, George Francis, 78–79
Karpov, 18, 192–193, 196
Kasparov, Garry, 191–193, 196–197
Keres, 192
key moments, 28–29
Khan, Sultan, 203
king-pawn openings, 215–217
knights, 243–246
Konig, 21
Korchnoi, 18
Kotov, Alexander, 122
Kramnik, Vladimir, 192, 197–198

L
language ability and chess, 182–184
Lasker, 139, 142, 206

lessons
  best age to start, 76–77
  over Internet, 53–54
  over telephone, 61–62
  too much/too little, 86–87
Lloyd, Sam, 265
logic, 130–131
long castling, 229
longest game, 258–260
losing games, 83–85
losing interest, 12–13
Luzhin Defense, The (Nabokov),
    73–74
Lyman, Shelby, 209

M
MacEnuity, David, 77
MacMurray, Donald, 258–259
man versus machine, 197–199
Manual of Chess (Lasker), 206
Margulies, Stuart, 183
Marshall, Carrie, 204
Marshall Chess Club, 204
Master level, as goal, 98–99
Master's of Chessboard (Reti),
    226–227
matches, 281
mathematics and chess, 180–182
MCO (Modern Chess Openings),
    218
Mednis, Edmar, 235, 237
Melville and chess, 205
memory and understanding,
    118–119
mental skills enlisted by chess players,
    184–186
middlegame, bypassing, 239–241
movies and chess, 210
music and chess, 181–182
My Chess Career (Capablanca),
    192
My Great Predecessors (Kasparov),
    191, 211–212
My System (Nimzowitsch), 10,
    35–36

N
Nabokov, Vladimir, 73–74
narrative of moves, 130–131
Nauck, 265
nerves, 5–6. *see also* self-doubt
new ideas, 241–242
Nikolic (I.)-Arsovic, 258
Nimzowitsch, 10, 35–36
notating games, 71–72
numerical assessments, 32–33
Nunn, John, 190

O
objectivity, 5, 139
odds, 257–258
online play compared to over-the
    board play, 154–158, 160
open games compared to closed
    games, 215–217
opening principles, 63
opening tips, general, 227
openings
  books on, 21, 218, 219, 226–227
  choosing, 220
  developing a repertoire, 51,
    223–227
  king-pawn, 96–97, 215–217
  Orangutan, 204
  playing Black, 221–222
  queen pawn, 215–217
  Sokolsky's, 204
  studying, 21, 224–227
  teaching, 62–63, 93–97
Orangutan Opening, 204
origin of chess, 176
original chess pieces, 176
over-the-board play compared to on-
    line play, 154–158, 160

P
Pandolfini
  most influential books, 189
  teaching methods, 58–59, 119–120
patience, 7–8
pawn promotion, 249–253

performance orientation, 140–142
pigs (as term for rooks), 261
planning, 112, 116
plateaus, 13–14, 17–18, 179
Play Like a Grandmaster (Kotov), 122
playing down, 26–27
playing for a draw, 173
playing to improve game, 30–31,
    33–35, 55, 71
postal chess. *see* correspondence chess
prizes, 90–91
problem solving, 109
prodigies, 182
psychological aspects of chess, 4–8,
    72, 138–139
puzzles, 4, 20, 54, 110, 114

Q
queen movement, 217
queen-pawn openings, 215–217
question and answer method,
    119–120

R
Rand, Ayn, 187–188
rating classes, 30, 31–32
rating decline, 35–36
ratings
  coaches and, 41–42
  online compared to over-the-board,
    154–155
  teachers and, 44
regimen for study, 14–15
Reshevsky, 183
resigning, 88–89, 186
Reti, Richard, 226–227
rivalries, 192–194
robots, 148
Ronn, Ionel, 151
rook, as pig, 261
Ruy Lopez Exchange Variation, 240

S
sacrifices, 127–128
Santasiere, I.M., 204

Santasiere's Folly, 204
Schenk, Gustav, 206
Secrets of Chess Intuition (Beliavsky),
    151
self study, 14–17, 27–28, 50–51,
    54–55
self-doubt, 4–5
self-reliance, 54–55
Sesame Street, 211
Short History of Chess, A (Davidson),
    176
skittles, 260–261
slowing down, 70–71, 85–86
software, 51, 55, 166–168, 192
Sokolsky's Opening, 204
Spassky, Boris, 187–188, 196
special education, 64–65
speed chess, 151–153, 158–160, 164,
    172
starting late, 98–104
Stein, Leonid, 203
strategy, 268–269
strength indicators, 275–276
strongest players, 195–197
study time, 2
studying, 269–270
  counterattack, 18
  endgame, 233–239, 274
  opening or endgame, 235–236
  openings, 21, 224–227
  using Internet, 218
  value of, 133–134, 274–275
stuffed chess pieces for children,
    211
style of play, 128–129
success, ingredients of, 180
switching sides, 165–166
symbols, 253–255

T
tactical improvement, 4, 122–123,
    231–233
tactical problems, 54
tactics study, 71
Tarrasch, 11, 236–238

teachers. *see also* coaches
  changing, 40–41
  evaluating, 44, 46–47, 52
  finding, 39–40, 51–52
  qualifications of, 44–46, 55–57
  ratings and, 44
  sampling, 82
  vacations and, 281–282
teaching materials, 64–65
teaching methods
  generally, 48–50, 58–59
  holistic approach, 237
  using computers, 146–147
  for young children, 76–83
telephone lessons, 61–62
television and chess, 207–209
The Passsionate Game (Schenk), 206
The Seventh Seal (Bergman), 207
theoretical ideas, studying, 218
Think Like a Grandmaster (Kotov), 122
thinking, 112–114, 116–117, 119–120
time limits, 153–154, 161–162
time trouble, 269–270
touching, 66–67
touch-move rule, 251–253
tournament decisions, 89–90, 97–98
tournament slump, 83–85
tournaments, 281

trading pieces, 105
training system, 25–26, 39
trophies, 65–66, 91–92

V
value of chess, 184–187
visualization, 11–12, 108, 110, 118, 128–131, 185

W
Waitzkin, 261
weaknesses, strengthening, 19–20
Web-based chess, 144–146
White or Black, 215
Wilson, Fred, 77
winning positions, 273
women's grandmaster title, 199–200
world champions course, 20–22
World Open, 140

X
X-Men (Singer), 210

Y
Yugoslav Attack, 229–230

Z
Zilbermints, 230–231

A C K N O W L E D G M E N T S

I have many people to thank for the best features of the *Q&A Way*. In addition to those whose questions were selected for the present volume, my gratefulness goes to the readership of the *Chesscafé* for all their emails and encouragement. I must also recognize Hanon Russell, the publisher and editor of the *Chesscafé* site, for going with the original column idea and for his constant support. I don't know how he's put up with my deadline anomalies, and I'm always stunned by the easy and impressive way he outguns me in our missives and verbal exchanges. I'm also appreciative of Jenny Olsson, for gathering and helping to shape the material; Barbara, Ralf and Erik Henning Thiede, for their many practical suggestions and valuable advice; and Roselyn Abrahams, Glenn Petersen, Carol Ann Caronia, and Idelle Pandolfini, for all their pertinent input and helpful thinking. I must also thank the McKay publishing team. Mike Klein copyedited the manuscript and provided numerous improvements. Burt Hochberg was behind the concept from the start. His hard work and perceptive insights were greatly valued. And Jena Pincott, my astute editor, captained the ship. Her professionalism, sensibility, and guiding intelligence steered the *Q&A Way* into port.

Great Titles from the McKay Chess Library

Title Information	Level of Play*
The Art of Defense in Chess ISBN: 0-679-14108-1	I $15.95/$23.95
The Art of Positional Play ISBN: 0-8129-3475-X	I-A $15.95/C$23.95
Basic Chess Endings ISBN: 0-8129-3493-8	I-A $24.95/C$37.95
Best Lessons of a Chess Coach ISBN: 0-8129-2265-4	B-I $16.95/C$24.95
The Chess Advantage in Black and White ISBN: 0-8129-3571-3	I-A $18.95/C$28.95
Chess for Juniors ISBN: 0-8129-1867-3	B-I $14.95/C$22.95
Chess Fundamentals ISBN: 0-679-14004-2	B $14.95/C$22.95
The Chess Kid's Book of Checkmate ISBN: 0-8129-3594-2	B-I $10.95/C$16.95
The Chess Kid's Book of Tactics ISBN: 0-8129-3509-8	I $10.95/C$16.95
The Chess Kid's Book of the King and Pawn Endgame ISBN: 0-8129-3510-1	I-A $9.95/C$14.95
Chess Openings the Easy Way ISBN: 0-8129-3498-9	B-I $15.95/C$23.95
How to Play Good Opening Moves ISBN: 0-8129-3474-1	B-I $12.95/C$19.95
The Ideas Behind the Chess Openings ISBN: 0-8129-1756-1	B-I $13.95/C$21.00
The Inner Game of Chess ISBN: 0-8129-2291-3	I-A $16.95/C$24.95

Judgment & Planning in Chess ISBN: 0-679-14325-4	I-A $12.95 /C$19.95
King Power in Chess ISBN: 0-8129-3636-1	I-A $18.95/C$26.95
The Middlegame in Chess ISBN: 0-8129-3484-9	I $18.95/$28.95
Modern Chess Openings 14th ed. ISBN: 0-8129-3084-3	I-A $29.95/$44.95
More Unbeatable Chess for Juniors ISBN: 0-8129-3657-4	I-A $14.95/C$21.00
Pawn Structure Chess ISBN: 0-8129-2529-7	I-A $16.00/C$24.00
The Q&A Way in Chess ISBN: 0-8129-3622-1	I $15.95/$22.95
Solitaire Chess ISBN: 0-8129-3656-6	A $15.95/C$23.95
Turning Advantage into Victory in Chess ISBN: 0-8129-3581-0	I-A $17.95/C$25.95
Unbeatable Chess Lessons for Juniors ISBN: 0-8129-3511-X	I-A $15.95/C$23.95
United States Chess Federation Official Rules of Chess, 5th ed. ISBN: 0-8129-3559-4	NO RATING $18.95/C$28.95
Winning Chess Tournaments for Juniors ISBN: 0-8129-3635-3	I-A $14.95/C$21.00
A World Champion's Guide to Chess ISBN: 0-8129-3653-1	B-I $17.95/C$25.95

*Key to levels of play: (B) = Beginner; (I) = Intermediate; (A) = Advanced
Available at your local bookseller.
To order by phone, call 1-800-733-3000.